American Statesmen

BENJAMIN FRANKLIN

BY

JOHN T. MORSE, JR.

AUTHOR OF "LIFE OF JOHN ADAMS," "LIFE OF JOHN QUINCY ADAMS"
"LIFE OF THOMAS JEFFERSON," ETC.

BOSTON AND NEW YORK

HOUGHTON MIFFLIN COMPANY

The Riverside Press Cambridge

PREFACE.

———◆———

Just as I am reading the last proof-sheet of this volume, its publishers send me a catalogue of their "Books of Biography." In it my eye inopportunely falls upon these discouraging words, quoted from the Hon. John Bigelow, concerning Parton's Life of Franklin: "The delightful work of Mr. Parton has left no place in English literature for another biography of this most illustrious of our countrymen." I am much of Mr. Bigelow's opinion. Mr. Parton has given us such an admirable biography, so exhaustive and so remarkably happy in setting the real man vividly before the reader, that I feel that I must give something between a reason and an apology for the existence of this volume. The fact is simply this: without a life of Franklin this series would have appeared as absurdly imperfect as a library of English fiction with Scott or Thackeray absent from the shelves. The volume was a necessity, and since Mr. Parton's work, even if it could be borrowed or stolen, would not fit the space, this little book has been written. No poor genie of oriental magic was ever squeezed into more disproportionately narrow quarters than is Franklin in these four hundred pages; but again necessity must bear the burden of responsibility.

The edition of Franklin's works referred to in this volume is that of Mr. John Bigelow, published by G. P. Putnam's Sons, New York, 1887–88.

The edition of Bancroft's History of the United States referred to is the earliest octavo edition.

JOHN T. MORSE, JR.

BEVERLY FARMS, *August* 9, 1889.

CONTENTS.

CHAPTER   PAGE

I. EARLY YEARS 1

II. A CITIZEN OF PHILADELPHIA: CONCERNMENT IN
PUBLIC AFFAIRS 17

III. REPRESENTATIVE OF PENNSYLVANIA IN ENGLAND:
RETURN HOME 58

IV. LIFE IN PHILADELPHIA 85

V. SECOND MISSION TO ENGLAND: I. 99

VI. SECOND MISSION TO ENGLAND: II. . . . 141

VII. SECOND MISSION TO ENGLAND: III. THE HUTCHIN-
SON LETTERS: THE PRIVY COUNCIL SCENE:
RETURN HOME 175

VIII. SERVICES IN THE STATES 202

IX. MINISTER TO FRANCE: I. DEANE AND BEAUMAR-
CHAIS: FOREIGN OFFICERS 217

X. MINISTER TO FRANCE: II. PRISONERS: TROUBLE
WITH LEE AND OTHERS 245

XI. MINISTER TO FRANCE: III. TREATY WITH FRANCE:
MORE QUARRELS 264

XII. FINANCIERING 300

XIII. HABITS OF LIFE AND OF BUSINESS: AN ADAMS IN-
CIDENT 333

XIV. PEACE NEGOTIATIONS: LAST YEARS IN FRANCE . 352

XV. AT HOME: PRESIDENT OF PENNSYLVANIA: THE
CONSTITUTIONAL CONVENTION: DEATH . . 397

BENJAMIN FRANKLIN.

CHAPTER I.

EARLY YEARS.

IT is a lamentable matter for any writer to find himself compelled to sketch, however briefly, the early years of Benjamin Franklin. That autobiography, in which the story of those years is so inimitably told, by its vividness, its simplicity, even by its straightforward vanity, and by the quaint charm of its old-fashioned but well-nigh faultless style, stands among the few masterpieces of English prose. It ought to have served for the perpetual protection of its subject as a copyright more sacred than any which rests upon mere statutory law. Such, however, has not been the case, and the narrative has been rehearsed over and over again till the American who is not familiar with it is indeed a curiosity. Yet no one of the subsequent narrators has justified his undertaking. Therefore because the tale has been told so often, and once has been told so well, and also in order that the stone which it is my lot to cast upon a cairn made up of so many failures may at least be only a small pebble,

I shall get forward as speedily as possible to that point in Franklin's career where his important public services begin, at the same time commending every reader to turn again for further refreshment of his knowledge to those pages which might well have aroused the envy of Fielding and Defoe.

Franklin came from typical English stock. For three hundred years, perhaps for many centuries more, his ancestors lived on a small freehold at Ecton in Northamptonshire, and so far back as record or tradition ran the eldest son in each generation had been bred a blacksmith. But after the strange British fashion there was intertwined with this singular fixedness of ideas a stubborn independence in thinking, courageously exercised in times of peril. The Franklins were among the early Protestants, and held their faith unshaken by the terrors of the reign of Bloody Mary. By the end of Charles the Second's time they were non-conformists and attendants on conventicles; and about 1682 Josiah Franklin, seeking the peaceful exercise of his creed, migrated to Boston, Massachusetts. His first wife bore him seven children, and died. Not satisfied, he took in second nuptials Abiah Folger, "daughter of Peter Folger, one of the first settlers of New England, of whom honorable mention is made by Cotton Mather," and justly, since in those dark days he was an active philanthropist towards the Indians, and an opponent of religious persecution.[1] This lady outdid

[1] Parton's *Life of Franklin*, i. 27.

her predecessor, contributing no less than ten children to expand the family circle. The eighth of
this second brood was named Benjamin, in memory
of his father's favorite brother. He was born in
a house on Milk Street, opposite the Old South
Church, January 6, old style, 17, new style, 1706.
Mr. Parton says that probably Benjamin "derived
from his mother the fashion of his body and the
cast of his countenance. There are lineal descendants of Peter Folger who strikingly resemble Franklin in these particulars; one of whom, a banker of
New Orleans, looks like a portrait of Dr. Franklin
stepped out of its frame." [1] A more important inheritance was that of the humane and liberal traits
of his mother's father.

In that young, scrambling village in the new
country, where all material, human or otherwise,
was roughly and promptly utilized, the unproduc-
tive period of boyhood was cut very short. Franklin's father speedily resolved to devote him, "as the
tithe of his sons, to the service of the church," and
so sent him to the grammar school. A droller
misfit than Franklin in an orthodox New England
pulpit of that era can hardly be imagined; but
since he was only seven years old when his father
endeavored to arrange his life's career, a misappre-
ciation of his fitnesses was not surprising. The
boy himself had the natural hankering of children
bred in a seaboard town for the life of a sailor.
It is amusing to fancy the discussions between this

---

[1] Parton's *Life of Franklin*, i. 31.

babe of seven years and his father, concerning his
occupation in life. Certainly the babe had not
altogether the worst of it, for when he was eight
years old his father definitively gave up the notion
of making him a preacher of the Gospel. At the
ripe age of ten he was taken from school, and set
to assist his father in the trade of tallow-chandler
and soap-boiler. But dipping wicks and pouring
grease pleased him hardly better than reconciling
infant damnation and a red-hot hell with the love-
liness of Christianity. The lad remained discon-
tented. His chief taste seemed to be for reading,
and great were the ingenuity and the self-sacrifice
whereby he secured books and leisure to read them.
The resultant of these several forces was at last
a suggestion from his father that he should take
up, as a sort of quasi-literary occupation, the trade
of a printer. James Franklin, an older brother of
Benjamin, was already of that calling. Benjamin
stood out for some time, but at last reluctantly
yielded, and in the maturity of his thirteenth year
this child set his hand to an indenture of apprenticeship which formally bound him to his brother
for the next nine years of his life.

Handling the types aroused a boyish ambition to
see himself in print. He scribbled some ballads,
one about a shipwreck, another about the capture
of a pirate; but he "escaped being a poet," as fortunately as he had escaped being a clergyman.
James Franklin seems to have trained his junior
with such fraternal cuffs and abuse as the elder

brothers of English biography and literature appear usually to have bestowed on the younger. But this younger one got his revenges. James published the "New England Courant," and, inserting in it some objectionable matter, was forbidden to continue it. Thereupon he canceled the indenture of apprenticeship, and the newspaper was thereafter published by Benjamin Franklin. A secret renewal of the indenture was executed simultaneously. This "flimsy scheme" gave the boy his chance. Secure that the document would never be produced, he resolved to leave the printing-house. But the influence of James prevented his getting employment elsewhere in the town. Besides this, other matters also harassed him. It gives an idea of the scale of things in the little settlement, and of the serious way in which life was taken even at its outset, to hear that this 'prentice lad of seventeen years had already made himself "a little obnoxious to the governing party," so as to fear that he might soon "bring himself into scrapes." For the inherited habit of freedom in religious speculation had taken a new form in Franklin, who was already a free-thinker, and by his "indiscreet disputations about religion" had come to be "pointed at with horror by good people as an infidel and atheist" — compromising, even perilous, names to bear in that Puritan village. Various motives thus combined to induce migration. He stole away on board a sloop bound for New York, and after three days arrived there, in October, 1723. He had but a trifling sum of money, and he knew no one in the strange city. He sought occupation in his trade, but got nothing better than advice to move on to Philadelphia; and thither he went. The story of this journeying is delightfully told in the autobiography, with the famous little scene wherein he figures with a loaf under each arm and munching a third while he walks " up Market Street, as far as Fourth Street, passing by the door of Mr. Read, my future wife's father; when she, standing at the door, saw me, and thought I made, as I certainly did, a most awkward, ridiculous appearance."

In Philadelphia Franklin soon found opportunity to earn a living at his trade. There were then only two printers in that town, ignorant men both, with scant capacity in the technique of their calling. His greater acquirements and ability, and superior knowledge of the craft, soon attracted attention. One day Sir William Keith, governor of the Province, appeared at the printing-office, inquired for Franklin, and carried him off " to taste some excellent Madeira " with himself and Colonel French, while employer Keimer, bewildered at the compliment to his journeyman, " star'd like a pig poison'd." Over the genial glasses the governor proposed that Franklin should set up for himself, and promised his own influence to secure for him the public printing. Later he wrote a letter, intended to induce Franklin's father to advance the necessary funds. Equipped with this document, Franklin

set out, in April, 1724, to seek his father's coöperation, and surprised his family by appearing unan-
nounced among them, not at all in the classic garb
of the prodigal son, but "having a genteel new suit
from head to foot, a watch, and my pockets lin'd
with near five pounds sterling in silver." But
neither his prosperous appearance nor the flattering
epistle of the great man could induce his hard-
headed parent to favor a scheme "of setting a boy
up in business, who wanted yet three years of being
at man's estate." The independent old tallow-
chandler only concluded that the distinguished
baronet "must be of small discretion." So Franklin returned with "some small gifts as tokens" of
parental love, much good advice as to "steady industry and prudent parsimony," but no cash in
hand. The gallant governor, however, said: "Since
he will not set you up, I will do it myself," and a
plan was soon concocted whereby Franklin was to
go to England and purchase a press and types with
funds to be advanced by Sir William. Everything
was arranged, only from day to day there was delay
in the actual delivery to Franklin of the letters of
introduction and credit. The governor was a very
busy man. The day of sailing came, but the documents had not come, only a message from the governor that Franklin might feel easy at embarking,
for that the papers should be sent on board
at Newcastle, down the stream. Accordingly, at
the last moment, a messenger came hurriedly on
board and put the packet into the captain's hands.

Afterward, when during the leisure hours of the voyage the letters were sorted, none was found for Franklin. His patron had simply broken an inconvenient promise. It was indeed a "pitiful trick" to "impose so grossly on a poor innocent boy." Yet Franklin, in his broad tolerance of all that is bad as well as good in human nature, spoke with good-tempered indifference, and with more of charity than of justice, concerning the deceiver. "It was a habit he had acquired. He wish'd to please everybody; and, having little to give, he gave expectations. He was otherwise an ingenious, sensible man, a pretty good writer, and a good governor for the people. . . . Several of our best laws were of his planning, and passed during his administration."

None the less it turned out that this contemptible governor did Franklin a good turn in sending him to London, though the benefit came in a fashion not anticipated by either. For Franklin, not yet much wiser than the generality of mankind, had to go through his period of youthful folly, and it was good fortune for him that the worst portion of this period fell within the eighteen months which he passed in England. Had this part of his career been run in Philadelphia its unsavory aroma might have kept him long in ill odor among his fellow-townsmen, then little tolerant of profligacy. But the "errata" of a journeyman printer in London were quite beyond the ken of provincial gossips.

He easily gained employment in his trade, at wages which left him a little surplus beyond his maintenance. This surplus, during most of the time, he and his comrades squandered in the pleasures of the town. Yet in one matter his good sense showed itself, for he kept clear of drink; indeed, his real nature asserted itself even at this time, to such a degree that we find him waging a temperance crusade in his printing-house, and actually weaning some of his fellow compositors from their dearly loved "beer." One of these, David Hall, afterward became his able partner in the printing business in Philadelphia. Amid much bad companionship he fell in with some clever men. His friend James Ralph, though a despicable, bad fellow, had brains and some education. At this time, too, Franklin was in the proselyting stage of infidelity. He published "A Dissertation on Liberty and Necessity, Pleasure and Pain," and the pamphlet got him some little notoriety among the free-thinkers of London, and an introduction to some of them, but chiefly of the class who love to sit in taverns and blow clouds of words. Their society did him no good, and such effervescence was better blown off in London than in Philadelphia.

But after the novelty of London life had worn off, it ceased to be to Franklin's taste. He began to reform somewhat, to retrench and lay by a little money; and after eighteen months he eagerly seized an opportunity which offered for returning home.

This was opened to him by a Mr. Denham, a good man and prosperous merchant, then engaged in England in purchasing stock for his store in Philadelphia. Franklin was to be his managing and confidential clerk, with the prospect of rapid advancement. At the same time Sir William Wyndham, ex-Chancellor of the Exchequer, endeavored to persuade Franklin to open a swimming school in London. He promised very aristocratic patronage; and as an opening for money-getting this plan was perhaps the better. Franklin almost closed with the proposition. He seems, however, to have had a little touch of homesickness, a preference, if not quite a yearning, for the colonies, which sufficed to turn the scale. Such was his third escape; he might have passed his days in instructing the scions of British nobility in the art of swimming! He arrived at home, after a tedious voyage, October 11, 1726. But almost immediately fortune seemed to cross him, for Mr. Denham and he were both taken suddenly ill. Denham died; Franklin narrowly evaded death, and fancied himself somewhat disappointed at his recovery, "regretting in some degree that [he] must now sometime or other have all that disagreeable work to go over again." He seems to have become sufficiently interested in what was likely to follow his decease, in this world at least, to compose an epitaph which has become world-renowned, and has been often imitated: —

THE BODY
OF
BENJAMIN FRANKLIN
(LIKE THE COVER OF AN OLD BOOK,
ITS CONTENTS TORN OUT,
AND STRIPT OF ITS LETTERING AND GILDING,)
LIES HERE, FOOD FOR WORMS,
YET THE WORK ITSELF SHALL NOT BE LOST,
FOR IT WILL, AS HE BELIEVED, APPEAR ONCE MORE,
IN A NEW
AND MORE BEAUTIFUL EDITION,
CORRECTED AND AMENDED
BY
THE AUTHOR.

But there was no use for this graveyard literature; Franklin got well, and recurred again to his proper trade. Being expert with the composing-stick, he was readily engaged at good wages by his old employer, Keimer. Franklin, however, soon suspected that this man's purpose was only to use him temporarily for instructing some green hands, and for organizing the printing-office. Naturally a quarrel soon occurred. But Franklin had proved his capacity, and forthwith the father of one Meredith, a fellow-journeyman under Keimer, advanced sufficient money to set up the two as partners in the printing business. Franklin managed the office, showing admirable enterprise, skill, and industry. Meredith drank. This allotment of functions soon produced its natural result. Two friends of Franklin lent him what capital he needed; he bought out Meredith and had the whole business for himself.

His zeal increased; he won good friends, gave general satisfaction, and absorbed all the best business in the Province.

At the time of the formation of the partnership the only newspaper of Pennsylvania was published by Bradford, a rival of Keimer in the printing business. It was "a paltry thing, wretchedly managed, no way entertaining, and yet was profitable to him." Franklin and Meredith resolved to start a competing sheet; but Keimer got wind of their plan, and at once " published proposals for printing one himself." He had got ahead of them, and they had to desist. But he was ignorant, shiftless, and incompetent, and after carrying on his enterprise for "three quarters of a year, with at most only ninety subscribers," he sold out his failure to Franklin and Meredith "for a trifle." To them, or rather to Franklin, "it prov'd in a few years extremely profitable." Its original name, "The Universal Instructor in all Arts and Sciences, and Pennsylvania Gazette" was reduced by the amputation of the first clause, and, relieved from the burden of its trailing title, it circulated actively throughout the Province, and further. Number 40, Franklin's first number, appeared October 2, 1729. Bradford, who was postmaster, refused to allow his post-riders to carry any save his own newspaper. But Franklin, whose morality was nothing if not practical, fought the devil with fire, and bribed the riders so judiciously that his newspaper penetrated whithersoever they went.

He says of it: " Our first papers made a quite different appearance from any before in the Province;
a better type, and better printed ; but some spirited
remarks of my writing, on the dispute then going
on between Governor Burnet and the Massachusetts Assembly, struck the principal people, occasioned the paper and the manager of it to be much
talked of, and in a few weeks brought them all to
be our subscribers." Later his articles in favor of
the issue of a sum of paper currency were so largely
instrumental in carrying that measure that the
profitable job of printing the money became his
reward. Thus advancing in prestige and prosperity, he was able to discharge by installments his indebtedness. " In order to secure," he says, " my
credit and character as a tradesman, I took care to
be not only in reality industrious and frugal, but to
avoid all appearances to the contrary." A characteristic remark. With Franklin every virtue had
its market value, and to neglect to get that value
out of it was the part of folly.

About this time the wife of a glazier, who occupied part of Franklin's house, began match-making
in behalf of a "very deserving" girl; and Franklin,
nothing loath, responded with " serious courtship."
He intimated his willingness to accept the maiden's
hand, provided that its fellow hand held a dowry,
and he named an hundred pounds sterling as his
lowest figure. The parents, on the other part, said
that they had not so much ready money. Franklin
civilly suggested that they could get it by mortgag-

ing their house; they firmly declined. The negotiation thereupon was abandoned. "This affair,"
Franklin continues, "having turned my thoughts
to marriage, I look'd round me and made overtures
of acquaintance in other places; but soon found
that, the business of a printer being generally
thought a poor one, I was not to expect money with
a wife, unless with such a one as I should not
otherwise think agreeable." Finding such difficulties in the way of a financial alliance, Franklin
appears to have bethought him of affection as a
substitute for dollars; so he blew into the ashes of
an old flame, and aroused some heat. Before going
to England he had engaged himself to Miss Deborah Read; but in London he had pretty well forgotten her, and had written to her only a single
letter. Many years afterward, writing to Catharine
Ray in 1755, he said: "The cords of love and
friendship . . . . in times past have drawn me . . .
back from England to Philadelphia." If the remark referred to an affection for Miss Read, it was
probably no more trustworthy than are most such
allegations made when lapsing years have given
a fictitious coloring to a remote past. If indeed
Franklin's profligacy and his readiness to marry
any girl financially eligible were symptoms attendant upon his being in love, it somewhat taxes the
imagination to fancy how he would have conducted
himself had he not been the victim of romantic
passion. Miss Read, meanwhile, apparently about
as much in love as her lover, had wedded another

man, "one Rogers, a potter," a good workman but worthless fellow, who soon took flight from his bride and his creditors. Her position had since become somewhat questionable; for there was a story that her husband had an earlier wife living, in which case of course her marriage with him was null. There was also a story that he was dead. But there was little evidence of the truth of either tale. Franklin, therefore, hardly knew what he was wedding, a maid, a widow, or another man's wife. Moreover the runaway husband "had left many debts, which his successor might be call'd upon to pay." Few men, even if warmly enamored, would have entered into the matrimonial contract under circumstances so discouraging; and there are no indications save the marriage itself that Franklin was deeply in love. Yet on September 1, 1730, the pair were wedded. Mrs. Franklin survived for forty years thereafter, and neither seems ever to have regretted the step. "None of the inconveniences happened that we had apprehended," wrote Franklin; "she proved a good and faithful helpmate; assisted me much by attending the shop; we throve together, and have ever mutually endeavored to make each other happy." A sensible, comfortable, satisfactory union it was, showing how much better is sense than sensibility as an ingredient in matrimony. Mrs. Franklin was a handsome woman, of comely figure, yet nevertheless an industrious and frugal one; later on in life Franklin boasted that he had "been clothed from head to foot in linen of [his] wife's manufacture." An early contribution of his own to the domestic *ménage* was his illegitimate son, William, born soon after his wedding, of a mother of whom no record or tradition remains. It was an unconventional wedding gift to bring home to a bride; but Mrs. Franklin, with a breadth and liberality of mind akin to her husband's, readily took the babe not only to her home but really to her heart, and reared him as if he had been her own offspring. Mr. Parton thinks that Franklin gave this excellent wife no further cause for suspicion or jealousy.

CHAPTER II.

So has ended the first stage, in the benign presence of Hymen. The period of youth may be regarded as over ; but the narrative thereof, briefly as
it has been given, is not satisfactory. One longs to
help out the outline with color, to get the expression as well as merely the features of the young
man who is going to become one of the greatest
men of the nation. Many a writer and speaker
has done what he could in this task, for Franklin
has been for a century a chief idol of the American
people. The Boston boy, the boy printer, the runaway apprentice, the young journeyman, friend-
less and penniless in distant London, are pictures
which have been made familiar to many generations of schoolboys ; and the trifling anecdote of
the bread rolls eaten in the streets of Philadelphia
has for its only rival among American historical
traditions the more doubtful story about George
Washington, the cherry-tree, and the little hatchet.

Yet, if plain truth is to be told, there was nothing unusual about this sunrise, no rare tints of
divine augury ; the luminary came up in every-day

fashion. Franklin had done much reading ; he had
taken pains to cultivate a good style in writing English ; he had practiced himself in dispute ; he had
adopted some odd notions, for example vegetarian-
ism in diet ; he had at times acquired some influence among his fellow-journeymen, and had used it
for good ; he had occasionally fallen into the society
of men of good social position , he had kept clear
of the prevalent habit of excessive drinking ; sometimes he had lived frugally and had laid up a little
money ; more often he had been wasteful ; he had
been very dissolute, and in sowing his wild oats he
had gone down into the mud. His autobiography
gives us a simple, vivid, strong picture, which we
accept as correct, though in reading it one sees that
the lapse of time since the occurrences narrated, together with his own success and distinction in life,
have not been without their obvious effect. By the
time he thought it worth while to write those pages,
Franklin had been taught to think very well of
himself and his career. For this reason he was,
upon the one hand, somewhat indifferent as to setting down what smaller men would conceal, confident that his fame would not stagger beneath the
burden of youthful wrong-doing ; on the other
hand, he deals rather gently, a little ideally, with
himself, as old men are wont to acknowledge with
condemnation tempered with mild forgiveness the
foibles of their early days. It is evident that, as
a young man, Franklin intermingled sense with
folly, correct living with dissipation, in a manner

that must have made it difficult for an observer to forecast the final outcome, and which makes it almost equally impossible now to form a satisfactory idea of him. He is not to be disposed of by placing him in any ready-made and familiar class. If he had turned out a bad man, there would have been abundance in his early life to point the moralist's warning tale; as he turned out a very reputable one, there is scarcely less abundance for panegyrists to expatiate upon. Certainly he was a man to attract some attention and to carry some weight, yet not more than many another of whom the world never hears. At the time of his marriage, however, he is upon the verge of development; a new period of his life is about to begin; what had been dangerous and evil in his ways disappears; the breadth, originality, and practical character of his mind are about to show themselves. He has settled to a steady occupation; he is industrious and thrifty; he has gathered much information, and may be regarded as a well-educated man; he writes a plain, forcible style; he has enterprise and shrewdness in matters of business, and good sense in all matters, — that is the chief point, his sound sense has got its full growth and vigor, and of sound sense no man ever had more. Very soon he not only prospers financially, but begins to secure at first that attention and soon afterward that influence which always follow close upon success in practical affairs. He becomes the public-spirited citizen; scheme after scheme of social and public improvement is suggested and carried forward by him, until he justly comes to be one of the foremost citizens of Philadelphia. The enumeration of what he did within a few years in this small new town and poor community will be found surprising and admirable.

His first enterprise, of a *quasi* public nature, was the establishment of a library. There were to be fifty subscribers for fifty years, each paying an entrance fee of forty shillings and an annual due of ten shillings. He succeeded only with difficulty and delay, yet he did succeed, and the results were important. Later a charter was obtained, and the number of subscribers was doubled. " This," he says, " was the mother of all the North American subscription libraries, now so numerous. . . . These libraries have improved the general conversation of the Americans, made the common traders and farmers as intelligent as most gentlemen from other countries, and perhaps have contributed in some degree to the stand so generally made throughout the colonies in defence of their privileges." " Reading became fashionable," he adds. But it was not difficult to cultivate the desire for reading ; that lay close to the surface. The boon which Franklin conferred lay rather in setting the example of a scheme by which books could be cheaply obtained in satisfactory abundance.

From the course of this business he drew one of those shrewd, practical conclusions which aided him so much in life. He says that he soon felt

" the impropriety of presenting one's self as the proposer of any useful project that might be supposed to raise one's reputation in the smallest degree above that of one's neighbors, when one has need of their assistance to accomplish that project. I therefore put myself as much as I could out of sight, and stated it as a scheme of a *number of friends*, who had requested me to go about and propose it." This method he found so well suited to the production of results that he habitually followed it in his subsequent undertakings. It was sound policy ; the self-abnegation helped success ; the success secured personal prestige. It was soon observed that when " a number of friends " or " a few gentlemen " were represented by Franklin, their purpose was usually good and was pretty sure to be carried through. Hence came reputation and influence.

In December, 1732, he says, " I first published my Almanack, under the name of *Richard Saunders*," price five pence, thereby falling in with a common custom among the colonial printers. Within the month three editions were sold ; and it was continued for twenty-five years thereafter with an average sale of 10,000 copies annually, until " Poor Richard " became a *nom de plume* as renowned as any in English literature. The publication ranks as one of the most influential in the world. Its " proverbial sentences, chiefly such as inculcated industry and frugality as the means of procuring wealth and thereby securing virtue," were sown like seed all over the land. The almanac went year after year, for quarter of a century, into the house of nearly every shopkeeper, planter, and farmer in the American provinces. Its wit and humor, its practical tone, its shrewd maxims, its worldly honesty, its morality of common sense, its useful information, all chimed well with the national character. It formulated in homely phrase and with droll illustration what the colonists more vaguely knew, felt, and believed upon a thousand points of life and conduct. In so doing it greatly trained and invigorated the natural mental traits of the people. " Poor Richard " was the revered and popular schoolmaster of a young nation during its period of tutelage. His teachings are among the powerful forces which have gone to shaping the habits of Americans. His terse and picturesque bits of the wisdom and the virtue of this world are familiar in our mouths to-day ; they moulded our great-grandparents and their children ; they have informed our popular traditions ; they still influence our actions, guide our ways of thinking, and establish our points of view, with the constant control of acquired habits which we little suspect. If we were accustomed still to read the literature of the almanac, we should be charmed with its humor. The world has not yet grown away from it, nor ever will. Addison and Steele had more polish but vastly less humor than Franklin. " Poor Richard " has found eternal life by passing into the daily speech of the peo-

ple, while the "Spectator" is fast being crowded
out of the hands of all save scholars in literature.
At this period of his life he wrote many short fugi-
tive pieces, which hold some of the rarest wit that
an American library contains. Few people suspect that the ten serious and grave-looking octavos,
imprinted "The Works of Benjamin Franklin,"
hide much of that delightful kind of wit that can
never grow old, but is as charming to-day as when
it came damp from the press a century and more
ago. How much of "Poor Richard" was actually
original is a sifting not worth while to make.
Franklin said: "I was conscious that not a tenth
part of the wisdom was my own which he ascribed
to me, but rather the gleanings that I had made of
the sense of all ages and nations." No profound
wisdom is really new, but only the expression of
it; and all that of "Poor Richard" had been fused
in the crucible of Franklin's brain.

But the famous almanac was not the only pulpit
whence Franklin preached to the people. He had
an excellent ideal of a newspaper. He got news
into it, which was seldom done in those days, and
which made it attractive; he got advertisements
into it, which made it pay, and which also was a
novel feature; indeed, Mr. Parton says that he
"originated the modern system of business advertis-
ing;" he also discussed matters of public interest.
Thus he anticipated the modern newspaper, but in
some respects improved in advance upon that which
he anticipated. He made his "Gazette" a vehicle

for disseminating information and morality, and he
carefully excluded from it "all libeling and personal abuse." The sheet in its every issue was
doing the same sort of work as "Poor Richard."
In a word, Franklin was a born teacher of men,
and what he did in this way in these his earlier
days gives him rank among the most distinguished
moralists who have ever lived.

What kind of morality he taught is well known.
It was human; he kept it free from entangling
alliances with any religious creed; its foundations
lay in common sense, not in faith. His own nature in this respect is easy to understand but difficult to describe, since the words which must be
used convey such different ideas to different persons. Thus, to say that he had the religious temperament, though he was skeptical as to all the
divine and supernatural dogmas of the religions of
mankind, will seem to many a self-contradiction,
while to others it is entirely intelligible. In his
boyhood one gets a flavor of irreverence which was
slow in disappearing. When yet a mere child he
suggested to his father the convenience of saying
grace over the whole barrel of salt fish, in bulk, as
the mercantile phrase would be. By the time that
he was sixteen, Shaftesbury and Collins, efficiently
aided by the pious writers who had endeavored to
refute them, had made him "a real doubter in many
points of our religious doctrine;" and while he was
still his brother's apprentice in Boston, he fell into
disrepute as a skeptic. Apparently he gathered

momentum in moving along this line of thought, until in England his disbelief took on for a time an extreme and objectionable form. His opinions then were "that nothing could possibly be wrong in the world; and that vice and virtue were empty distinctions, no such things existing." But the pamphlet, already mentioned, in which he expressed these views, was the outburst of a youthful free-thinker not yet accustomed to his new ideas; not many years passed over his head before it "appear'd not so clever a performance as [he] once thought it;" and in his autobiography he enumerates it among the "errata" of his life.

It was not so very long afterward that he busied himself in composing prayers, and even an entire litany, for his own use. No Christian could have found fault with the morals therein embodied; but Christ was entirely ignored. He even had the courage to draw up a new version of the Lord's Prayer; and he arranged a code of thirteen rules after the fashion of the Ten Commandments; of these the last one was: "Imitate Jesus and So-crates." Except during a short time just preced-ing and during his stay in London he seems never to have been an atheist; neither was he ever quite a Christian; but as between atheism and Chris-tianity he was very much further removed from the former than from the latter. He used to call himself a deist, or theist; and said that a deist was as much like an atheist as chalk is like char-coal. The evidence is abundant that he settled down into a belief in a personal God, who was good, who concerned himself with the affairs of men, who was pleased with good acts and displeased with evil ones. He believed also in immortality and in rewards in a life to come. But he supported none of these beliefs upon the same basis on which Christians support them.

Unlike the infidel school of that day he had no antipathy even to the mythological portions of the Christian religion, no desire to discredit it, nor ambition to distinguish himself in a crusade against it. On the contrary, he was always resolute to live well with it. His mind was too broad, his habit of thought too tolerant, to admit of his antagonizing so good a system of morals because it was intertwined with articles of faith which he did not believe. He went to church frequently, and always paid his contribution towards the expenses of the society; but he kept his commendation only for those practical sermons which showed men how to become virtuous. In like manner the instruction which he himself inculcated was strictly confined to those virtues which promote the welfare and happiness of the individual and of society. In fact he recognized none other; that which did not advance these ends was but a spurious pretender to the title of virtue.

One is tempted to make many quotations from Franklin's writings in this connection; but two or three must suffice. In 1743 he wrote to his sister : —

"There are some things in your New England doctrine and worship which I do not agree with; but I do not therefore condemn them, or desire to shake your belief or practice of them. We may dislike things that are nevertheless right in themselves. I would only have you make me the same allowance, and have a better opinion both of morality and your brother."

In 1756 he wrote to a friend : —

"He that for giving a draught of water to a thirsty person should expect to be paid with a good plantation, would be modest in his demands compared with those who think they deserve Heaven for the little good they do on earth. . . . For my own part, I have not the vanity to think I deserve it, the folly to expect it, nor the ambition to desire it; but content myself in submitting to the will and disposal of that God who made me, who hitherto has preserved and blessed me, and in whose fatherly goodness I may well confide. . . . .

"The faith you mention has doubtless its use in the world; I do not desire it to be diminished, nor would I endeavor to lessen it in any man. But I wish it were more productive of good works than I have generally seen it. I mean real good works, — works of kindness, charity, mercy, and public spirit; not holiday-keeping, sermon-reading or hearing, performing church ceremonies, or making long prayers, filled with flatteries and compliments despised even by wise men and much less capable of pleasing the Deity. The worship of God is a duty, the hearing and reading of sermons may be useful; but if men rest in hearing and praying, as too many do, it is as if a tree should value itself in being watered and putting forth leaves, tho' it never produced any fruit."

Throughout his life he may be said to have very slowly moved nearer and nearer to the Christian faith, until at last he came so near that many of those somewhat nondescript persons who call themselves "liberal Christians" might claim him as one of themselves. But if a belief in the divinity of Christ is necessary to make a "Christian," it does not appear that Franklin ever fully had the qualification. When he was an old man, in 1790, President Stiles of Yale College took the freedom of interrogating him as to his religious faith. It was the first time that any one had ever thus ventured. His reply[1] is interesting: "As to Jesus of Nazareth," he says, "I think his system of morals and his religion, as he left them to us, the best the world ever saw, or is like to see." But he thinks they have been corrupted. "I have, with most of the present dissenters in England, some doubts as to his divinity; though it is a question I do not dogmatize upon, having never studied it, and think it needless to busy myself with it now, when I expect soon an opportunity of knowing the truth with less trouble. I see no harm, however, in its being believed, if that belief has the good consequences, as probably it has, of making his doctrines more respected and more observed; especially as I do not see that the Supreme takes it amiss by distinguishing the unbelievers in his government of the world with any peculiar marks of his displeasure." His God was substantially the God of

[1] *Works,* x. 192.

Christianity; but concerning Christ he was generally reticent and non-committal.

Whatever were his own opinions, which undoubtedly underwent some changes during his life, as is the case with most of us, he never introduced Christianity, as a faith, into any of his moral writings. A broad human creature, with a marvelous knowledge of mankind, with a tolerance as far-reaching as his knowledge, with a kindly liking for all men and women; withal a prudent, shrewd, cool-headed observer in affairs, he was content to insist that goodness and wisdom were valuable, as means, towards good repute and well-being, as ends. He urges upon his nephew, about to start in business as a goldsmith, "*perfect honesty;*" and the reason he gives for his emphasis is, that the business is peculiarly liable to suspicion, and if a man is "once detected in the smallest fraud . . . at once he is ruined." The character of his argument was always simple. He usually began with some such axiom as the desirability of success in one's enterprises, or of health, or of comfort, or of ease of mind, or a sufficiency of money; and then he showed that some virtue, or collection of virtues, would promote this result. He advocated honesty upon the same principle upon which he advocated that women should learn to keep accounts, or that one should hold one's self in the background in the presentation of an enterprise such as his public library; that is to say, his advocacy of a cardinal virtue, of acquiring a piece of knowledge, or of adopting a

certain method of procedure in business, ran upon
the same line, namely, the practical usefulness of
the virtue, the knowledge, or the method, for increasing the probability of a practical success in
worldly affairs. Among the articles inculcating
morality which he used to put into his newspaper
was a Socratic Dialogue, "tending to prove that
whatever might be his parts and abilities, a vicious
man could not properly be called a man of sense."

He was forever at this business; it was his nature
to teach, to preach, to moralize. With creeds he
had no concern, but took it as his function in life
to instruct in what may be described as *useful
morals*, the gospel of good sense, the excellence of
common humanity. About the time in his career
which we have now reached this tendency of his
had an interesting development in its relationship
to his own character. He "conceiv'd the bold and
arduous project of arriving at moral perfection."
It is impossible to recite the details of his scheme,
but the narration constitutes one of the most entertaining and characteristic parts of the autobiography. Such a plan could not long be confined in its
operation to himself alone; the teacher must teach;
accordingly he designed to write a book, to be
called "The Art of Virtue," a title with which he
was greatly pleased, as indicating that the book was
to show "the means and manner of obtaining virtue" as contradistinguished from the "mere exhor-
tation to be good, that does not instruct or indicate
the means." A receipt book for virtues! Practi-

cal instructions for acquiring goodness! Nothing could have been more characteristic. One of his Busy-Body papers, February 18, 1728, begins with the statement that: "It is said that the Persians, in their ancient constitution, had public schools in which virtue was taught as a liberal art, or science;" and he goes on to laud the plan highly. Perhaps this was the origin of the idea which subsequently became such a favorite with him. It was his

"design to explain and enforce this doctrine: that vicious actions are not hurtful because they are forbidden, but forbidden because they are hurtful, the nature of man alone considered; that it was therefore every one's interest to be virtuous who wished to be happy even in this world; and I should . . . have endeavored to convince young persons that no qualities were so likely to make a poor man's fortune as those of probity and integrity."

Long years afterward, in 1760, he wrote about it to Lord Kames: —

"Many people lead bad lives that would gladly lead good ones, but do not know *how* to make the change. . . . To expect people to be good, to be just, to be temperate, etc., without *showing* them *how* they should *become* so seems like the ineffectual charity mentioned by the apostle, which consists in saying to the hungry, the cold, and the naked, 'Be ye fed, be ye warmed, be ye clothed,' without showing them how they should get food, fire, or clothing. . . . To acquire those [virtues] that are wanting, and secure what we acquire, as well as those we have naturally, is the subject of *an art*. It is as properly an art as painting, navigation, or architecture. If a man would become a painter, navigator, or architect, it is not enough that he is *advised* to be one, that he is *convinced* by the arguments of his adviser that it would be for his advantage to be one, and that he resolves to be one; but he must also be taught the principles of the art, be shown all the methods of working, and how to acquire the habit of using properly all the instruments. . . . My 'Art of Virtue' has also its instruments, and teaches the manner of using them."

He was then full of zeal to give this instruction. A year later he said: "You will not doubt my being serious in the intention of finishing my "Art of Virtue." It is not a mere ideal work. I planned it first in 1732. . . .The materials have been growing ever since. The form only is now to be given." He even says that "experiments" had been made "with success;" one wonders how; but he gives no explanation. Apparently Franklin never definitely abandoned this pet design; one catches glimpses of it as still alive in his mind, until it seems to fade away in the dim obscurity of extreme old age. He said of it that it was only part of "a great and extensive project that required the whole man to execute," and his countrymen never allowed Franklin such uninterrupted possession of himself.

A matter more easy of accomplishment was the drawing up a creed which he thought to contain "the essentials of every known religion," and to be "free of everything that might shock the professors of any religion." He intended that this should serve as the basis of a sect, which should practice his rules for self-improvement. It was at first to consist of "young and single men only," and great caution was to be exercised in the admission of members. The association was to be called the "Society of the Free and Easy;" "free, as being, by the general practice and habit of the virtues, free from the dominion of vice; and particularly by the practice of industry and frugality free from debt, which exposes a man to confinement and a species of slavery to his creditors." It is hardly surprising to hear that this was one of the very few failures of Franklin's life. In 1788 he professed himself "still of the opinion that it was a practicable scheme." One hardly reads it without a smile nowadays, but it was not so out of keeping with the spirit and habits of those times. It indicates at least Franklin's appreciation of the power of fellowship, of association. No man knew better than he what stimulus comes from the sense of membership in a society, especially a secret society. He had a great fondness for organizing men into associations, and a singular aptitude for creating, conducting, and perpetuating such bodies. The Junto, a child of his active brain, became a power in local public affairs, though organized and conducted strictly as a "club of mutual improvement." He formed it among his "ingenious acquaintance" for the discussion of "queries on any point of morals, politics, or natural philosophy." He found his model, without doubt, in the "neighborhood

benefit societies," established by Cotton Mather,
during Franklin's boyhood, among the Boston
churches, for mutual improvement among the members.[1] In time there came a great pressure for an
increase of the number of members ; but Franklin
astutely substituted a plan whereby each member
was to form a subordinate club, similar to the original, but having no knowledge of its connection
with the Junto. Thus sprang into being five or six
more, "The Vine, The Union, The Band, etc.,"
"answering, in some considerable degree, our views
of influencing the public opinion upon particular
occasions." When Franklin became interested in
any matter, he had but to introduce it before the
Junto for discussion ; straightway each member
who belonged to any one of the other societies
brought it up in that society. Thus through so
many active-minded and disputatious young men
interest in the subject speedily percolated through
a community of no greater size than Philadelphia.
Franklin was the tap-root of the whole growth, and
sent his ideas circulating throughout all the wide-
spreading branches. He tells us that in fact he
often used this efficient machinery to much advantage in carrying through his public and *quasi* public measures. Thus he anticipated more powerful
mechanisms of the like kind, such as the Jacobin
Club ; and he himself, under encouraging circumstances, might have wielded an immense power as
the creator and occult, inspiring influence of some
great political society.

---

[1] Parton's *Life of Franklin*, i. 47.

Besides his didactic newspaper, his almanac even more didactic, the Junto, the subscription library, the Society of the Free and Easy, his system of religion and morals, and his scheme for acquiring all the virtues, Franklin was engaged in many other matters. He learned French, Italian, and Spanish; and in so doing evolved some notions which are now beginning to find their way into the system of teaching languages in our schools and colleges. In 1736 he was chosen clerk to the General Assembly, and continued to be reëlected during the next fourteen years, until he was chosen a member of the legislature itself. In 1737 he was appointed postmaster of Philadelphia, an office which he found "of great advantage, for, tho' the salary was small, it facilitated the correspondence that improv'd my newspaper, increased the number demanded, as well as the advertisements to be inserted, so that it came to afford me a considerable income. My old competitor's newspaper declined proportionably, and I was satisfied without retaliating his refusal, while postmaster, to permit my papers being carried by the riders."

Soon afterward he conferred a signal benefit on his countrymen by inventing an "open stove for the better warming of rooms, and at the same time saving fuel,"— the Franklin stove, or, as he called it, "the Pennsylvania fireplace." Mr. Parton warmly describes it as the beginning of "the American stove system, one of the wonders of the industrial world." Franklin refused to take out a patent for

it, " from a principle which has ever weighed with
me on such occasions, viz. : That as we enjoy great
advantages from the inventions of others, we should
be glad of an opportunity to serve others by any
invention of ours; and this we should do freely
and generously." This lofty sentiment, wherein
the philanthropist got the better of the man of
business, overshot its mark ; an iron-monger of
London, who did not combine philosophy and philanthropy with his trade, made " some small
changes in the machine, which rather hurt its
operation, got a patent for it there, and made a little fortune by it."

A little later Franklin founded a philosophical
society, not intended to devote its energies to abstractions, but rather to a study of nature, and the
spread of new discoveries and useful knowledge in
practical affairs, especially in the way of farming
and agriculture. Franklin always had a fancy for
agriculture, and conferred many a boon upon the
tillers of the soil. A good story, which may be
true, tells how he showed the fertilizing capacity of
plaster of paris. In a field by the roadside he
wrote, with plaster, THIS HAS BEEN PLASTERED ;
and soon the brilliant green of the letters carried
the lesson to every passer-by.

In 1743 Franklin broached the idea of an academy; but the time had not quite come when the
purse-strings of well-to-do Pennsylvanians could be
loosened for this purpose, and he had no success.
It was, however, a project about which he was much

in earnest, and a few years later he returned to it
with better auspices. He succeeded in getting it
under weigh by means of private subscriptions. It
soon vindicated its usefulness, drew funds and en-
dowments from various sources, and became the
University of Pennsylvania. Franklin tells an
amusing story about his subsequent connection
with it. Inasmuch as persons of several religious
sects had contributed to the fund, it was arranged
that the board of trustees should consist of one
member from each sect. After a while the Moravian died; and his colleagues, having found him obnoxious to them, resolved not to have another of
the same creed. Yet it was difficult to find any
one who did not belong to, and therefore unduly
strengthen, some sect already represented. At
length Franklin was mentioned as being "*merely
an honest man*, and of no sect at all." The recommendation secured his election. It was always a
great cause of his success and influence that nothing could be alleged against his correct and respectable exterior and prudent, moderate deportment.

He now endeavored to reorganize the system, if
system it can be called, of the night-watch in Philadelphia. His description of it is picturesque: —

"It was managed by the constables of the respective
wards, in turn; the constable warned a number of
housekeepers to attend him for the night. Those who
chose never to attend paid him six shillings to be ex-
cus'd, which was supposed to be for hiring substitutes,
but was, in reality, much more than was necessary for

that purpose, and made the constableship a place of profit; and the constable, for a little drink, often got such ragamuffins about him as a watch, that respectable house-keepers did not choose to mix with. Walking the rounds, too, was often neglected, and most of the nights spent in tippling."

But even Franklin's influence was overmatched by this task. An abuse, nourished by copious rum, strikes its roots deep, and many years elapsed before this one could be eradicated.

In another enterprise Franklin shrewdly enlisted the boon-companion element on his side, with the result of immediate and brilliant success. He began as usual by reading a paper before the Junto, and through this intervention set the people thinking concerning the utter lack of any organization for extinguishing fires in the town. In consequence the Union Fire Company was soon established, the first thing of the kind in the city. Franklin continued a member of it for half a century. It was thoroughly equipped and efficiently conducted. An item in the terms of association was that the members should spend a social evening together once a month. The example was followed; other companies were formed, and fifty years later Franklin boasted that since that time the city had never "lost by fire more than one or two houses at a time; and the flames have often been extinguished before the house in which they began has been half consumed."

About this time he became interested in the matter of the public defenses, and wrote a pamphlet, "Plain Truth," showing the helpless condition of Pennsylvania as against the French and their Indian allies. The result was that the people were alarmed and aroused. Even the Quakers winked at the godless doings of their fellow-citizens, while the enrollment and drill of a volunteer force went forward, and funds were raised for building and arming a battery. Franklin suggested a lottery, to raise money, and went to New York to borrow guns. He was very active and very successful; and though the especial crisis fortunately passed away without use being made of these preparations, yet his energy and efficiency greatly enhanced his reputation in Pennsylvania.

That Franklin had been prospering in his private business may be judged from the facts that in 1748 he took into partnership David Hall, who had been a fellow journeyman with him in London ; and that his purpose was substantially to retire and get some "leisure . . . for philosophical studies and amusements." He cherished the happy but foolish notion of becoming master of his own time. But his fellow-citizens had purposes altogether inconsistent with those pleasing and comfortable plans which he sketched so cheerfully in a letter to his friend Colden in September, 1748. The Philadelphians, whom he had taught thrift, were not going to waste such material as he was. "The publick," he found, "now considering me as a man of leisure, laid hold of me for their purposes; every

part of our civil government, and almost at the
same time, imposing some duty upon me. The
governor put me into the commission of the peace;
the corporation of the city chose me of the common
council, and soon after an alderman; and the citizens at large chose me a burgess to represent them
in the Assembly." This last position pleased him
best, and he turned himself chiefly to its duties,
with the gratifying result, as he records, that the
" trust was repeatèd every year for ten years, without my ever asking any elector for his vote, or signifying, either directly or indirectly, any desire of
being chosen."

The next year he was appointed a commissioner
to treat with the Indians, in which business he had
so much success as can ever attend upon engagements with savages. He gives an amusing account
of the way in which all the Indian emissaries got
drunk, and of their quaint apology: that the Great
Spirit had made all things for some use; that
" when he made rum, he said, ' Let this be for the
Indians to get drunk with;' *and it must be so.*"

In 1751 he assisted Dr. Bond in the foundation
of his hospital. The doctor at first tried to carry
out his scheme alone, but could not. The tranquil
vanity of Franklin's narration is too good to be
lost: " At length he came to me, with the compliment that he found there was no such thing as
carrying a public-spirited project through, without
my being concerned in it. ' For,' says he, ' I am
often asked by those to whom I propose subscrib-

ing, Have you consulted Franklin upon this business? and what does he think of it? And when I
tell them that I have not (supposing it rather out
of your line), they do not subscribe, but say they
will consider of it.'" It is surprising that this artful and sugar-tongued doctor, who evidently could
read his man, had not been more successful with
his subscription list. With Franklin, at least, he
was eminently successful, touching him with a con-
summate skill which brought prompt response and
coöperation. The result was as usual. Franklin's
hand knew the way to every Philadelphian merchant's pocket. Respected as he was, it may be
doubted whether he was always sincerely welcomed
as he used to move from door to door down those
tranquil streets, with an irresistible subscription
paper in his hand. In this case private subscriptions were eked out by public aid. The legislature was applied to for a grant. The country
members objected, said that the benefit would be
local, and doubted whether even the Philadelphians
wanted it. Thereupon Franklin drew a bill, by
which the State was to give £2,000 upon condition
that a like sum should be raised from private
sources. This was soon done. Franklin regarded
his device as a novelty and a ruse in legislation.
He complacently says: "I do not remember any of
my political manœuvres, the success of which gave
me at the time more pleasure, or wherein, after
thinking of it, I more easily excused myself for
having made some use of cunning." Simple times,

in which such an act could be described as a "ma-
nœuvre" and " cunning !."

He further turned his attention to matters of
local improvement. He got pavements laid ; and
even brought about the sweeping of the streets
twice in each week. Lighting the streets came almost simultaneously ; and in connection with this
he showed his wonted ingenuity. Globes open only
at the top had heretofore been used, and by reason
of the lack of draught, they became obscured by
smoke early in the evening. Franklin made them
of four flat panes, with a smoke-funnel, and crevices
to admit the air beneath. The Londoners had
long had the method before their eyes, every evening, at Vauxhall ; but had never got at the notion
of transferring it to the open streets.

For a long while Franklin was employed by the
postmaster-general of the colonies as "his comp-
troller in regulating several offices and bringing the
officers to account." In 1753 the incumbent died,
and Franklin and Mr. William Hunter, jointly,
were appointed his successors. They set to work
to reform the entire postal service of the country.
The first cost to themselves was considerable, the
office falling more than £900 in debt to them during the first four years. But thereafterward the
benefit of their measures was felt, and an office
which had never before paid anything to that of
Great Britain came, under their administration,
" to yield three times as much clear revenue to the
crown as the post - office of Ireland." Franklin

narrates that in time he was displaced " by a freak
of the ministers," and in happy phrase adds,
" Since that imprudent transaction, they have received from it — not one farthing ! " In this connection it may be worth while to quote Franklin's
reply to a request to give a position to his nephew,
a young man whom he liked well, and otherwise
aided. " If a vacancy should happen, it is very
probable he may be thought of to supply it ; but it
is a rule with me not to remove any officer that
behaves well, keeps regular accounts, and pays
duly ; and I think the rule is founded on reason
and justice."

At this point in his autobiography he records,
with just pride, that he received the degree of
Master of Arts, first from Yale College and afterward from Harvard. " Thus, without studying in
any college, I came to partake of their honors.
They were conferred in consideration of my improvements and discoveries in the electric branch
of natural philosophy."

An interesting page in the autobiography concerns events in the year 1754. There were distinct
foreshadowings of that war between England and
France which soon afterward broke out, beginning
upon this side of the water earlier than in Europe ;
and the lords of trade ordered a congress of commissioners from the several colonies to assemble
at Albany for a conference with the chiefs of
the Six Nations. They came together June 19,
1754. Franklin was a deputy from Pennsylvania ;

and on his way thither he "projected and drew a
plan for the union of all the colonies under one
government, so far as might be necessary for defense and other important general purposes." It
was not altogether a new idea; in 1697 William
Penn had suggested a commercial union and an
annual congress. The journal of the congress
shows that on June 24th it was unanimously voted
that a union of the colonies was "absolutely necessary for their security and defense." The Massachusetts delegation alone had been authorized to
consider the question of a union, and they had
power to enter into a confederation "as well in
time of peace as of war." Franklin had already
been urging this policy by writings in the Gazette,
and now, when the ideas of the different commissioners were brought into comparison, his were
deemed the best. His outline of a scheme, he says,
"happen'd to be preferr'd," and, with a few amendments, was accordingly reported. It was a league
rather than a union, somewhat resembling the
arrangement which came into existence for the
purposes of the Revolution. But it came to nothing; "its fate," Franklin said, "was singular."
It was closely debated, article by article, and having at length been "pretty unanimously accepted,
it came before the colonial assemblies for ratification." But they condemned it; "there was too
much prerogative in it," they thought. On the
other hand, the board of trade in England would
not approve it because it had "too much of the

democratic." All which led Franklin to " suspect that it was really the true medium." He himself acknowledged that one main advantage of it would be " that the colonies would, by this connection, learn to consider themselves, not as so many independent states, but as members of the same body; and thence be more ready to afford assistance and support to each other," etc. It was already the *national idea* which lay, not quite formulated, yet distinct enough in his mind. It was hardly to be expected that the home government would fail to see this tendency, or that they would look upon it with favor. Franklin long afterward indulged in some speculations as to what might have been the consequences of an adoption of his scheme, namely : united colonies, strong enough to defend themselves against the Canadian French and their Indian allies ; no need, therefore, of troops from England ; no pretext, therefore, for taxing the provinces ; no provocation, therefore, for rebellion. " But such mistakes are not new ; history is full of the errors of states and princes. . . . The best public measures are seldom *adopted from previous wisdom but forc'd by the occasion.*" But this sketch of what might have been sounds over-fanciful, and the English were probably right in thinking that a strong military union, with home taxation, involved more of danger than of safety for the future connection between the colonies and the mother country.

There was much uneasiness, much planning,

theorizing, and discussing going on at this time about the relationship between Great Britain and her American provinces ; earlier stages of that talk which kept on growing louder, more eager, and more disputatious, until it was swallowed up in the roar of the revolutionary cannon. Among others, Shirley, governor of Massachusetts, concocted a scheme and showed it to Franklin. By this an assembly of the governors of all the colonies, attended by one or two members of their respective councils, was to have authority to take such measures as should seem needful for defense, with power to draw upon the English treasury to meet expenses, the amount of such drafts to be " re-imbursed by a tax laid on the colonies by act of Parliament." This alarming proposition at once drew forth three letters from Franklin, written in December, 1754, and afterward published in the " London Chronicle " in December, 1766. His position amounted to this : that the business of self-defense and the expense thereof were matters neither beyond the abilities of the colonies, nor outside their willingness, and should therefore be managed by them. Their loyalty could be trusted ; their knowledge must be the best; on the other hand, governors were apt to be untrustworthy, self-seeking, and ignorant of provincial affairs. But the chief emphasis of his protest falls against taxation without representation. He says : —

" That it is supposed an undoubted right of Englishmen not to be taxed but by their own consent, given through their representatives.

"That the colonists have no representatives in Parliament.

"That compelling the colonists to pay money without their consent would be rather like raising contributions in an enemy's country, than taxing of Englishmen for their own public benefit.

"That it would be treating them as a conquered people, and not as true British subjects."

And so on ; traversing beforehand the same ground soon to be so thoroughly beaten over by the patriot writers and speakers of the colonies. In a very few years the line of argument became familiar, but for the present Franklin and a very few more were doing the work of suggestion and instruction for the people at large, teaching them by what logic their instinctive convictions could be maintained.

He further ingeniously showed that the colonists were already heavily taxed in ways from which they could not escape. Taxes paid by British artificers came out of the colonial consumers, and the colonists were compelled to buy only from Britain those articles which they would otherwise be able to buy at much lower prices from other countries. Moreover, they were obliged to sell only in Great Britain, where heavy imposts served to curtail the net profits of the producer. Even such manufactures as could be carried on in the colonies were forbidden to them. He concluded : —

"These kinds of secondary taxes, however, we do not complain of, though we have no share in the laying or disposing of them ; but to pay immediate, heavy taxes, in the laying, appropriation, and disposition of which we have no part, and which perhaps we may know to be as unnecessary as grievous, must seem hard measures to Englishmen, who cannot conceive that by hazarding their lives and fortunes in subduing and settling new countries, extending the dominion and increasing the commerce of the mother nation, they have forfeited the native rights of Britons, which they think ought rather to be given to them, as due to such merit, if they had been before in a state of slavery."

A third letter discussed a proposition advanced by Shirley for giving the colonies representation in Parliament. Franklin was a little skeptical, and had no notion of being betrayed by a kiss. A real unification of the two communities lying upon either side of the Atlantic, and even a close approximation to proportionate representation, would constitute an excellent way out of the present difficulties. But he saw no encouragement to hope for this.

In fact, the project of laying direct internal taxes upon the colonies by act of Parliament was taking firm root in the English mind, and colonial protests could not long stay the execution of the scheme. Even such grants of money as were made by some of the colonial legislatures were vetoed, on the ground that they were connected with encroachments, schemes for independence, and an assumption of the right to exercise control in the matter of the public finances.[1] The Penns rejoiced.

[1] Bancroft, *Hist. U. S.*, iv. 176.

Thomas Penn wrote, doubtless with a malicious chuckle : " If the several assemblies will not make provision for the general service, an act of Parliament may oblige them here." He evidently thought that it would be very wholesome if government should become incensed and severe with the recalcitrants.

During his discussion with Shirley, Franklin had been upon a visit to Boston. He " left New England," he says, " slowly, and with great reluctance ; " for he loved the country and the people. He returned home to be swept into the hurly-burly of military affairs. War appropriations came hard from the legislature of the Quaker province ; but the occasion was now at hand when come they must. In the autumn of 1755 £60,000 were voted, chiefly for defense, and Franklin was one of the committee in charge of the expenditure. The border was already unsafe, and formal hostilities on a large scale were close at hand. France and England must fight it out for the possession of the new continent, which, boundless as it then seemed, was yet not big enough to admit of their both dwelling in it. France had been steadily pressing upon the northern and western frontiers of the British colonies, and she now held Crown Point, Niagara, the fort on the present site of Pittsburg, and the whole valley of the Ohio River. It seemed that she would confine the English to the strip along the coast which they already occupied. It is true that she offered to relinquish the Ohio valley to the savages, to be a neutral belt between the European nations on either side of it. But the proposal could not be accepted; the French were much too clever in managing the Indians. Moreover, it was felt that they would never permanently desist from advancing. Then, too, the gallant Braddock was on his way across seas, with a little army of English regulars. Finally, the disproportion between the English and French in the New World was too great for the former to rest satisfied with a compromise. There were about 1,165,000 whites in the British Provinces, and only about 80,000 French in Canada. The resources, also, of the former were in every respect vastly greater. These iron facts must tell; were already telling. Throughout this last deadly grapple, now at hand, the French were in desperate earnest. History records few struggles wherein the strength of a combatant was more utterly spent, with more entire devotion, than was the case with these Canadian - French provinces. Every man gave himself to the fight, so literally that no one was left to till the fields, and erelong famine began its hideous work among the scanty forces. The English and Americans, on the other hand, were far from conducting the struggle with the like temper as the French; yet with such enormous advantages as they possessed, if they could not conquer a satisfactory peace in course of time, they ought to be ashamed of themselves. So no composition could be arranged; the Seven Years' War began, and to open it with becoming *éclat* Braddock debarked, a gorgeous spectacle in red and gold. Yet still there had as yet been in Europe no declaration of hostilities between England and France; on the contrary, the government of the former country was giving very fair words to that of the latter; and in America the British professed only to intend " to repel encroachments." [1]

Franklin had to take his share of the disasters attendant upon the fatal campaign of Braddock. According to his notion that foolish officer and his two ill-behaved regiments should never, by good rights, have been sent to the provinces at all; for the colonists, being able and willing to do their own fighting, should have been allowed to undertake it. But eleven years before this time the Duke of Bedford had declared it a dangerous policy to enroll an army of 20,000 provincials to serve against Canada, " on account of the independence it might create in those provinces, when they should see within themselves so great an army, possessed of so great a country by right of conquest." This anxiety had been steadily gaining ground. The home government did not choose " to permit the union of the colonies, as proposed at Albany, and to trust that union with their defense, lest they should thereby grow too military and feel their own strength, suspicions and jealousies being at this time entertained of them." So it was because the shadow of the Revolutionary War already darkened the visions of English statesmen that the gallant array of sol-

[1] Bancroft, *Hist. U. S.*, iv. 182.

diery, with the long train of American attendants, had to make that terrible march to failure and death.

The Assembly of the Quaker province was sadly perturbed lest this arbitrary warrior, encamped hard by in Virginia, should " conceive violent prejudices against them, as averse to the service." In their alarm they had recourse to Franklin's shrewd wit and ready tongue. Accordingly, he visited Braddock under pretense of arranging for the transmission of mails during the campaign, stayed with him several days, and dined with him daily. There were some kinds of men, perhaps, whom Braddock appreciated better than he did Indians; nor is it a slight proof of Franklin's extraordinary capacity for getting on well with every variety of human being that he could make himself so welcome to this testy, opinionated military martinet, who in every particular of nature and of training was the precise contrary of the provincial civilian.

Franklin's own good will to the cause, or his ill-luck, led him into an engagement, made just before his departure, whereby he undertook to procure horses and wagons enough for the transportation of the ordnance and all the appurtenances of the camp. It was not a personal contract upon his part to furnish these; he was neither to make any money, nor to risk any; he was simply to render the gratuitous service of inducing the Pennsylvania farmers to let out their horses, wagons, and drivers to the general. It was a difficult task, in which the emissaries of Braddock had utterly failed in Virginia. But Franklin conceived the opportunities to be better in his own Province, and entered on the business with vigor and skill. Throughout the farming region he sent advertisements and circulars, cleverly devised to elicit what he wanted, and so phrased as to save him harmless from personal responsibility for any payment. Seven days' pay was to be " advanced and paid in hand " by him, the remainder to be paid by General Braddock, or by the paymaster of the army. He said, in closing his appeal : " I have no particular interest in this affair, as, except the satisfaction of endeavoring to do good, I shall have only my labor for my pains."

But he was not to get off so easily ; for, he says, " the owners, . . . alleging that they did not know General Braddock, or what dependence might be had on his promise, insisted on my bond for the performance, which I accordingly gave them." This was the more patriotic because Franklin was by no means dazzled by the pomp and parade of the doughty warrior, but on the contrary, reflecting on the probable character of the campaign, he had " conceived some doubts and some fears for the event." What happened every one knows. The losses of wagons and horses in the slaughter amounted to the doleful sum of £20,000; " which to pay would have ruined me," wrote Franklin. Nevertheless the demands began at once to pour in upon him, and suits were instituted. It was a grievous affair, and the end was by no means clear. It was easily possible that in place of his fortune, sacrificed in the public service, he might have only the sorry substitute of a claim against the government. But after many troubled weeks he was at length relieved of the heaviest portion of his burden, through General Shirley's appointment of a commission to audit and pay the claims for actual losses. Other sums due him, representing considerable advances which he had made at the outset in the business, and later for provisions, remained unpaid to the end of his days. The British government in time probably thought the Revolution as efficient as a statute of limitations for barring that account. At the moment, however, Franklin not only lost his money, but had to suffer the affront of being supposed even to be a gainer, and to have filled his own pockets. He indignantly denied that he had "pocketed a farthing;" but of course he was not believed. He adds, with delicious humor : " and, indeed, I have since learnt that immense fortunes are often made in such employments." Those, however, were simple, provincial days. In place of the money which he did not get, also of the further sum which he actually lost, he had to satisfy himself with the consolation derived from the approbation of the Pennsylvania Assembly, while also Braddock's dispatches gave him a good name with the officials in England, which was of some little service to him.

A more comical result of the Braddock affair was that it made Franklin for a time a military

man and a colonel. He had escaped being a clergyman and a poet, but he could not escape that
common fate of Americans, the military title, the
prevalence of which, it has been said, makes "the
whole country seem a retreat of heroes." It befell
Franklin in this wise: immediately after Braddock's defeat, in the panic which possessed the
people and amid the reaction against professional
soldiers, recourse was had to plain good sense,
though unaccompanied by technical knowledge.
No one, as all the Province knew, had such sound
sense as Franklin, who was accordingly deputed to
go to the western frontier with a small volunteer
force, there to build three forts for the protection
of the outlying settlements. "I undertook," he
says, "this military business, though I did not conceive myself well qualified for it." It was a service involving much difficulty and hardship, with
some danger; General Braddock would have made
a ridiculous failure of it; Franklin acquitted himself well. What he afterward wrote of General
Shirley was true of himself: "For, tho' Shirley
was not bred a soldier, he was sensible and sagacious in himself, and attentive to good advice from
others, capable of forming judicious plans, and
quick and active in carrying them into execution."
In a word, Franklin's military career was as creditable as it was brief. He was called forward at
the crisis of universal dismay; he gave his popular
influence and cool head to a peculiar kind of service, of which he knew much by hearsay, if nothing

by personal experience; he did his work well; and, much stranger to relate, he escaped the delusion that he was a soldier. So soon as he could do so, that is to say after a few weeks, he returned to his civil duties. But he had shown courage, intelligence, and patriotism in a high degree, and he had greatly increased the confidence reposed in him by his fellow-citizens.

Beyond those active military measures which the exigencies of the time made necessary, Franklin fell in with, if he did not originate, a plan designed to afford permanent protection in the future. This was to extend the colonies inland. His notions were broad, embracing much both in space and time. He thought " what a glorious thing it would be to settle in that fine country a large, strong body of religious, industrious people. What a security to the other colonies and advantage to Britain by increasing her people, territory, strength, and commerce." He foretold that "perhaps in less than another century " the Ohio valley might " become a populous and powerful dominion, and a great accession of power either to England or France." Having this scheme much at heart, he drew up a sort of prospectus "for settling two western colonies in North America; " " barrier colonies " they were called by Governor Pownall, who was warm in the same idea, and sent a plan of his own, together with Franklin's, to the home government.

It is true that these new settlements, regarded strictly as bulwarks, would have been only a change of "barrier," an advancement of frontier; they themselves would become frontier instead of the present line, and would be equally subject to Indian and French assaults. Still the step was in the direction of growth and expansion; it was advancing and aggressive, and indicated an appreciation of the enormous motive power which lay in English colonization. Franklin pushed it earnestly, interested others in it, and seemed at one time on the point of securing the charters. But the conquest of Canada within a very short time rendered defensive colonization almost needless, and soon afterward the premonitions and actual outbreak of the Revolution put an end to all schemes in this shape.

CHAPTER III.

IT was not possible to make a world-wide reputation in the public affairs of the Province of Pennsylvania; but so much fame as opportunity would admit of had by this time been won by Franklin. In respect of influence and prestige among his fellow-colonists none other came near to him. Meanwhile among all his crowding occupations he had found time for those scientific researches towards which his heart always yearned. He had flown his famous kite; had entrapped the lightning of the clouds; had written treatises, which, having been collected into a volume, " were much taken notice of in England," made no small stir in France, and were " translated into the Italian, German, and Latin languages." A learned French abbé, " preceptor in natural philosophy to the royal family, and an able experimenter," at first controverted his discoveries and even questioned his existence. But after a little time this worthy scientist became " assur'd that there really existed such a person as Franklin at Philadelphia," while other distinguished scientific men of Europe united in the adoption of his theories. Kant called him the Prometheus of modern times. Thus, in one way and another, his name had probably already come to be more widely known than that of any other living man who had been born on this side of the Atlantic. It might have been even much more famous, had he been more free to follow his own bent, a pleasure which he could only enjoy in a very limited degree. In 1753 he wrote: "I am so engaged in business, public and private, that those more pleasing pursuits [philosophical enquiries] are frequently interrupted, and the chain of thought necessary to be closely continued in such disquisitions is so broken and disjointed that it is with difficulty I satisfy myself in any of them." Similar complaints occur frequently, and it is certain that his extensive philosophical labors were all conducted in those mere cracks and crannies of leisure scantily interspersed amid the hours of a man apparently overwhelmed with the functions of active life.

He was now selected by the Assembly to encounter the perils of crossing the Atlantic upon an important mission in behalf of his Province. For a long while past the relationship between the Penns, unworthy sons of the great William, and now the proprietaries, on the one side, and their *quasi* subjects, the people of the Province, upon the other, had been steadily becoming more and more strained, until something very like a crisis had been reached. As usual in English and Anglo-American communities, it was a quarrel over dollars, or rather over pounds sterling, a question of taxation, which was producing the alienation. At bottom, there was the trouble which always pertains to absenteeism; the proprietaries lived in England, and regarded their vast American estate, with about 200,000 white inhabitants, only as a source of revenue. That mercantile community, however, with the thrift of Quakers and the independent temper of Englishmen, had a shrewd appreciation of, and an obstinate respect for, its own interests. Hence the discussions, already of threatening proportions.

The chief point in dispute was, whether or not the waste lands, still directly owned by the proprietaries, and other lands let by them at quitrents, should be taxed in the same manner as like property of other owners. They refused to submit to such taxation ; the Assembly of Burgesses insisted. In ordinary times the proprietaries prevailed ; for the governor was their nominee and removable at their pleasure ; they gave him general instructions to assent to no law taxing their holdings, and he naturally obeyed his masters. But since governors got their salaries only by virtue of a vote of the Assembly, it seems that they sometimes disregarded instructions, in the sacred cause of their own interests. After a while, therefore, the proprietaries, made shrewd by experience, devised the scheme of placing their unfortunate sub-rulers under bonds. This went far towards settling the matter. Yet in such a crisis and stress as were now present in the colony, when exceptionally large sums had to be raised, and great sacrifices and sufferings endured, and when little less than the actual existence of the Province might be thought to be at stake, it certainly seemed that the rich and idle proprietaries might stand on the same footing with their poor and laboring subjects. They lived comfortably in England upon revenues estimated to amount to the then enormous sum of £20,000 sterling; while the colonists were struggling under unusual losses, as well as enormous expenses, growing out of the war and Indian ravages. At such a time their parsimony, their " incredible meanness," as Franklin called it, was cruel as well as stupid. At last the Assembly flatly refused to raise any money unless the proprietaries should be burdened like the rest. All should pay together, or all should go to destruction together. The Penns too stood obstinate, facing the not less resolute Assembly. It was indeed a deadlock! Yet the times were such that neither party could afford to maintain its ground indefinitely. So a temporary arrangement was made, whereby of £60,000 sterling to be raised the proprietaries agreed to contribute £5,000, and the Assembly agreed to accept the same in lieu or commutation for their tax. But neither side abandoned its principle. Before long more money was needed, and the dispute was as fierce as ever.

The burgesses now thought that it would be well to carry a statement of their case before the

king in council and the lords of trade. In
February, 1757, they named their speaker, Isaac
Norris, and Franklin to be their emissaries " to
represent in England the unhappy situation of the
Province," and to seek redress by an act of Parliament. Norris, an aged man, begged to be excused; Franklin accepted. His son was given
leave of absence, in order to attend him as his
secretary. During the prolonged and bitter con-
troversies Franklin had been the most prominent
member of the Assembly on the popular side. He
had drawn many of the addresses, arguments, and
other papers; and his familiarity with the business,
therefore, no less than his good judgment, shrewdness, and tact united to point him out as the man
for the very unpleasant and difficult errand.

A portion of his business also was to endeavor to
induce the king to resume the Province of Pennsylvania as his own. A clause in the charter had
reserved this right, which could be exercised on
payment of a certain sum of money. The colonists
now preferred to be an appanage of the crown
rather than a fief of the Penns. Oddly enough,
some of the provincial governors were suggesting
the like measure concerning other provinces; but
from widely different motives. The colonists
thought a monarch better than private individuals,
as a master; while the governors thought that only
the royal authority could enforce their theory of
colonial government. They angrily complained
that the colonies would do nothing voluntarily; a

most unjust charge, as was soon to be seen; for in the Seven Years' War the colonists did three quarters of all that was done. What the governors really meant was that the colonies would not raise money and turn it over to other persons to spend for them.

It must be acknowledged that the prospects for the success of this mission were not good. Almost simultaneously with Franklin's appointment, the House of Commons resolved that " the claim of right in a colonial Assembly to raise and apply public money, by its own act alone, is derogatory to the crown, and to the rights of the people of Great Britain." This made Thomas Penn jubilant. " The people of Pennsylvania," he said, " will soon be convinced . . . that they have not a right to the powers of government they claim." [1]

Franklin took his passage in a packet - ship, which was to sail from New York forthwith. But the vessel was subject to the orders of Lord Loudoun, newly appointed governor of the Province of New York, and a sort of military over-lord over all the governors, assemblies, and people of the American provinces. His mission was to organize, to introduce system and submission, and above all else to overawe. But he was no man for the task ; not because his lordship was not a dominant character, but because he was wholly unfit to transact business. Franklin tried some negotiations with him, and got no satisfaction or conclusion.

[1] Bancroft, *Hist. U. S.*, iv. 255.

The ship which waited upon the will of this noble procrastinator had a very doubtful future. Every day at nine o'clock his lordship seated himself at his desk, and stayed there writing industriously, hour after hour, upon his despatches; every day he foretold with much accuracy and positiveness of manner that these would surely be ready, and the ship would inevitably sail, on the next day. Thus week after week glided by, and still he uttered the same prediction, " to-morrow, and to-morrow, and to-morrow." Yet in spite of this wonderful industry of the great man his letters never got written, so that, says Franklin, " it was about the beginning of April that I came to New York, and I think it was the end of June before we sail'd." Even then the letters were not ready, and for two days the vessel had to accompany his lordship's fleet on the way towards Louisburg, before she got leave to go upon her own proper voyage. It is entertaining to hear that this same lord, during his stay in America, detained other packets for other letters, until their bottoms got so foul and worm-eaten that they were unseaworthy. He was irreverently likened by those who waited on his pleasure to " St. George on the signs, always on horseback, and never rides on." He was at last removed by Mr. Pitt, because that energetic minister said " that he never heard from him, and could not know what was doing."

Escaping at last from a detention more tedious, if less romantic, than any which ever befell Ulysses,

Franklin steered for England. The vessel was " several times chas'd " by French cruisers, and later was actually within a few lengths of being wrecked on the Scilly rocks. Franklin wrote to his wife that if he were a Roman Catholic he should probably vow a chapel to some saint; but, as he was not, he should much like to vow a light-house. At length, however, he came safely into Falmouth, and on July 27, 1757, arrived in London.

Immediately he was taken to see Lord Granville, president of the council; and his account of the interview is too striking not to be given entire. His lordship, he says,

" received me with great civility ; and after some questions respecting the present state of affairs in America and discourse thereupon, he said to me : ' You Americans have wrong ideas of the nature of your constitution ; you contend that the king's instructions to his governors are not laws, and think yourselves at liberty to regard or disregard them at your own discretion. But these instructions are not like the pocket instructions given to a minister going abroad, for regulating his conduct on some trifling point of ceremony. They are first drawn up by judges learned in the laws; they are then considered, debated, and perhaps amended, in council, after which they are signed by the king. They are then, so far as they relate to you, the *law of the land*, for the king is the *legislator of the colonies*.' I told his lordship this was new doctrine to me. I had always understood from our charters that our laws were to be made by our assemblies, to be presented indeed to the king for his royal assent; but that being once given, the king could not repeal or alter them. And as the assemblies could not make permanent laws without his assent, so neither could he make a law for them without theirs. He assured me I was totally mistaken. I did not think so, however ; and his lordship's conversation having somewhat alarmed me as to what might be the sentiments of the court concerning us, I wrote it down as soon as I returned to my lodgings." [1]

Granville also defended the recent act of Parliament laying " grievous restrictions on the export of provisions from the British colonies," the intent being to distress the American possessions of France by famine. His lordship said: " America must not do anything to interfere with Great Britain in the European markets." Franklin replied : " If we plant and reap, and must not ship, your lordship should apply to Parliament for transports to bring us all back again."

Next came an interview with the proprietaries. Each side declared itself disposed towards " reasonable accommodations ; " but Franklin supposed that " each party had its own ideas of what should be meant by *reasonable.*" Nothing came of all this palaver ; which only meant that time was being wasted to no better purpose than to show that the two parties were " very wide, and so far from each other in [their] opinions as to discourage all hope of agreement." But this had long been evident. The lawyer of the proprietaries was then

[1] *Works*, i. 295, 296 ; see also an account, substantially the same, in letter to Bowdoin, January 13, 1772.

put forward. He was a " proud, angry man," with a " mortal enmity " toward Franklin ; for the two had exchanged buffets more than once already, and the " proud angry man " had been hit hard. It had been his professional duty, as counsel for the Penns, to prepare many papers to be used by their governor in the course of their quarrels with the Assembly. It had usually fallen to Franklin's lot to draft the replies of the Assembly, and by Franklin's own admission these documents of his, like those which they answered, were " often tart and sometimes indecently abusive." Franklin now found his old antagonist so excited that it seemed best to refuse to have any direct dealings with him.

The proprietaries then put their interests in charge of Attorney-General Pratt, afterwards Lord Camden, and the Solicitor-General Charles Yorke, afterward Lord Chancellor. These legal lumina- ries consumed " a year, wanting eight days " before they were in a condition to impart light; and dur- ing that period Franklin could of course achieve nothing with the proprietaries. After all, the pro- prietaries ignored and insulted him, and made further delay by sending a message to the Assem- bly of Pennsylvania, wherein they complained of Franklin's " rudeness," and professed themselves " willing to accommodate matters," if a " person of candour " should be sent to treat with them. The only reply to their message came in the pointed and intelligible shape of an act " taxing the pro- prietary estate in common with the estates of the people." Much disturbed, the proprietaries now obtained a hearing before the king in council. They requested his majesty to set aside this tax act, and several other acts which had been passed within two years by the Assembly. Of these other acts some were repealed, according to the prayer of the proprietaries ; but more were allowed to stand. These were, however, of comparatively little consequence ; the overshadowing grievance for the Penns lay in this taxation of their property. Concerning this it was urged by their counsel that the proprietaries were held in such odium by the people that, if left to the popular " mercy in apportioning the taxes, they would be ruined." The other side, of course, vehemently denied that there was the slightest ground for such a suspicion.

In June, 1760, the board of trade rendered a report very unfavorable to the Assembly. Their language showed that they had been much affected by the appearance of popular encroachments, and by the allegations of an intention on the part of the colonists " to establish a democracy in place of his majesty's government." Their advice was to bring " the constitution back to its proper principles ; to restore to the crown, in the person of the proprietaries, its just prerogative ; to check the growing influence of assemblies, by distinguishing, what they are perpetually confounding, the executive from the legislative power." News of this alarming document reached Franklin just as he was about to start upon a trip through Ireland.

It put an end to that pleasure; he had to set to work on the moment, with all the zeal and by all the means he could compass, to counteract this fulmination. Just how he achieved so difficult an end is not recorded; but it appears that he suc- ceeded in securing a further hearing, in the pro- gress of which Lord Mansfield " rose, and beckon- ing me, took me into the clerk's chambers, . . . and asked me, if I was really of opinion that no injury would be done to the proprietary estate in the execution of the act. I said : Certainly. ' Then,' says he, ' you can have little objection to enter into an engagement to assure that point.' I answered : None at all." Thereupon a paper of this purport, binding personally upon Franklin and upon Mr. Charles, the resident agent of the Province, was drawn up, and was duly executed by them both; and on August 28th the lords filed an amended report, in which they said that the act taxing the proprietary estates upon a common basis with those of other owners was " fundamen- tally wrong and unjust and ought to be repealed, *unless* six certain amendments were made therein." These amendments were, in substance, the under- takings entered into in the bond of the colonial agents. Franklin soon afterward had occasion to review this whole business. He showed that of the six amendments, five were immaterial, since they only expressed with greater clearness the intent of the Assembly. He admitted that the sixth was of more consequence. It seems that £100,000 had been voted, appropriated, raised and, expended, chiefly for the defense of the colony. The manner of doing this was to issue paper money to this amount, to make it legal tender, and then to retire it by the proceeds of the tax levy. The proprietaries insisted that they could not be compelled to receive their rents in this money, and the lords now found for them. Franklin acknowledged that herein perhaps the lords were right and the Assembly wrong; but he added this scathing paragraph: —

"But if he cannot on these considerations quite excuse the Assembly, what will he think of those honourable proprietaries, who, when paper money was issued in their colony for the *common defense* of their vast estates with those of the people, could nevertheless wish to be exempted from their share of the unavoidable disadvantages. Is there upon earth a man besides, with any conception of what is honest, with any notion of honor, with the least tincture in his veins of the gentleman, but would have blushed at the thought, but would have rejected with disdain such undue preference, if it had been offered him? Much less would he have struggled for it, moved heaven and earth to obtain it, resolved to ruin thousands of his tenants by a repeal of the act, rather than miss of it, and enforce it afterwards by an audaciously wicked instruction, forbidding aids to his king, and exposing the Province to destruction, unless it was complied with. And yet, these are honourable men!"

This was, however, altogether a subordinate issue.

The struggle had really been conducted to determine whether the proprietary estate should be
taxed like other estates, and the decision upheld
such taxation. This was a complete triumph for
the Assembly and their representative. " But let
the proprietaries and their discreet deputies hereafter recollect and remember," said Franklin, " that
the same august tribunal, which censured some of
the modes and circumstances of that act, did at the
same time establish and confirm the grand principle of the act, namely : ' That the proprietary
estate ought, with other estates, to be taxed ; ' and
thereby did, in effect, determine and pronounce
that the opposition so long made in various shapes
to that just principle, by the proprietaries, was
' fundamentally *wrong* and *unjust !* ' "

It was a long while before the Assembly found
leisure to attend to that engagement of their agents
which stipulated for an investigation to see whether
the proprietaries had not been unduly and exces-
sively assessed. But at length, after having had
the spur of reminder constantly applied to their
laggard memories, they appointed a committee to
inquire and report concerning the valuations made
by the tax-gatherers.

This committee reported that —

" there has not been any injustice done to the proprietaries, or attempts made to rate or assess any part of
their estates higher than the estates of the like kind belonging to the inhabitants are rated and assessed ; but,

on the contrary, . . . their estates are rated, in many instances, below others."

So the matter ended.

Franklin had been detained a little more than three years about this business. At its conclusion he anticipated a speedy return home; but he had to stay yet two years more to attend to sundry matters smaller in importance, but which were advanced almost as slowly. Partly such delay was because the aristocrats of the board of trade and the privy council had not the habits of business men, but consulted their own noble convenience in the transaction of affairs; and partly it was because procrastination was purposely employed by his opponents, who harassed him and blocked his path by every obstacle, direct and indirect, which they could put in his way. For they seemed to hope for some turn in affairs, some event, or some too rapid advance of the popular party in America, which should arouse the royal resentment against the colonists and so militate on their side. Delay was easily brought about by them. They had money, connections, influence, and that familiarity with men and ways which came from their residence in England; while Franklin, a stranger on an unpopular errand, representing before an aristocratic government a parcel of tradespeople and farmers who lived in a distant land and were charged with being both niggardly and disaffected, found that he could make only difficult and uncertain progress. He was like one who sails a race not only against hostile winds and tides, but also in strange waters where the shoals and rocks are unknown, and where invisible currents ceaselessly baffle his course. His lack of personal importance hampered him exasperatingly. Thus during his prolonged stay he repeatedly made every effort in his power to obtain an audience of William Pitt. But not even for once could he succeed. A provincial agent, engaged in a squabble about taxing proprietary lands, was too small a man upon too small a business to consume the precious time of the great prime minister, who was endeavoring to dominate the embroilments and intrigues of all Europe, to say nothing of the machinations of his opponents at home. So the subalterns of Mr. Pitt met Franklin, heard what he had to say, sifted it through the sieve of their own discretion, and bore to the ears of their principal only such compends as they thought worthy of attention.

But the vexation of almost endless delay had its alleviations, apparently much more than enough to offset it. Early in September, 1757, that is to say some five or six weeks after his landing, Franklin was taken very ill of an intermittent fever, which lasted for eight weeks. During his convalescence he wrote to his wife that the agreeable conversation of men of learning, and the notice taken of him by persons of distinction, soothed him under this painful absence from family and friends; yet these solaces would not hold him there another week, were it not for duty to his country and the

hope of being able to do it service. But after the
early homesickness wore off, a great attachment for
England took its place. He found himself a man
of note among scientists there, who gave him a
ready welcome and showed a courteous and flattering recognition of his high distinction in their pursuits. Thence it was easy to penetrate into the
neighboring circle of literature, wherein he made
warm personal friends, such as Lord Kames, David
Hume, Dr. Robertson, and others. From time to
time he was a guest at many a pleasant country
seat, and at the universities. He found plenty of
leisure, too, for travel, and explored the United
Kingdom very thoroughly. When he went to Edinburgh he was presented with the freedom of the
city; and the University of St. Andrews conferred
on him the degree of Doctor of Laws; later, Oxford did the same. He even had time for a trip
into the Low Countries. As months and finally
years slipped away, with just enough of occupation
of a dignified character to save him from an annoying sense of idleness, with abundant opportunities
for social pleasure, and with a very gratifying deference shown towards himself, Franklin, who liked
society and did not dislike flattery, began to think
the mother country no such bad place. For an intellectual and social career London certainly had
advantages over Philadelphia. Mr. Strahan, the
well-known publisher of those days, whom Franklin
used affectionately to call Straney, became his close
friend, and was very insistent with him that he

should leave the Provinces and take up a permanent residence in England. He baited his hook with an offer of his son in marriage with Franklin's daughter Sarah. He had never seen Sarah, but he seems to have taken it for granted that any child of her father must be matrimonially satisfactory. Franklin wrote home to his wife that the young man was eligible, and that there were abundant funds in the Strahan treasury; but that he did not suppose that she would be able to overcome her terror of the ocean voyage. Indeed this timidity on the part of his wife was more than once put forward by him as if it were really the feather which turned the scale in the choice of his future residence.

Franklin himself also was trying his hand at match-making. He had taken a great fancy to a young lady by the name of Mary Stevenson, with whom, when distance prevented their meeting, he kept up a constant correspondence concerning points of physical science. He now became very pressing with his son William to wed this learned maiden; but the young man possibly did not hold a taste for science to be the most winning trait in woman; at any rate, having bestowed his affections elsewhere, he refused to transfer them. So Franklin was compelled to give up his scheme, though with an extreme reluctance, which he expressed to the rejected damsel with amusing openness. Had either of these matrimonial bonds been made fast, it is not improbable that Franklin would have lived out the rest of his life as a friend of the colonies in England. But his lot was otherwise cast; a second time he escaped, though narrowly, the prospect of dying an Englishman and the subject of a king. At the moment he was not altogether glad that matters worked thus. On August 17, 1762, he wrote from Portsmouth to Lord Kames : —

"I am now waiting here only for a wind to waft me to America ; but cannot leave this happy island and my friends in it without extreme regret, though I am going to a country and a people that I love. I am going from the old world to the new; and I fancy I feel like those who are leaving this world for the next : grief at the parting ; fear of the passage ; hope of the future. These different passions all affect their minds at once; and these have *tendered* me down exceedingly."

And six days later, from the same place, he wrote to Strahan : "I cannot, I assure you, quit even this disagreeable place, without regret, as it carries me still farther from those I love, and from the opportunities of hearing of their welfare. The attraction of reason is at present for the other side of the water, but that of inclination will be for this side. You know which usually prevails. I shall probably make but this one vibration and settle here forever. Nothing will prevent it, if I can, as I hope I can, prevail with Mrs. F. to accompany me, especially if we have a peace." Apparently the Americans owe a great debt of gratitude to Mrs. Franklin's fearfulness of the untrustworthy Atlantic.

Before dismissing this stay of Franklin in England a word should be said concerning his efforts for the retention of Canada by the British, as spoils of war. The fall of Quebec, in the autumn of 1759, practically concluded the struggle in America. The French were utterly spent; they had no food, no money; they had fought with desperate courage and heroic self-devotion; they could honestly say that they had stood grimly in the last trench, and had been slaughtered there until the starved and shattered remnant could not find it in their exhausted human nature longer to conduct a contest so thoroughly finished. In Europe, France was hardly less completely beaten. At the same time the singular position of affairs existed that the triumphant conqueror was even more resolutely bent upon immediate peace than were the conquered. George III., newly come to the throne, set himself towards this end with all the obstinacy of his resolute nature. It became a question of terms, and eager was the discussion thereof. The colonies were profoundly interested, for a question sharply argued was: whether England should retain Guadaloupe or Canada. She had conquered both, but it seemed to be admitted that she must restore one. It was even then a comical bit of political mathematics to establish anything like an equation between the two, nor could it possibly have been done with reference to intrinsic values. It was all very well to dilate upon the sugar crop of the island, its trade, its fertility, its harborage.

Every one knew that Canada could outweigh all these things fifty times over. But into the Guadaloupe scale was dropped a weighty consideration, which was clearly stated in an anonymous pamphlet attributed to William Burke. This writer said : —

"If the people of our colonies find no check from Canada, they will extend themselves almost without bound into the inland parts. They will increase infinitely from all causes. What the consequence will be, to have a numerous, hardy, independent people, possessed of a strong country, communicating little or not at all with England, I leave to your own reflections. By eagerly grasping at extensive territory we may run the risk, and in no very distant period, of losing what we now possess. A neighbor that keeps us in some awe is not always the worst of neighbors. So that, far from sacrificing Guadaloupe to Canada, perhaps, if we might have Canada without any sacrifice at all, we ought not to desire it. There should be a balance of power in America. . . . The islands, from their weakness, can never revolt ; but, if we acquire all Canada, we shall soon find North America itself too powerful and too populous to be governed by us at a distance."

From many other quarters came the same warning predictions.[1]

Franklin watched the controversy with deep interest and no small anxiety. As the argument grew heated he could no longer hold his hand ; he cast into the Canadian scale an able pamphlet, in-

[1] Bancroft, *Hist. U. S.*, iv. 363–365.

genuous in the main if not in all the details. It is not worth while to rehearse what he had to say upon mercantile points, or even concerning the future growth of a great American empire. What he had really to encounter was the argument that it was sound policy to leave Canada in possession of the French. Those who pretended to want Guadaloupe did not so much really want it as they did wish to have Canada remain French. To make good this latter point they had to show, first, that French ownership involved no serious danger to the English possessions; second, that it brought positive advantages. To the first proposition they said that the French had fully learned their lesson of inferiority, and that a few forts on the frontier would easily overawe the hostile Indians. To the second proposition, they elaborated the arguments of William Burke. Franklin replied that the war-parties of braves would easily pass by the forts in the forests, and after burning, pillaging, murdering, and scalping, would equally easily and safely return. Nothing save a Chinese wall the whole length of the western frontier would suffice for protection against savages. Then, with one of those happy illustrations of which he was a master, he said: "In short, long experience has taught our planters that they cannot rely upon forts as a security against Indians ; the inhabitants of Hackney might as well rely upon the Tower of London, to secure them against highwaymen and house-breakers." The admirable simile could neither be answered nor forgotten.

Concerning the positive desirability of leaving the French as masters of Canada to "check" the growth of the colonies, Franklin indignantly exclaimed: "It is a modest word, this '*check*' for massacring men, women, and children!" If Canada is to be "restored on this principle, . . . will not this be telling the French in plain terms, that the horrid barbarisms they perpetrate with Indians on our colonists are agreeable to us; and that they need not apprehend the resentment of a government with whose views they so happily concur." But he had the audacity to say that he was abundantly certain that the mother country could never have any occasion to dread the power of the colonies. He said: —

"I shall next consider the other supposition, that their growth may render them *dangerous*. Of this, I own, I have not the least conception, when I consider that we have already *fourteen separate governments* on the maritime coast of the continent; and, if we extend our settlements, shall probably have as many more behind them on the inland side." By reason of the different governors, laws, interests, religions and manners of these, "their jealousy of each other is so great, that, however necessary a union of the colonies has long been, for their common defence and security against their enemies, and how sensible soever each colony has been of that necessity, yet they have never been able to effect such a union among themselves, nor even to agree in requesting the mother country to establish it for them." If they could not unite for self-defence against the French and the murderous savages, "can it reasonably be supposed there is any danger of their uniting against their own nation, which protects and encourages them, with which they have so many connexions and ties of blood, interest, and affection, and which, it is well known, they all love much more than they love one another?

"In short there are so many causes that must operate to prevent it, that I will venture to say a union amongst them for such a purpose is not merely improbable, it is impossible. And if the union of the whole is impossible, the attempt of a part must be madness. . . . When I say such a union is impossible, I mean without the most grievous tyranny and oppression. . . . *The waves do not rise but when the winds blow.* . . . What such an administration as the Duke of Alva's in the Netherlands might produce, I know not; but this, I think, I have a right to deem impossible."

We read these words, even subject to the mild saving of the final sentences, with some bewilderment. Did their shrewd and well-informed writer believe what he said? Was he casting this political horoscope in good faith? Or was he only uttering a prophecy which he desired, if possible, and for his own purposes, to induce others to believe? If he was in earnest, Attorney-General Pratt was a better astrologer. "For all what you Americans say of your loyalty," he said to Franklin, "and notwithstanding your boasted affection, you will one day set up for independence." "No such idea," said Franklin, "is entertained by the Americans, or ever will be, unless you grossly abuse them." "Very true," said Pratt; "that I see will happen, and will produce the event." [1] Choiseul, the able French minister, expressed his wonder that the "great Pitt should be so attached to the acquisition of Canada," which, being in the hands of France, would keep the "colonies in that dependence which they will not fail to shake off the moment Canada shall be ceded." [2] Vergennes saw the same thing not less clearly; and so did many another.

If Franklin was really unable to foresee in this business those occurrences which others predicted with such confidence, at least he showed a grand conception of the future, and his vision took in more distant and greater facts and larger truths of statesmanship than were compassed by the British ministers. Witness what he wrote to Lord Kames : —

"I have long been of opinion that the foundations of the future grandeur and stability of the British empire lie in America. . . . I am therefore by no means for restoring Canada. If we keep it, all the country from the St. Lawrence to the Mississippi will in another century be filled with British people. Britain itself will become vastly more populous by the immense increase to its commerce; the Atlantic sea will be covered with your trading ships ; and your naval power, thence continually increasing, will extend your influence round the whole globe, and awe the world."

[1] Bancroft, *Hist. U. S.*, iv. 380.
[2] Ibid., iv. 399.

Whatever regret Franklin may have felt at not being able to remain in England was probably greatly mitigated if not entirely dissipated by the cordial reception which he met with at home. On December 2, 1762, he wrote to Strahan that the reports of the diminution of his friends were all false; that ever since his arrival his house had been full of a succession of them from morning till night, congratulating him on his return. The Assembly honored him with a vote of thanks, and also voted him £3,000 towards defraying his expenses. It was, of course, much less than he had expended during an absence of nearly six years; but it seems that he considered that, since much of his time had been passed in the enjoyment of an agreeable leisure, he should bear a corresponding part of the expense. While on the sea he had been chosen unanimously, as indeed had been done in each year of his absence, a member of that body; and he was told that, if he had not got so privately into town, he should have been met by an escort of 500 horsemen. All this must have been very gratifying.

A different kind of tribute, somewhat indirect, but none the less intelligible, was at the same time paid to him by the British government. In the autumn of 1762 his illegitimate son, William Franklin, was appointed governor of New Jersey. This act created a great storm of wrath from some of the provincial aristocratic party, and was vehemently railed at as an "indignity," a "dishonor

and disgrace," an " insult." After all, it failed of
its obvious purpose. The government shot brought
down the wrong bird, common carrion, while the
one aimed at never swerved in the slightest from
his course. William, whom no one cared for in
the least, became a confirmed royalist, and ultimately, as a Tory refugee, for years continued to
absorb a pension for which he could return no
adequate consideration. So far as Benjamin
Franklin was concerned, he was at first much
pleased ; but his political views and course were
not in the slightest degree affected. On the contrary, as the scheme developed, and the influence
on the younger man became apparent, the final result was an alienation between father and son,
which was only partially healed so late as 1784,
just before the former returned from Europe for
the last time.

CHAPTER IV.

LIFE IN PHILADELPHIA.

WHEN Franklin came home he was fifty-six years old. By nature he was physically indolent, and fifteen years ago he had given proof of his desire for the command of his own time by retiring from a lucrative business. But his forecasting of a tranquil, social career in Philadelphia, with science as his chief and agreeable occupation, was still to continue a day-dream, interrupted only by some thoughts of an English home. "Business, public and private, consumes all my time; I must return to England for repose. With such thoughts I flatter myself, and need some kind friend to put me often in mind that old trees cannot safely be transplanted." Thus he wrote to Mary Stevenson, the young lady whom he had hoped to have as a daughter-in-law.

His first labor in the provinces came in the shape of a journey about the country to supervise and regulate the postal business. Upon this errand he went 1,600 miles, which was no slight matter as travel was conducted in those days. He started in the spring of 1763, and did not get back until November. Upon his return he found himself at once immersed in public affairs.   In October, 1763, Governor Hamilton was superseded by John Penn, nephew of the proprietary Thomas Penn.

"Never," said Franklin, "did any administration open with a more promising prospect than this of Governor Penn. He assured the people in his first speeches of the proprietaries' paternal regard for them, and their sincere dispositions to do everything that might promote their happiness. As the proprietaries had been pleased to promote a son of the family to the government, it was thought not unlikely that there might be something in these professions ; for that they would probably choose to have his administration made easy and agreeable, and to that end might think it prudent to withdraw those harsh, disagreeable, and unjust instructions, with which most of his predecessors had been hampered. The Assembly therefore believed fully and rejoiced sincerely. They showed the new governor every mark of respect and regard that was in their power. They readily and cheerfully went into everything he recommended to them."

Moreover, the first event of public importance after Governor Penn's advent had, in its early stage, the effect of drawing him very closely to Franklin. Some of the settlers on the frontier, infuriated beyond the control of reason by the Indian marauding parties, gathered together for the purpose of slaughter. If they had directed their vengeance against the braves, and even all the occupants of the villages of the wilderness, they might have been excused though their vindictive rage led them to retaliate by the same barbarities which the red men had practiced towards the whites. Unfortunately, instead of courageously turning their faces towards the forests, they turned their backs in that direction, where only there was any enemy to be feared, and in a safe expedition they wreaked a deadly, senseless, cowardly, and brutal vengeance on an unoffending group of twenty old men, women and children, living peacefully and harmlessly near Lancaster. The infamous story is familiar in the annals of Pennsylvania, as the "Paxton massacre," because the "Paxton boys," the perpetrators, came from the Scotch-Irish settlement bearing that name.

Franklin's indignation was great, and he expressed it forcibly in a pamphlet. But many, even of the class which should have felt with him, were in such a temper that they would condemn no act done against an Indian. Encouraged by the prevalence of this feeling, this same band, swelled to a numerous and really formidable force, had the audacity to start for Philadelphia itself, with the avowed purpose of massacring there a small body of civilized Christian Indians, who had fled thither for safety under the charge of their Moravian missionary, and against whom not a complaint could be made. Panic reigned in the City of Brotherly Love, little competent to cope with imminent violence. In the crisis citizens and governor could conceive no more hopeful scheme than an appeal to Franklin, which was made at once and urgently. The governor himself actually took up his residence in Franklin's house, and stayed there till the threat of trouble passed over, speaking, writing, and ordering only at Franklin's dictation — a course which had in it; more of sense than of dignity. The appeal was made in the right quarter. Already profoundly moved in this matter, Franklin was prompt and zealous to save his city from a shameful act, and the Indians from barbarous murder. His efforts soon gathered, and after a fashion organized, a body of defenders probably somewhat more numerous than the approaching mob. Yet a collision would have been most unfortunate, whatever the result ; and to avert it Franklin took it upon him to go in person to meet the assailants. His courage, coolness, and address prevailed ; he succeeded in satisfying the " Paxton boys " that they were so greatly outnumbered, that, far from attacking others, they could only secure their own safety by instant dispersion. Thus by the resources and presence of mind of one man Philadelphia was saved from a day of which the bloody stain could never have been effaced from her good fame.

But Franklin seemed for a while to reap more of hostility than of gratitude for his gallant and honorable conduct in this emergency. Governor Penn was an ignoble man, and after the danger was over he left the house, in which he had certainly played a rather ignominious part, with those feelings toward his host which a small soul inevitably

cherishes toward a greater under such circumstances. Moreover, there were very many among
the people who had more of sympathy with the
" Paxton boys " than with the wise and humane
man who had thwarted them. " For about forty-
eight hours," Franklin wrote to one of his friends,
" I was a very great man; " but after " the fighting face we put on " caused the insurgents to turn
back, " I became a less man than ever ; for I had,
by this transaction, made myself many enemies
among the populace," a fact of which the governor
speedily took advantage. But without this episode
enmity between Penn and Franklin was inevitable.
They served masters whose ends were wide apart;
upon the one side avaricious proprietaries of little
foresight and judgment, upon the other side a people jealous of their rights and unwilling to leave to
any one else the definition and interpretation of
them.

Soon it became known that the instructions of
the new governor differed in no substantial particular from those of his predecessors. The procession
of vetoes upon the acts of the Assembly resumed
its familiar and hateful march. A militia bill was
thus cut off, because, instead of leaving with the
governor the nomination of regimental officers, it
stipulated that the rank and file should name three
persons for each position, and that the governor
should choose one of these, — an arrangement bad
in itself, but perhaps well suited to the habits and
even the needs of the Province at that time. A tax

bill met the like fate, because it did not discriminate in favor of the located lands of the proprietaries by rating their best lands at no higher valuation than the worst lands of other persons. Soon it was generally felt that matters were as bad as ever, and with scantier chances of improvement. Then " all the old wounds broke out and bled afresh; all the old grievances, still unredressed, were recollected ; despair succeeded of seeing any peace with a family that could make such returns to all overtures of kindness." The aggrieved party revived its scheme for a transfer of the government from the proprietaries to the crown, and Franklin threw himself into the discussion with more of zeal and ardor than he had often shown.

While the debates upon this subject waxed hot in the Assembly, it was moved and carried that that body should adjourn for a few weeks, in order that members might consult their constituents and sound the public feeling. During this recess it may be conceived that neither side was slack in its efforts. Franklin for his share contributed a pamphlet, entitled " Cool Thoughts on the Present Situation of our Public Affairs." " Mischievous and distressing," he said, as the frequent disputes " have been found to both proprietaries and people, it does not appear that there is any prospect of their being extinguished, till either the proprietary purse is unable to support them, or the spirit of the people so broken that they shall be willing to submit to anything rather than continue them."

With a happy combination of shrewdness and moderation he laid the blame upon the intrinsic nature of a proprietary government. " For though it is not unlikely that in these as well as in other disputes there are faults on both sides, every glowing coal being apt to inflame its opposite ; yet I see no reason to suppose that all proprietary rulers are worse men than other rulers, nor that all people in proprietary governments are worse people than those in other governments. I suspect, therefore, that the cause is radical, interwoven in the constitution, and so become the very nature, of proprietary governments ; and will therefore produce its effects as long as such governments continue." It indicated a broad and able mind, and one well under control, to assume as a basis this dispassionate assertion of a general principle, amid such personal heats as were then inflaming the passions of the whole community. His conclusion held one of his admirable similes which had the force of argument : " There seems to remain then but one remedy for our evils, a remedy approved by experience, and which has been tried with success by other provinces ; I mean that of an immediate *Royal Government*, without the intervention of proprietary powers, which, like unnecessary springs and movements in a machine, are so apt to produce disorder."

Further, he held out a bait to the crown : —

" The expression, *change of government*, seems indeed to be too extensive, and is apt to give the idea of a

general and total change of our laws and constitution.
It is rather and only a *change of governor* — that is, instead of self-interested proprietaries, a gracious king.
His majesty, who has no views but for the good of the
people, will thenceforth appoint the governor, who, un-
shackled by proprietary instructions, will be at liberty
to join with the Assembly in enacting wholesome laws.
At present, when the king desires supplies of his faithful
subjects, and they are willing and desirous to grant them,
the proprietaries intervene and say : ' Unless our private
interests in certain particulars are served, *nothing shall
be done.*' This insolent tribunal VETO has long encum-
bered our public affairs and been productive of many
mischiefs."

He then drew a petition " to the king's most excellent majesty in council," which humbly showed
" That the government of this Province by proprietaries has, by long experience, been found inconvenient, attended by many difficulties and ob-
structions to your majesty's service, arising from
the intervention of proprietary private interests in
public affairs, and disputes concerning those interests. That the said proprietary government is weak,
unable to support its own authority, and maintain
the common internal peace of the Province ; great
riots have lately arisen therein. . . . And these
evils are not likely to receive any remedy here, the
continual disputes between the proprietaries and
people, and their mutual jealousies and dislikes,
preventing." Wherefore his majesty was asked
to be " graciously pleased to resume the govern-

ment of this Province, . . . permitting your duti-
ful subjects therein to enjoy, under your majesty's
more immediate care and protection, the privileges
that have been granted to them by and under your
royal predecessors."

The result of feeling the public pulse showed
that it beat very high and strong for the proposed
change. Accordingly the resolution to present the
petition was now easily carried. But again the
aged speaker, Norris, found himself called upon to
do that for which he had not the nerve. He resigned the speakership; Franklin was chosen in
his place and set the official signature to the document.

Another paper by Franklin upon the same subject, and of considerable length, appeared in the
shape of a preface to a speech delivered in the Assembly by Joseph Galloway in answer to a speech
on the proprietary side by John Dickinson, which
speech, also with a long preface, had been printed.
In this pamphlet he reviewed all the recent history
of the Province. He devoted several pages to a
startling exposition of the almost incredible usage
which had long prevailed, whereby bills were left
to accumulate on the governor's table, and then
were finally signed by him in a batch, only upon
condition that he should receive, or even sometimes
upon his simultaneously receiving, a considerable
douceur. Not only had this been connived at by
the proprietaries, but sometimes these payments
had been shared between the proprietaries and the

governors. This topic Franklin finally dismissed
with a few lines of admirable sarcasm : " Do not,
my courteous reader, take pet at our proprietary
constitution for these our bargain and sale proceedings in legislation. It is a happy country where
justice, and what was your own before, can be had
for ready money. It is another addition to the
value of money, and, of course, another spur to industry. Every land is not so blessed." Many
quotations from this able state paper have already
been made in the preceding pages, though it is so
brilliant a piece of work that to quote is only to
mutilate. Its argument, denunciation, humor, and
satire are interwoven in a masterly combination.
The renowned " sketch in the lapidary style," prepared for the gravestone of Thomas and Richard
Penn, with the introductory paragraphs, constitutes
one of the finest assaults in political literature.[1] It
is unfortunately impossible to give any adequate
idea or even abstract of a document which covers
so much ground and with such variety of treatment. It had of course a powerful effect in stimulating the public sentiment, and it was especially
useful in supplying formidable arguments to those
of the popular way of thinking ; drawing their
weapons from this armory, they felt themselves
invincible.

But it must not be supposed that all this while
Franklin was treading the velvet path of universal

---

[1] Franklin's animosity against the Penns was mitigated in later
years. See Franklin's *Works,* viii. 273.

popularity, amid the unanimous encouragement of his fellow-citizens, and with only the frowns of the proprietary officials to disturb his serenity. By one means and another the proprietaries mustered a considerable party in the Province, and the hatred of all these men was concentrated upon Franklin with extreme bitterness. He said that he was "as much the butt of party rage and malice," and was as much pelted with hostile prints and pamphlets, as if he were prime minister. Neither was the notion of a royal government looked upon with liking even by all those who were indignant against the present system. Moreover many persons still remained ill-disposed towards him by reason of his opinions and behavior during the Paxton outbreak. The combination against him, made up of all these various elements, felt itself powerful enough for mischief, and found its opportunity in the election to the Assembly occurring in the autumn of 1764. The polls were opened on October 1, at nine o'clock in the morning. The throng was dense, and the column of voters could move but slowly. At three o'clock of the following morning, the voting having continued during the night, the friends of the " new ticket," that is to say of the new candidate, moved to close the polls. The friends of the " old ticket " opposed this motion and unfortunately prevailed. They had a " reserve of the aged and lame," who had shunned the crowd and were now brought in chairs and litters. Thus in three hours they increased their score by some two hun-

dred votes. But the other side was not less enter-
prising, and devoting the same extension of time to
scouring Germantown and other neighborhoods,
they brought in near five hundred additional votes
upon their side. It was apparently this strange
blunder of the political managers for the " old
ticket " party that was fatal to Franklin, for when
the votes were all counted he was found to be beaten
by a balance against him of twenty-five. He had
therefore evidently had a majority at the hour
when his friends prevented the closing of the polls.
He " died like a philosopher. But Mr. Galloway
agonized in death like a Mortal Deist, who has no
Hopes of a Future Existence." [1]

But the jubilation of the proprietary party over
this signal victory was soon changed into mourning.
For within a few days the new Assembly was in
session, and at once took into consideration the appointment of Dr. Franklin as its agent to present to the king in council another petition for a
royal government. The wrath of the other side
blazed forth savagely. " No measure," their leader,
Dickinson, said, was " so likely to inflame the resentments and embitter the discontents of the people." He " appealed to the heart of every member
for the truth of the assertion that no man in Pennsylvania is at this time so much the object of public
dislike as he that has been mentioned. To what
a surprising height this dislike is carried among

---

[1] Parton's *Life of Franklin*, i. 451, quoting *Life of Joseph Reed*,
i. 37.

vast numbers" he did "not choose to repeat." He said that within a few hours of the nomination hundreds of the most reputable citizens had protested, and if time were given thousands "would crowd to present the like testimony against [him]. Why then should a majority of this House single out from the whole world the man most obnoxious to his country to represent his country, though he was at the last election turned out of the Assembly, where he had sat for fourteen years? Why should they exert their power in the most disgusting manner, and throw pain, terror, and displeasure into the breasts of their fellow-citizens?" The excited orator then threw out a suggestion to which this vituperation had hardly paved a way of roses; he actually appealed to Franklin to emulate Aristides, and not be worse than "the dissolute Otho," and to this end urged that he should distinguish himself in the eyes of all good men by "voluntarily declining an office which he could not accept without alarming, offending, and disturbing his country." "Let him, from a private station, from a smaller sphere, diffuse, as I think he may, a beneficial light; but let him not be made to move and blaze like a comet, to terrify and to distress." [1] The popular majority in the Assembly withstood Mr. Dickinson's rhetoric, and, to quote the forcible language of Bancroft, "proceeded to an act which in its consequences was to influence the world." That is to say, they carried the appointment. Franklin

[1] Parton's *Life of Franklin,* i. 451, 452.

likewise set aside Dickinson's seductive counsels, and accepted the position.

It is not in human nature to be so extravagantly abused in times of intense excitement, and wholly to hold one's peace. Even the cool temper of Dr. Franklin was incited to a retort; his defense was brief and dignified, in a very different tone from that of the aspersions to which it replied; and it carries that influence which always belongs to him who preserves moderation amid the passions of a fierce controversy.[1]

[1] See, for example, Franklin's *Works*, iii. 361, 362.

CHAPTER V.

FRANKLIN so hastened his preparations that he was ready to depart again for England in twelve days after his election. There was no money in the provincial treasury; but some of the well-to-do citizens, in expectation of reimbursement, raised by subscription £1,100. He took only £500. A troop of three hundred mounted citizens escorted him from the city sixteen miles down the river to the ship, and "filled the sails with their good wishes." This parade, designed only as a friendly demonstration, was afterward made a charge against him, as an assumption of pomp and a display of popularity. If it had been deliberately planned, it would have been ill-advised; but it took him by surprise, and he could not prevent it. The ship cast anchor in St. Helen's Road, Isle of Wight, on December 9, 1764. He forthwith hastened to London, and installed himself in the familiar rooms at No. 7 Craven Street, Strand. In Philadelphia, when the news came of the safe arrival of this "man the most obnoxious to his country," the citizens kept the bells ringing until midnight.

So altogether the prospect now seemed agreeable in whatever direction Dr. Franklin chose to look. He was in quarters in which he was at least as much at home as he could feel in his house at Philadelphia; Mrs. Stevenson, his landlady, and her daughter Mary, whom he had sought to persuade his son to marry, upon the excellent ground of his own great affection for her, not only made him comfortable but saved him from homesickness; old and warm friends welcomed him; the pleasures of London society again spread their charms before him. Without the regrets and doubts which must have attended the real emigration which he had been half inclined to make, he seemed to be reaping all the gratification which that could have brought him. At the same time he had also the pride of receiving from the other side of the Atlantic glowing accounts of the esteem in which he was held by a controlling body of those who were still his fellow-citizens there. But already there had shown itself above the horizon a cloud which rapidly rose, expanded, and obscured all this fair sky. . Franklin came to England in the anticipation of a short stay, and with no purpose beyond the presentation and urging of the petition for the change of government. Somewhat less than ten months, he thought, would suffice to finish this business. In fact, he did not get home for ten years, and this especial errand, which had seemed all that he had to do, soon sank into such comparative insignificance that, though not actually forgotten, it could not secure attention. He conscientiously made repeated efforts to keep the petition in the memory of the English ministry, and to obtain action upon it; but his efforts were vain; that body was absorbed by other affairs in connection with the troublesome American colonies,— affairs which gave vastly more perplexity and called for much more attention than were becoming in the case of provinces that should have been submissive as well-behaved children. Franklin himself found his own functions correspondingly enlarged. Instead of remaining simply an agent charged with urging a petition which brought him in conflict only with private persons, like himself subjects of the king, he found his position rapidly change and develop until he became really the representative of a disaffected people maintaining a cause against the monarch and the government of the great British Empire. It was the "Stamp Act" which effected this transformation.

Scarcely had the great war with France been brought to a close by the treaty of 1763, bringing such enormous advantages to the old British possessions in America, before it became apparent that among the fruits some were mingled that were neither sweet nor nourishing. The war had moved the colonies into a perilous foreground. Their interests had cost much in men and money, and had been worth all that they had cost, and more; the benefits conferred upon them had been immense, yet were recognized as not being in excess of their real importance, present and future. Worst of all, the magnitude of their financial resources had been made apparent; without a murmur, without visible injury to their prosperity, they had voluntarily raised large sums by taxation. Meanwhile the English treasury had been put to enormous charges, and the English people groaned beneath the unwonted tax burdens which they had to bear. The attention of British financiers, even before the war was over, was turned toward the colonies, as a field of which the productive capacity had never been developed.

So soon as peace brought to the government leisure to adjust domestic matters in a thorough manner, the scheme for colonial taxation came to the front. "America . . . became the great subject of consideration; . . . and the minister who was charged with its government took the lead in public business." [1] This minister was at first Charles Townshend, than whom no man in England, it was supposed, knew more of the transatlantic possessions. His scheme involved a standing army of 25,000 men in the provinces, to be supported by taxes to be raised there. In order to obtain this revenue he first gave his care to the revision of the navigation act. Duties which had been so high that they had never been collected he now proposed to reduce and to enforce. This was designed to be only the first link in the chain, but before he could forge others he had to go out of office with the Bute ministry. The change in the

[1] Bancroft, *Hist. U. S.*, iv. 28.

cabinet, however, made no change in the colonial policy; that was not " the wish of this man or that man," but apparently of nearly all English statesmen.

So in March, 1763, George Grenville, in the treasury department, took up the plan which Townshend had laid down. Grenville was commercially-minded, and his first efforts were in the direction of regulating the trade of the colonies so as to carry out with much more stringency and thoroughness than heretofore three principles: first, that England should be the only shop in which a colonist could purchase; second, that colonists should not make for themselves those articles which England had to sell to them; third, that the people of different colonies should not trade with each other even to the indirect or possible detriment of the trade of either with England. Severely as these restrictions bore upon the colonists, they were of that character, as relating to external trade, which no colonist denied to lie within the jurisdiction of Parliament. But they were not enough; they must be supplemented; and a stamp act was designed as the supplement. On March 9, 1764, Grenville stated his intention to introduce such a bill at the next session; he needed the interval for inquiries and preparation. It was no very novel idea. It " had been proposed to Sir Robert Walpole; it had been thought of by Pelham; it had been almost resolved upon in 1755; it had been pressed upon Pitt: it seems, beyond a doubt, to have been a part of the system adopted in the ministry of Bute, and it was sure of the support of Charles Townshend. Knox, the agent of Georgia, stood ready to defend it. . . . The agent of Massachusetts favored raising the wanted money in that way." Little opposition was anticipated in Parliament, and none from the king. In short, " everybody, who reasoned on the subject, decided for a stamp tax." [1] Never did any bill of any legislature seem to come into being with better auspices. Some among the colonial agents certainly expressed ill feeling towards it; but Grenville silenced them, telling them that he was acting " from a real regard and tenderness " towards the Americans. He said this in perfect good faith. His views both of the law and of the reasons for the law were intelligent and honest; he had carefully gathered information and sought advice; and he had a profound belief alike in the righteousness and the wisdom of the measure.

News of what was in preparation in England reached Pennsylvania in the summer of 1764, shortly before Franklin sailed. The Assembly debated concerning it; Franklin was prominent in condemning the scheme ; and a resolution protesting against it was passed. It was made part of Franklin's duty in London to urge upon Grenville these views of Pennsylvania. But when he arrived he found that the grinding at the mills of government was going on much too evenly to be disturbed

[1] Bancroft, *Hist. U. S.*, iv. 155.

by the introduction of any such insignificant foreign
substance as a colonial protest. Nevertheless he
endeavored to do what he could. In company with
three other colonial agents he had an interview
with Grenville, February 2, 1765, in which he urged
that taxation by act of Parliament was needless,
inasmuch as any requisition for the service of the
king always had found, and always would find, a
prompt and liberal response on the part of the
Assembly. Arguments, however, and protests
struck ineffectually against the solid wall of Grenville's established purpose. He listened with a civil
appearance of interest and dismissed his visitors
and all memory of their arguments together. On
the 13th of the same month he read the bill
in Parliament; on the 27th it passed the Commons; on March 8th, the Lords; and on March
22d it was signed by a royal commission; the
insanity of the king saved him from placing his
own signature to the ill - starred law. In July
Franklin wrote to Charles Thomson : —

"Depend upon it, my good neighbor, I took every
step in my power to prevent the passing of the Stamp
Act. Nobody could be more concerned and interested
than myself to oppose it sincerely and heartily. But the
tide was too strong against us. The nation was provoked
by American claims of independence, and all parties
joined in resolving by this act to settle the point. We
might as well have hindered the sun's setting. That we
could not do. But since it is down, my friend, and it
may be long before it rises again, let us make as good a

night of it as we can. We can still light candles. Frugality and industry will go a great way towards indemnifying us. Idleness and pride tax with a heavier hand than kings and parliaments. If we can get rid of the former, we may easily bear the latter."

In such a temper was he at this time, and so remained until he got news of the first mutterings of the storm in the colonies. His words show a discouragement and despondency unusual with him; but what attracts remark is the philosophical purpose to make the best even of so bad a business, the hopeless absence of any suggestion of a further opposition, and that his only advice is patient endurance. Unquestionably he did conceive the matter to be for the time settled. The might of England was an awful fact, visible all around him; he felt the tremendous force of the great British people; and he saw their immense resources every day as he walked the streets of busy, prosperous London. As he recalled the infant towns and scattered villages of the colonies, how could he contemplate forcible resistance to an edict of Parliament and the king? Had Otis, Adams, Henry, Gadsden, and the rest seen with their bodily eyes what Franklin was seeing every day, their words might have been more tempered. Even a year later, in talk with a gentleman who said that so far back as 1741 he had expressed an opinion that the colonies " would one day release themselves from England," Franklin answered, " with his earnest, expressive, and intelligent face : " " Then you were mistaken ; the

Americans have too much love for their mother country ; " and he added that " secession was impossible, for all the American towns of importance, Boston, New York, and Philadelphia, were exposed to the English navy. Boston could be destroyed by bombardment." Near the same time he said to Ingersoll of Connecticut, who was about departing for the colonies : " Go home and tell your countrymen to get children as fast as they can." By no means without forebodings for the future, he was yet far from fancying that the time had come when physical resistance was feasible. It seemed still the day for arguments, not for menaces.

To Franklin in this frame of mind, never doubting that the act would be enforced, there was brought a plausible message from Grenville. The minister desired " to make the execution of the act as little inconvenient and disagreeable to America as possible," and to this end he preferred to nominate as stamp distributers " discreet and reputable " residents in the Province, rather than to send over strangers from Great Britain. Accordingly he solicited a nomination from Franklin of some " honest and responsible " man in Philadelphia. Franklin readily named a trustworthy merchant of his acquaintance, Mr. Hughes. The Stamp Act itself hardly turned out a greater blunder for Grenville than this well-meant suggestion was near turning out for Franklin. When the Philadelphians got news of the passage of the act, the preparations for its enforcement, the nomination of Mr.

Hughes, and the fact that he had been suggested by Franklin, the whole city rose in a wild frenzy of rage. Never was such a sudden change of feeling. He who had been their trusted companion was now loudly reviled as a false and truckling traitor. He was said to have deserted his own, and to have gone over to the minister's side; to have approved the odious law, and to have asked that a position under it might be given to his friend. The mobs ranging the streets threatened to destroy the new house, in which he had left his wife and daughter. The latter was persuaded to seek safety in Burlington; but Mrs. Franklin, with admirable courage, stayed in the house till the danger was over. Some armed friends stood ready to assist if the crisis should come, but fortunately it passed by. All sorts of stories were spread concerning Franklin, — even that it was he who had "*planned* the Stamp Act;" and that he was endeavoring also to get the Test Act introduced into the colonies! A caricature represented the devil whispering into his ear: "Ben, you shall be my agent throughout my dominions."

Knowing Franklin's frame of mind, it is easy to fancy the surprise with which he learned of the spirit which had blazed forth in the colonies, and of the violent doings in many places; and we may imagine the pain and mortification with which he heard of the opinions expressed by his fellow-citizens concerning his own action. He said little at the time, so far as we know; but many years afterwards he gave a narrative of his course in language which was almost apologetic and deprecatory. A pen in his fingers became a sympathetic instrument, and betrays sometimes what his moderate language does not distinctly state. The intense, bitter condemnation vented by his constituents, who so lately had been following his lead, but who now reviled a representative who had misrepresented them in so vital an affair, cut its way deep.

The gap between him and them did indeed seem a wide one. In the colonies there was universal wrath, oftentimes swelling into fury ; in some places mobs, much sacking of houses, hangings and burnings in effigy ; compulsion put upon kings' officers publicly to resign their offices ; wild threats and violence ; obstruction to the distribution of the stamped paper ; open menaces of forcible resistance, even of secession and rebellion ; a careful estimating of the available armed forces among the colonies ; the proposal for a congress of colonies to promote community of action, to protest, and to consult for the common cause ; disobedient resolutions by legislatures ; a spreading of the spirit of colonial union by the general cry of " Join or die ; " agreements not to import or use articles of English manufacture, with other sunderings of commercial relations. Far behind this mad procession, of which the more moderate divisions were marshalled by Otis, Sam Adams, and Gadsden, and soon also by John Adams and Patrick Henry, and by many other well-known "patriots," Franklin appeared to be a laggard in the rear distance, with disregarded arguments and protests, with words of moderation, even counsels of submission, nay, actually with a sort of connivance in the measure by the nomination of an official under it.

Yet the intervening space was not so great as it appeared. There was nothing in the counsels of the reasonable and intelligent " patriots " which was repugnant to Franklin's opinions. So soon as he saw the ground upon which they had placed themselves, he made haste to come into position with them. It was fortunate indeed that the transient separation was closed again before it could lead to the calamity of his removal from his office. For no man or even combination of men, whom it was possible to send from the provinces, could have done them the services which Franklin was about to render. Besides the general power of his mind, he had peculiar fitnesses. He was widely known and very highly esteemed in England, where he moved in many circles. Among members of the nobility, among men high in office, among members of Parliament, among scientific men and literary men, among men of business and affairs, and among men who made a business of society, he was always welcome. In that city in which dinners constituted so important an element in life, even for the most serious purposes, he was the greatest of diners-out; while at the coffee-houses, clubs, and in the old-fashioned tavern circles no companion was more highly esteemed than he. He consorted not only with friends of the

colonies, but was, and for a long time continued to
be, on intimate terms of courteous intercourse also
with those who were soon to be described as their
enemies. Each and all, amid this various and extensive acquaintance, listened to him with a respect
no tithe of which could have been commanded by
any other American then living. The force of his
intelligence, the scope of his understanding, the
soundness of his judgment, had already been appreciated by men accustomed to study and to estimate
the value of such traits. His knowledge of American affairs, of the trade and business of the provinces, of the characteristics of the people in different parts of the country, were very great, because
of his habit of shrewd observation, of his taste for
practical matters, and of his extensive travels and
connections as postmaster. Add to this that he had
a profound affection for the mother country, which
was not only a tradition and a habit, but a warm
and lively attachment nourished by delightful personal experience, by long residence and numerous
friendships, by gratifying appreciation of and compliments to himself. No one could doubt his sincerity when he talked of his love for England as a
real and influential sentiment. At the same time
he was an American and a patriot. Though he had
failed to anticipate the state of feeling which the
Stamp Act begot, it was his only failure of this
kind; generally he spoke the sentiments of the colonists with entire truth and sympathy. He was
one who could combine force with moderation in

the expression of his views, the force being all the greater for the moderation; he had an admirable head to conceive an argument, a tongue and pen to state it clearly and pointedly. He had presence of mind in conversation, was ready and quick at fence; he was widely learned; he was a sounder political economist than any member of the English government; above all, he had an unrivaled familiarity with the facts, the arguments, and the people on both sides of the controversy; he kept perfect control of his temper, without the least loss of earnestness; and had the rare faculty of being able to state his own side with plain force, and yet without giving offense. Such were his singular qualifications, which soon enabled him to perform the greatest act of his public life.

Matters came by degrees into better shape for the colonies. In politics any statesman has but to propose a measure to find it opposed by those who oppose him. So what had seemed an universal willingness to levy internal taxes upon the colonies soon lost this aspect. No sooner did the news from the angry colonies bring the scheme into prominence than the assaults upon it became numerous, and enemies of Grenville became friends of America. Arguments so obvious and so strong as those against the measure were eagerly made the most of by the opponents of the men who were in office. Among these opponents was Pitt, that formidable man before whom all trembled. Gout had disabled him, but who could tell when he might get sufficient respite to return and deal havoc? Yet in spite of all that was said, the ministry seemed impregnable. Grenville was very able, always of a stubborn temper, and in this especial case convinced to the point of intensity that the right lay with him; moreover, he was complete master in Parliament, where his authority seemed still to increase steadily. No man was sanguine enough to see hope for the colonies, when suddenly an occurrence, which in this age could not appreciably affect the power of an English premier, snapped Grenville's sway in a few days. This was only the personal pique of the king, irritated by complaints made by the Duke of Bedford about the favorite, Bute. For such a cause George III. drove out of office, upon grounds of his own dislike, a prime minister and cabinet with whom he was in substantial accord upon the most important public matters then under consideration, and although it was almost impossible to patch together any tolerably congruous or competent body of successors.

Pitt endeavored to form a cabinet, but was obliged, with chagrin, to confess his inability. At last the Duke of Cumberland succeeded in forming the so-called Rockingham Cabinet, a weak combination, but far less unfavorable than its predecessor towards America. The Marquis of Rockingham, as prime minister, had Edmund Burke as his private secretary; while General Conway, one of the very few who had opposed the Stamp Act, now actually received the southern department of state within which the colonies were included. Still there seemed little hope for any undoing of the past, which probably would never have been wrung from this or any British ministry so long as all the discontent was on the other side of three thousand miles of ocean. But this was ceasing to be the case. The American weapon of non-importation was proving most efficient. In the provinces the custom of wearing mourning was abandoned; no one killed or ate lamb, to the end that by the increase of sheep the supply of wool might be greater; homespun was now the only wear; no man would be seen clad in English cloth. In a word, throughout America there was established what would now be called a thorough and comprehensive " boycott " against all articles of English manufacture. So very soon the manufacturers of the mother country began to find themselves the only real victims of the Stamp Act. In America it was inflicting no harm, but rather was encouraging economy, enterprise, and domestic industry; while the sudden closing of so enormous a market brought loss and bankruptcy to many an English manufacturer and warehouseman. Shipping, too, was indirectly affected. An outcry for the change of a disastrous policy swelled rapidly in the manufacturing and trading towns; and erelong the battle of the colonists was being fought by allies upon English soil, who were stimulated by the potent impulse of self-preservation. These men cared nothing for the principle at stake, nothing for the colonists personally; but they cared for the business by which they sustained their own homes, and they were resolved that the destroying Stamp Act should be got out of their way. Such an influence was soon felt. Death also came in aid of the Americans, removing in good time the Duke of Cumberland, the merciless conqueror of Culloden, who now was all ready to fight it out with the colonies, and only thus lost the chance to do so.

Beneath the pressure of these events concession began to be talked of, though at first of course its friends were few and its enemies many. Charles Townshend announced himself able to contemplate with equanimity the picture of the colonies relapsing " to their primitive deserts." But the trouble was that little deserts began to spot the face of England ; and still the British merchant, who seldom speaks long in vain, was increasing his clamor, and did not fancy the prospect of rich trading fields reduced to desolation. In January, 1766, too, the dreaded voice of Pitt again made itself heard in St. Stephen's, sending forth an eloquent harangue for America: "The Americans are the sons, not the bastards, of England. As subjects they are entitled to the common right of representation, and cannot be bound to pay taxes without their consent. Taxation is no part of the governing power.[1] The taxes are a voluntary gift and grant by the Com-

[1] Grenville had laid down the proposition that England was " the sovereign, the supreme legislative power over America," and that " taxation is a part of that sovereign power."

mons alone. In an American tax what do we do?
We, your Majesty's Commons of Great Britain,
give and grant to your Majesty — what? Our
own property? No! we give and grant to your
Majesty the property of your Majesty's commons
in America. It is an absurdity in terms." [1] "The
idea of a virtual representation of America in this
House is the most contemptible that ever entered
into the head of man." "I never shall own the
justice of taxing America internally until she en-
joys the right of representation." Not very many
men in either house of Parliament would go the
full logical length of Pitt's argument; but men
who held views quite opposite to his as to the law-
ful authority of Parliament to lay this tax were
beginning to feel that they must join him in getting it out of the way of domestic prosperity in
England. It seemed to them a mistaken exercise of an unquestionable right. They were prepared to correct the mistake, which could be done
without abandoning the right. As this feeling visibly gained ground the ministry gathered courage
to consider the expediency of introducing a bill to
repeal the act. Could the king have had his way
they would not have survived in office to do so.
He would have had their ministerial heads off, as he
had stricken those of their immediate predecessors.
But efforts which he made to find successors for
them were fruitless, and so they remained in places
which no others could be induced to fill. Pitt was

[1] Bancroft, *Hist. U. S.*, v. 385–387.

sounded, to see whether he would ally himself with them ; but he would not. Had he been gained the fight would not have come simply upon the repeal of the act as unsatisfactory, but as being contrary to the constitution of England. The narrower battle-ground was selected by Rockingham.

The immediate forerunner in Parliament of the repeal of the Stamp Act was significant. A resolution was introduced into the House of Lords, February 3, 1766, that the " king in Parliament has full power to bind the colonies and people of America in all cases whatsoever." The debate which followed showed what importance this American question had assumed in England ; the expression of feeling was intense, the display of ability very great. Lord Camden and Lord Mansfield encountered each other ; but the former, with the best of the argument, had much the worst of the division. One hundred and twenty-five peers voted for the resolution, only five against it. In the Commons, Pitt assailed the resolution, with no better success than had attended Camden. No one knew how many voted Nay, but it was " less than ten voices, some said five or four, some said but three." [1] Immediately after this assertion of a principle, the same Parliament prepared to set aside the only application of it which had ever been attempted. It was well understood that the repeal of the Stamp Act was close at hand.

It was at this juncture that Franklin, who had

[1] Bancroft, *Hist. U. S.*, v. 417.

been by no means idle during the long struggle,
appeared as a witness in that examination which
perhaps displayed his ability to better advantage
than any other single act in his life. It was between February 3 and 13, 1766, that he and others
were summoned to give testimony concerning the
colonies at the bar of the House of Commons
sitting in committee of the whole. The others
have been forgotten, but his evidence never will be.
The proceeding was striking; there were some of
the cleverest and most experienced men in England
to question him; no one of them singly was his
match; but there were many of them, and they
conducted an examination and a cross-examination
both in one; that is to say, those who wished to
turn a point against him might at any moment
interpose with any question which might suddenly
confuse or mislead him. But no man was ever
better fitted than Franklin to play the part of a
witness, and no record in politics or in law can
compare with the report of his testimony. Some
persons have endeavored to account for, which
means of course to detract from, its extraordinary
merit by saying that some of the questions and
replies had been prearranged; but it does not
appear that such prearrangement went further
than that certain friendly interrogators had discussed the topics with him so as to be familiar with
his views. Every lawyer does this with his witnesses. Nor can it be supposed that the admirable
replies which he made to the enemies of America

were otherwise than strictly impromptu. He had thorough knowledge of the subject; he was in perfect control of his head and his temper; his extraordinary faculty for clear and pithy statement never showed to better advantage; he was, as always, moderate and reasonable; but above all the wonderful element was the quick wit and ready skill with which he turned to his own service every query which was designed to embarrass him; and this he did not in the vulgar way of flippant retort or disingenuous twistings of words or facts, but with the same straightforward and tranquil simplicity of language with which he delivered evidence for the friendly examiners. Burke likened the proceeding to an examination of a master by a parcel of schoolboys.

Franklin used to say, betwixt plaint and humor, that it always seemed to him that no one ever gave an abbreviation or an abstract of anything which he had written, without very nearly spoiling the original. This would be preëminently true of an abstract of this examination; abbreviation can be only mutilation. It ranged over a vast ground, — colonial history and politics, political economy, theories and practice in colonial trade, colonial commerce and industry, popular opinions and sentiment, and the probabilities of action in supposed cases. His answers made a great stir; they were universally admitted to have substantially advanced the day of repeal. They constituted the abundant armory to which the friends of the colonies resorted

for weapons offensive and defensive, for facts and
for ideas. He himself, with just complacency, remarked : " The then ministry was ready to hug me
for the assistance I afforded them." The "Gentleman's Magazine" said : —

"From this examination of Dr. Franklin the reader
may form a clearer and more comprehensive idea of the
state and disposition in America, of the expediency or
inexpediency of the measure in question, and of the
character and conduct of the minister who proposed it,
than from all that has been written upon the subject in
newspapers and pamphlets, under the titles of essays,
letters, speeches, and considerations, from the first
moment of its becoming the subject of public attention
until now. The questions in general are put with great
subtlety and judgment, and they are answered with such
deep and familiar knowledge of the subject, such precision and perspicuity, such temper and yet such spirit,
as do the greatest honor to Dr. Franklin, and justify the
general opinion of his character and abilities."

Like praises descended from every quarter.

One interesting fact clearly appears from this
examination : that Franklin now fully understood
the colonial sentiment, and was thoroughly in
accord with it. Being asked whether the colonists
"would submit to the Stamp Act, if it were modi-
fied, the obnoxious parts taken out, and the duty
reduced to some particulars of small moment," he
replied with brief decision : " No, they will never
submit to it." As to how they would receive "a
future tax imposed on the same principle," he said,

with the same forcible brevity: "Just as they do this : they would not pay it." *Q.* "Can anything less than a military force carry the Stamp Act into execution? *A.* I do not see how a military force can be applied to that purpose. *Q.* Why may it not? *A.* Suppose a military force sent into America, they will find nobody in arms. What are they then to do? They cannot force a man to take stamps who chooses to do without them. They will not find a rebellion; they may indeed make one. *Q.* If the act is not repealed, what do you think will be the consequences? *A.* A total loss of the respect and affection the people of America bear to this country, and of all the commerce that depends on that respect and affection. *Q.* How can the commerce be affected? *A.* You will find that if the act is not repealed, they will take a very little of your manufactures in a short time. *Q.* Is it in their power to do without them? *A.* The goods they take from Britain are either necessaries, mere conveniences, or superfluities. The first, as cloth, etc., with a little industry they can make at home; the second they can do without until they are able to provide them among themselves; and the last, which are much the greatest part, they will strike off immediately." This view of the willingness and capacity of the colonists to forego English importations he elsewhere elaborated fully. The English merchants knew to their cost that he spoke the truth.

With reference to the enforcement of claims

in the courts, he was asked whether the people would not use the stamps "rather than remain . . . unable to obtain any right or recover by law any debt?" He replied: "It is hard to say what they would do. I can only judge what other people will think, and how they will act, by what I feel within myself. I have a great many debts due to me in America, and I would rather they should remain unrecoverable by any law than submit to the Stamp Act."

A few weeks later he wrote: "I have some little property in America. I will freely spend nineteen shillings in the pound to defend my right of giving or refusing the other shilling. And, after all, if I cannot defend that right, I can retire cheerfully with my family into the boundless woods of America, which are sure to afford freedom and subsistence to any man who can bait a hook or pull a trigger." The picture of Dr. Franklin, the philosopher, at the age of sixty-one, "cheerfully" sustaining his family in the wilderness by the winnings of his rod and his rifle stirs one's sense of humor; but the paragraph indicates that he was in strict harmony with his countrymen, who were expressing serious resolution with some rhetorical exaggeration, in the American fashion.

The main argument of the colonies: that under the British constitution there could be no taxation without representation, was of course introduced into the examination; and Franklin seized the occasion to express his theory very ingeniously.

Referring to the fact that, by the Declaration of
Rights, no money could " be raised on the subject
but by consent of Parliament," the subtle question
was put : How the colonists could think that they
themselves had a right to levy money for the crown?
Franklin replied : " They understand that clause
to relate only to subjects within the realm ; that no
money can be levied on *them* for the crown but by
consent of Parliament. The colonies are not supposed to be within the realm ; they have assemblies
of their own, which are their parliaments." This
was a favorite theory with him, in expounding
which he likened the colonies to Ireland, and to
Scotland before the union. Many sentences to
the same purport occur in his writings ; for example :
" These writers against the colonies all bewilder
themselves by supposing the colonies *within* the
realm, which is not the case, nor ever was." " If
an Englishman goes into a foreign country, he is
subject to the laws and government he finds there.
If he finds no government or laws there, he is subject there to none, till he and his companions, if he
has any, make laws for themselves ; and this was
the case of the first settlers in America. Otherwise,
if they carried the English laws and power of Parliament with them, what advantage could the Puri-
tans propose to themselves by going ? " " The colonists carried no law with them ; they carried only
a power of making laws, or adopting such parts of
the English law or of any other law as they should
think suitable to their circumstances." [1] Radical

---

[1] To same purport see, also, *Works*, iv. 300.

doctrines these, which he could not reasonably expect would find favor under any principles of government then known in the world. To the like effect were other assertions of his, made somewhat later: "In fact, the British empire is not a single state; it comprehends many." "The sovereignty of the crown I understand. The sovereignty of the British legislature out of Britain I do not understand." "The king, and not the King, Lords, and Commons collectively, is their sovereign; and the king with their respective parliaments is their only legislator."[1] "The Parliament of Great Britain has not, never had, and of right never can have, without consent given either before or after, power to make laws of sufficient force to bind the subjects of America in any case whatever, and particularly in taxation." The singular phrase "the subjects of America" is worth noting. In 1769, still reiterating the same principle, he said: "We are free subjects of the king; and fellow-subjects of one part of his dominions are not sovereigns over fellow-subjects in any other part."

It is a singular fact that Franklin long cherished a personal regard towards the king, and a faith in his friendly and liberal purposes towards the colonies. Indignation against the Parliament was offset by confidence in George III. Even so late as the spring of 1769, he writes to a friend in America: "I hope nothing that has happened,

---

[1] Concerning this theory, see Fiske's *The Beginnings of New England*, 266.

or may happen, will diminish in the least our loyalty to our sovereign, or affection for this nation in
general. I can scarcely conceive a king of better
disposition, of more exemplary virtues, or more
truly desirous of promoting the welfare of all his
subjects. The experience we have had of the
family in the two preceding mild reigns, and the
good temper of our young princes, so far as can
yet be discovered, promise us a continuance of this
felicity." Of the British people too he thought
kindly. But for the Parliament he could find no
excuse. He admitted that it might be "decent"
indeed to speak in the "public papers" of the
"wisdom and the justice of Parliament;" nevertheless, the ascription of these qualities to the present Parliament certainly was not true, whatever
might be the case as to any future one. The next
year found him still counseling that the colonies
should hold fast to their allegiance to their king,
who had the best disposition towards them, and
was their most efficient bulwark against "the arbitrary power of a corrupt Parliament." In the
summer of 1773, he was seeking excuses for the
king's adherence to the principle that Parliament
could legally tax the colonies: "when one con-
siders the king's situation," with all his ministers,
advisers, judges, and the great majority of both
houses holding this view, when "one reflects how
necessary it is for him to be well with his Parliament," and that any action of his countenancing
a doctrine contrary to that of both the Lords and

the Commons " would hazard his embroiling himself with those powerful bodies," Franklin was of
opinion that it seemed " hardly to be expected from
him that he should take any step of that kind."
But this was the last apology which he uttered for
George III.   He was about to reach the same estimation of that monarch which has been adopted
by posterity.   Only a very little later he writes :
" Between you and me, the late measures have
been, I suspect, very much the king's own, and he
has in some cases a great share of what his friends
call *firmness*."   Thus tardily, reluctantly, and at
first gently, the kindly philosopher began to admit
to himself and others the truth as to his Majesty's
disposition and character.

Some persons in England, affected by the powerful argument of non-representation, proposed that
the colonies should be represented in Parliament ;
and about the time of the Stamp Act the possibility
of such an arrangement was seriously discussed.
Franklin was willing to speak kindly of a plan
which was logically unobjectionable, and which involved the admission that the existing condition was
unjust; but he knew very well that it would never
develop into a practicable solution of the problem,
and in fact it soon dropped out of men's minds.
January 6, 1766, he wrote that in his opinion the
measure of an *Union*, as he shrewdly called it, was
a wise one ; " but," he said, " I doubt it will
hardly be thought so here until it is too late to
attempt it.   The time has been when the colonies

would have esteemed it a great advantage, as well as honor, to be permitted to send members to Parliament, and would have asked for that privilege if they could have had the least hopes of obtaining it. The time is now come when they are indifferent about it, and will probably not ask it, though they might accept it, if offered them ; and the time will come when they will certainly refuse it. But if such an Union were now established (which methinks it highly imports this country to establish), it would probably subsist so long as Britain shall continue a nation. This people, however, is too proud, and too much despises the Americans to bear the thought of admitting them to such an equitable participation in the government of the whole." [1] Haughty words these, though so tranquilly spoken, and which must have startled many a dignified Briton : behold ! a mere colonist, the son of a tallow chandler, is actually declaring that those puny colonies of simple " farmers, husbandmen, and planters " were already " indifferent " about, and would soon feel in condition to " refuse," representation in such a body as the Parliament of England ; also that it " highly imported " Great Britain to *seek* amalgamation while yet it could be had ! But Franklin meant what he said, and he repeated it more than once, very earnestly. He resented that temper, of which he saw so much on every side, and which he clearly described by saying

[1] To same purport see letter to Evans, May 9, 1766, *Works*, iii. 464.

that every individual in England felt himself to be "part of a sovereign over America."

Men of a different habit of mind of course reiterated the shallow and threadbare nonsense about "virtual," or as it would be called nowadays, constructive, representation of the colonies, likening them to Birmingham, Manchester, and other towns which sent no members to Parliament — as if problems in politics followed the rule of algebra, that negative quantities, multiplied, produce a positive quantity. But Franklin concerned himself little about this unreasonable reasoning, which indeed soon had an effect eminently disagreeable to the class of men who stupidly uttered it. For it was promptly replied that if there were such large bodies of unrepresented Englishmen, it betokened a wrong state of affairs in England also. If English freeholders have not the right of suffrage, said Franklin, "they are injured. Then rectify what is amiss among yourselves, and do not make it a justification of more wrong." [1] Thus that movement began which in time brought about parliamentary reform, another result of this American disturbance which was extremely distasteful to that stratum of English society which was most strenuous against the colonists.

Still another point which demanded elucidation was: why Parliament should not have the power to lay internal taxes just as much as to levy duties. Grenville said: "External and internal taxes are

[1] See also to same purport, *Works,* iv. 157.

the same in effect, and only differ in name;" and
the authority of Parliament to lay external taxes
had never been called in question. Franklin's examiners tried him upon this matter: Can you
show that there is any kind of difference between
the two taxes, to the colony on which they are laid?
He answered: "I think the difference is very
great. An *external* tax is a duty laid on commodities imported; that duty is added to the first cost
and other charges on the commodity, and, when it
is offered for sale, makes a part of the price. If
the people do not like it at that price, they refuse
it; they are not obliged to pay for it. But an
internal tax is forced from the people without their
consent, if not laid by their own representatives.
The Stamp Act says, we shall have no commerce,
make no exchange of property with each other,
neither purchase, nor grant, nor recover debts; we
shall neither marry nor make our wills; unless we
pay such and such sums." It was suggested that
an external tax might be laid on the necessaries
of life, which the people must have; but Franklin
said that the colonies were, or very soon would be,
in a position to produce for themselves all necessaries. He was then asked what was the difference "between a duty on the importation of goods
and an excise on their consumption?" He replied
that there was a very material one; the excise, for
reasons given, seemed unlawful. "But the sea is
yours; you maintain by your fleets the safety of
navigation in it, and keep it clear of pirates; you

may have, therefore, a natural and equitable right to some toll or duty on merchandises carried through that part of your dominions, towards defraying the expense you are at in ships to maintain the safety of that carriage." This was a rather narrow basis on which to build the broad and weighty superstructure of the British Custom House; but it was not to be expected that Franklin should supply any better arguments upon that side of the question. It was obvious that Grenville's proposition might lead to two conclusions. He said: External and internal taxation are in principle substantially identical; we have the right to the former; therefore we must have the right to the latter. It was a quick reply: Since you have not a right to the latter, you cannot have a right to the former. But Franklin, being a prudent man, kept within his intrenchments, and would not hazard increasing the opposition to the colonial claims by occupying this advanced ground. He hinted at it, nevertheless: "At present the colonists do not reason so; but in time they possibly may be convinced by these arguments;" and so they were.

Franklin also in his examination, and at many other times and places, had something to say as to the willingness of the colonies to bear their full share of public burdens. He spoke with warmth and feeling, but with an entire absence of boastfulness or rodomontade. He achieved his purpose by simply recalling such facts as that the colonies in the late war had kept 25,000 troops in the field; that they had raised sums of money so large that even the English Parliament had seen that they were exceeding any reasonable estimate of their capacity, and had voted some partial restitution to them; and that they had received thanks, official and formal yet apparently sincere, for their zeal and their services. Few Englishmen knew these things. So, too, he said, the Americans would help the mother country in an European war, so far as they could; for they regarded themselves as a part of the empire, and really had an affection and loyalty towards England.

On February 21, 1766, General Conway moved for leave to introduce into the House of Commons a bill to repeal the Stamp Act. The motion was carried. The next day the House divided upon the repealing bill: 275 for repeal, 167 against it. The minority were willing greatly to modify the act; but insisted upon its enforcement in some shape. The anxious merchants, who were gathered in throngs outside, and who really had brought about the repeal, burst into jubilant rejoicing. A few days later, March 4th and 5th, the bill took its third reading by a vote of 250 yeas against 122 nays. In the House of Lords, upon the second reading, 73 peers voted for repeal, 61 against it. Thirty-three peers thereupon signed and recorded their protest. At the third reading no division was had, but a second protest, bearing 28 signatures, was

entered.   On March 18th the king, whose position
had been a little enigmatical, but who at last had
become settled in opposition to the bill, unwillingly
placed his signature to it, and ever after regretted
having done so.

When the good news reached the provinces great
indeed was the gladness of the people.   They
heeded little that simultaneously with the repeal a
resolve had been carried through declaratory of the
principle on which the Stamp Act had been based.
The assertion of the right gave them at this moment " very little concern," since they hugged a
triumphant belief that no further attempt would be
made to carry that right into practice.   The people
of Philadelphia seemed firmly persuaded that the
repeal was chiefly due to the unwearied personal
exertions of their able agent.   They could not recall their late distrust of him without shame, and
now replaced it with boundless devotion.   In the
great procession which they made for the occasion
" the sublime feature was a barge, forty feet long,
named FRANKLIN, from which salutes were fired
as it passed along the streets." [1]   That autumn the
old ticket triumphed again at the elections for
members of the Assembly.   Franklin's own pleasant way of celebrating the great event was by sending to his wife " a new gown," with the message,
referring, of course, to the anti-importation league:
that he did not send it sooner, because he knew that
she would not like to be finer than her neighbors,
unless in a gown of her own spinning.

[1] Parton's *Life of Franklin*, i. 481.

No American will find it difficult to conceive the utter ignorance concerning the colonies which then prevailed in England; about their trade, manufactures, cultivated products, natural resources, about the occupations, habits, manners, and ideas of their people, not much more was known than Americans now know concerning the boers of Cape Colony or the settlers of New Zealand. In his examination before the Commons, in many papers which he printed, by his correspondence, and by his conversation in all the various companies which he frequented, Franklin exerted himself with untiring industry to shed some rays into this darkness. At times the comical stories which he heard about his country touched his sense of humor, with the happy result that he would throw off some droll bit of writing for a newspaper, which would delight the friends of America and make its opponents feel very silly even while they could not help laughing at his wit. A good one of these was the paper in which he replied, among other things, to the absurd supposition that the Americans could not make their own cloth, because American sheep had little wool, and that little of poor quality: "Dear sir, do not let us suffer ourselves to be amused with such groundless objections. The very tails of the American sheep are so laden with wool that each has a little car or wagon on four little wheels to support and keep it from trailing on the ground. Would they caulk their ships, would they even litter their horses, with wool, if it were not both plenty and cheap? And what signifies the dearness of labor when an English shilling passes for five and twenty?" and so on. It is pleasant to think that then, as now, many a sober Britisher, with no idea that a satirical jest at his own expense was hidden away in this extravagance, took it all for genuine earnest, and was sadly puzzled at a condition of things so far removed from his own experience.

Very droll is the account of how nearly a party of clever Englishmen were taken in by the paper which purported to advance the claim of the king of Prussia to hold England as a German province, and to levy taxes therein, supported by precisely the same chain of reasoning whereby Britain claimed the like right in respect of the American colonies. This keen and witty satire had a brilliant success, and while Franklin prudently kept his authorship a close secret, he was not a little pleased to see how well his dart flew. In one of his letters he says : —

"I was down at Lord le Despencer's when the post brought that day's papers. Mr. Whitehead was there, too, who runs early through all the papers, and tells the company what he finds remarkable. . . . We were chatting in the breakfast parlor, when he came running in to us, out of breath, with the paper in his hand. 'Here,' says he, 'here's news for ye ! Here's the king of Prussia claiming a right to this kingdom !' All stared, and I as much as anybody ; and he went on to read it. When he had read two or three paragraphs, a gentleman present said : 'Damn their impudence ! I daresay we shall hear by the next post that he is upon his march with 100,000 men to back this.' Whitehead, who is very shrewd, soon after began to smoke it, and looking in my face said, ' I 'll be hanged if this is not some of your American jokes upon us.' "

Then, amid much laughter, it was admitted to be " a fair hit." Of a like nature was his paper setting out " Rules for reducing a great Empire to a small one," which prescribed with admirable satire such a course of procedure as English ministries had pursued towards the American provinces. Lord Mansfield honored it with his condemnation, saying that it was " very able and very artful indeed; and would do mischief by giving here a bad impression of the measures of government."

Yet this English indifference to transatlantic facts could not always be met in a laughing mood. It was too serious, too unfortunate, too obstinately persisted in to excite only ridicule. It was deplorable, upon the very verge of war, and incredible too, after all the warnings that had been had, that there should be among Englishmen such an utter absence of any desire to get accurate knowledge. In 1773 Franklin wrote: " The great defect here is, in all sorts of people, a want of attention to what passes in such remote countries as America; an unwillingness to read anything about them, if it appears a little lengthy; and a disposition to postpone a consideration even of the things which they know they must at last consider." Such ignorance, fertilized by ill will, bore the only fruit which could grow in such soil : abuse and vilification. Yet all the while the upper classes in France, with their eyes well open to a condition of things which seemed to threaten England, were keen enough in their desire for knowledge, translating all Franklin's papers, and keeping up constant communication with him through their embassy. Patient in others of those faults of vehemence and prejudice which had no place in his own nature, Franklin endured long the English provocations and retorted only with a wit too perfect to be personal, with unanswerable arguments, and with simple recitals of facts. But we shall see, later on, that there came an occasion, just before his departure, when even his temper gave way. It was not surprising, for the blood-letting point had then been reached by both peoples.

Franklin's famous examination and his other efforts in behalf of the colonies were appreciated by his countrymen outside of Pennsylvania. He was soon appointed agent also for New Jersey, Georgia, and Massachusetts. The last office was conferred upon him in the autumn of 1770, by no means without a struggle. Samuel Adams, a man as narrow as Franklin was broad, as violent as Franklin was calm, as bigoted a Puritan as Franklin was liberal a Free-thinker, felt towards Franklin that distrust and dislike which a limited but intense mind often cherishes towards an intellect whose vast scope and noble serenity it cannot comprehend. Adams accordingly strenuously opposed the appointment. It was plausibly suggested that Franklin already held other agencies, and that policy would advise " to enlarge the number of our friends." It was meanly added that he held an office under the crown, and that his son was a royal governor. Other ingenious, insidious, and personal objections were urged. Fortunately, however, it was in vain to array such points against Franklin's reputation. Samuel Cooper wrote to him that, though the House had certainly been much divided, " yet such was their opinion of your abilities and integrity, that a majority readily committed the affairs of the Province at this critical season to your care." By reason of this combination of agencies, besides his own personal capacity and prestige, Franklin seemed to become in the eyes of the English the representative of all America. In spite of the unpopularity attaching to the American cause, the position was one of some dignity, greatly enhanced by the respect inspired by the ability with which Franklin filled it, ability which was recognized no less by the enemies than by the friends of the provinces. It was also a position of grave responsibility; and it ought to have been one of liberal emolument, but it was not. The sum of his four salaries should have been £1,200 ; but only Pennsylvania and New Jersey actually paid him. Massachusetts would have paid, but the bills making the appropriations were obstinately vetoed by the royalist governor.[1]

Yet this matter of income was important to him, and it was at no slight personal sacrifice that he was now serving his country. He had a moderate competence, but his expenses were almost doubled by living thus apart from his family, while his affairs suffered by reason of his absence. For a while he was left unmolested in the post-mastership, and in view of all the circumstances it must be confessed that the ministry behaved very well to him in this particular. Rumors which occasionally reached his ears made him uncomfortably aware how precarious his tenure of this position really was. His prolonged absence certainly gave an abundantly fair pretext for his removal; still advantage was not taken of it. Some of his enemies, as he wrote in December, 1770, by plentiful abuse endeavored to provoke him to resign; but they found him sadly " deficient in that Christian virtue of resignation." It was not until 1774, after the episode of the Hutchinson letters and the famous hearing before the privy council, that he was actually displaced. If this forbearance of the ministry was attributable to magnanimity, it stands out in prominent inconsistence with the general course of official life in England at that time. Probably no great injustice would be done in suggesting a baser motive. The ministry doubtless aimed at one or both of two things: to keep a certain personal hold upon him, which might, insensibly to himself, mollify his actions; and to dis-

credit him among his countrymen by precisely such
fleers as had been cast against him in the Massachusetts Assembly.   More than once they sought
to seduce him by offers of office ; it was said that
he could have been an under-secretary of state, had
he been willing to qualify himself for the position
by modifying his views on colonial questions.
More than once, too, gossip circulated in America
that some such bargain had been struck, a slander which was cruel and ignoble indeed, when the
opportunity and temptation may be said to have
been present any and every day during many years
without ever receiving even a moment of doubtful
consideration.   Yet for this the English ministry
are believed not to have been wholly responsible,
since some of these tales are supposed to have been
the unworthy work of Arthur Lee of Virginia.
This young man, a student at one of the Inns of
Court in London, was appointed by the Massachusetts Assembly as a successor to fill Franklin's
place whenever the latter should return to Pennsylvania.   For at the time it was anticipated that
this return would soon occur ; but circumstances
interfered and prolonged Franklin's usefulness
abroad during several years more.   The heir apparent, who was ambitious, could not brook the
disappointment of this delay ; and though kindly
treated and highly praised by the unsuspicious
Franklin, he gave nothing but malice in return.
It is perhaps not fully proved, yet it is certainly

well suspected by historians, that his desire to wreak injury upon Franklin became such a passion as caused him in certain instances to forget all principles of honor, to say nothing of honesty.

CHAPTER VI.

SECOND MISSION TO ENGLAND: II.

IN order to continue the narrative of events with due regard to chronological order it is necessary to revert to the repeal of the Stamp Act. The repealing act was fully as unpopular in England as the repealed act had been in America. It was brought about by no sense of justice, by no good will toward the colonists, but solely by reason of the injury which the law was causing in England, and which was forced upon the reluctant consideration of Parliament by the urgent clamor of the suffering merchants; also perhaps in some degree by a disinclination to send an army across the Atlantic, and by the awkward difficulty suggested by Franklin when he said that if troops should be sent they would find no rebellion, no definite form of resistance, against which they could act. The repeal, therefore, though carried by a large majority, was by no means to be construed as an acknowledgment of error in an asserted principle, but only as an unavoidable admission of a mistake in the application of that principle. The repealing majority grew out of a strange coalition of men of the most opposite ways of thinking concerning the fundamental question. For example, Charles Townshend was a repealer, yet all England did not hold a man who was more wedded than was Townshend to the idea of levying internal taxes in the colonies by act of Parliament. The notion had been his own mischievous legacy to Grenville, but he now felt that it had been clumsily used by his legatee. Many men agreed with him, and the prevalence of this opinion was made obvious by the passage, almost simultaneously, of the resolution declaratory of the right of parliamentary taxation. But the solace of an empty assertion was wholly inadequate to heal the deep wound which English pride had received. The great nation had been fairly hounded into receding before the angry resistance of a parcel of provincials dwelling far away across the sea; the recession was not felt to be an act of magnanimity or generosity or even of justice, but only a bitter humiliation and indignity. Poor Grenville, the responsible adviser of the blundering and unfortunate measure, lost almost as much prestige as Franklin gained. It was hard luck for him; he was as honest in his convictions as Franklin was in the opposite faith, and he was a far abler minister than the successor charged to undo his work. But his knowledge of colonial facts was very insufficient, and the light in which he viewed them was hopelessly false. Franklin had a knowledge immeasurably greater, and was almost incapable of an error of judgment; of all the reputation which was won or lost in this famous contest he gathered the lion's share; he was the hero of the colonists; his ability was recognized impartially by both the contending parties in England, and he was marked as a great man by those astute French statesmen who were watching with delight the opening of this very promising rift in the British empire.

Anger, like water, subsides quickly after the tempest ceases. As each day in its flight carried the Stamp Act and the repeal more remotely into past history, the sanguine and peaceably minded began to hope that England and the colonies might yet live comfortably in union. It only seemed necessary that for a short time longer no fresh provocation should revive animosities which seemed composing themselves to slumber. The colonists tried to believe that England had learned wisdom; Englishmen were cautious about committing a second blunder. In such a time Franklin was the best man whom his countrymen could have had in England. His tranquil temperament, his warm regard for both sides, his wonderful capacity for living well with men who could by no means live well with each other, his social tact, and the respect which his abilities inspired, all combined to enable him now more than ever to fill admirably the position of colonial representative. The effect of such an influence is not to be seen in any single noteworthy occurrence, but is known by a thousand lesser indications, and it is unquestionable that no American representative even to this day has ever

been held in Europe in such estimation as was accorded to Franklin at this time.   He continued
writing and instructing upon American topics, but
to what has already been said concerning his services and opinions abroad, there is nothing of importance to be added occurring within two or three
years after the repeal.   While, however, he played
the often thankless part of instructor to the English, he had the courage to assume the even less
popular rôle of a moderator towards the colonists.
He made it his task to soothe passion and to preach
reason.   He did not do this as a trimmer; never
was one word of compromise uttered by him
throughout all these alarming years.   But he
dreaded that weakness which is the inevitable reaction from excess ; and he was supremely anxious
to secure that trustworthy strength which is impossible without moderation.   What he profoundly
wished was that the " fatal period " of war and
separation should be as much as possible " postponed, and that whenever this catastrophe shall
happen it may appear to all mankind that the fault
has not been ours."   Yet he fell far short of the
Christian principle of turning to the smiter the
other cheek.   He wished the colonists to keep a
steady front face, and only besought them not to
rush forward so foolishly fast as to topple over, of
which ill-considered violence there was much danger.   Of course the usual result of such efforts
overtook him.   He wrote somewhat sadly, in 1768 :
" Being born and bred in one of the countries, and

having lived long and made many agreeable connections of friendship in the other, I wish all prosperity to both; but I have talked and written so
much and so long on the subject, that my acquaintance are weary of hearing and the public of reading any more of it, which begins to make me weary
of talking and writing; especially as I do not find
that I have gained any point in either country, except that of rendering myself suspected by my impartiality; — in England of being too much an
American, and in America of being too much an
Englishman." More than once he repeated this
last sentence with much feeling. But whatever
there was of personal discouragement or despondency in this letter was only a temporary frame of
mind. Dr. Franklin never really slackened his
labors in a business which he had so much at heart
as this of the relationship of the colonies to the
mother country. Neither, it is safe to say, did he
ever bore any one by what he wrote or by what he
said, though his witty effusions in print were usually anonymous, and only some of his soberer and
argumentative papers announced their paternity.

The agony with which the repeal of the Stamp
Act was effected racked too severely the feeble
joints of the Rockingham ministry, and that ill-
knit body soon began to drop to pieces. A new
incumbent was sought for the department which
included the colonies, but that position seemed to
be shunned with a sort of terror; no one loved
office enough to seek it in this niche; no one could

expect comfort in a chamber haunted by such rest-less ghosts. Early in July, at the earnest solicita-tion of the king, Pitt endeavored not so much to form a new ministry as to revamp the existing one. He partially succeeded, but not without difficulty. The result seemed to promise well for the colonies, since the new cabinet contained their chief friends: Pitt himself, Shelburne, Camden, Conway, names all justly esteemed by America. Yet all these were fully offset by the audacious Charles Towns-hend, the originator and great apostle of the scheme of colonial taxation, whom Pitt, much against his will, had been obliged to place in the perilous post of chancellor of the exchequer. It was true that Lord Shelburne undertook the care of the colonies, and that no Englishman cherished better dispo-sitions towards them; but he had to encounter two difficulties, neither of which could be overcome. The one was that Townshend's views were those which soon proved not only to be coincident with those of the king, but also to be popular in Parlia-ment; the other was that, while he had the admin-istration of colonial affairs, Townshend had the function of introducing schemes of taxation. So long as he remained in office he administered all the business of the colonies in the spirit of liberal reform. No reproach was ever brought against his justice, his generosity, his enlightened views of government. But unfortunately all that he had to do, being strictly in the way of *administration*, such as the restraining over-loyal governors, the amelioration of harsh legislation, and universal moderation in language and behavior, could avail comparatively little so long as Townshend, whom Pitt used to call " the incurable," could threaten and bring in obnoxious revenue measures.

Shelburne had the backing of Pitt; but, by ill luck, so soon as the cabinet was formed, Pitt ceased to be Pitt, and became the Earl of Chatham; and with the loss of his own name he lost also more than half of his power. Moreover the increasing infirmities of his body robbed him of efficiency and impaired his judgment. He was utterly unable to keep in subordination his reckless chancellor of the exchequer, betwixt whom and himself no good will had ever existed. On the other hand, this irrepressible Townshend had a far better ally in George III., who sympathized in his purposes, gave him assistance which was none the less powerful for being indirect and occult, and who hated and ingeniously thwarted Shelburne. Moreover, as has been said, it was a popular delusion that Townshend had exceptionally full and accurate knowledge concerning American affairs. His self-confident air, making assurance of success, won for him one half of the battle by so sure a presage of victory. He lured the members of the House by showing them a considerable remission in their own taxes, provided they would stand by his scheme of replacing the deficit by an income from the colonies; and he boldly assured his delighted auditors that he knew " the mode by which a revenue could be drawn from America without offense." He was of the thoughtless class which learns no lesson. He still avowed himself "a firm advocate of the Stamp Act," and with cheerful scorn he "laughed at the absurd distinction between internal and external taxes." He did not expect, he merrily said, alluding to the distinction just conferred upon Chatham, to have *his* statue erected in America. The reports of his speeches kept the colonial mind disquieted. The act requiring the provinces in which regiments were quartered to provide barracks and rations for the troops at the public expense was a further irritation. Shelburne sought to make the burden as easy as possible, but Townshend made Shelburne's duties as hard as possible. Of what use were the minister's liberality and moderation, when the chancellor of the exchequer evoked alarm and wrath by announcing insolently that he was for governing the Americans as subjects of Great Britain, and for restraining their trade and manufactures in subordination to those of the mother country! So the struggle went on within the ministry as well as without it; but the opponents of royal prejudice were heavily handicapped; for the king, though stupid in general, had some political skill and much authority. His ill-concealed personal hostility to his "enemy," as he called Shelburne, threatened like the little cloud in the colonial horizon. Nor was it long before Chatham, a dispirited wreck, withdrew himself entirely from all active participation in affairs, shut himself up at Hayes, and refused to be seen by any one who wished to talk on business.

On May 13, 1767, colonial agents and merchants trading to America were refused admission to hear the debates in the House of Commons. Upon that day Townshend was to develop his scheme. By way, as it were, of striking a keynote, he proposed that the Province of New York should be restrained from enacting any legislation until it should comply with the "billeting act," against which it had heretofore been recalcitrant. He then sketched a scheme for an American board of commissioners of customs. Finally he came to the welcome point of the precise taxes which he designed to levy: he proposed duties on wine, oil, and fruits, imported directly into the colonies from Spain and Portugal; also on glass, paper, lead, colors, and china, and three pence per pound on tea. The governors and chief justices, most of whom were already appointed by the king, but who got their pay by vote of the colonial assemblies, were hereafter to have fixed salaries, to be paid by the king from this American revenue. Two days later the resolutions were passed, directing the introduction of bills to carry out these several propositions, and a month later the bills themselves were passed.

Meantime the cabinet was again getting very rickety, and many heads were busy with suggestions for patching it in one part or another. With Chatham in retreat and the king in the ascendant, it seemed that Townshend had the surest seat. But there is one risk against which even monarchs cannot insure their favorites, and that risk now fell out against Townshend. He died suddenly of a fever, in September, 1767. Lord North succeeded him, destined to do everything which his royal master desired him to do, and bitterly to repent it. A little later, in December, the king scored another success ; Shelburne was superseded in the charge of the colonies by the Earl of Hillsborough, who reëntered the board of trade as first commissioner, and came into the cabinet with the new title of secretary of state for the colonies.

Hillsborough was an Irish peer, with some little capacity for business, but of no more than moderate general ability. He also was supposed, altogether erroneously, to possess a little more knowledge, or, as it might have been better expressed, to be shackled with a little less ignorance, concerning colonial affairs than could be predicated of most of the noblemen who were eligible for public office. America had acquired so much importance that the reputation of familiarity with its condition was an excellent recommendation for preferment. Franklin wrote that this change in the ministry was " very sudden and unexpected ; " and that " whether my Lord Hillsborough's administration will be more stable than others have been for a long time, is quite uncertain ; but as his inclinations are rather favorable towards us (so far as he thinks consistent with what he supposes the unquestionable rights of Britain), I cannot but wish it may continue."

It was Franklin's temperament to be hopeful, and he also purposely cultivated the wise habit of not courting ill fortune by anticipating it. In this especial instance, however, he soon found that his hopefulness was misplaced. Within six months he discovered that this new secretary looked upon the provincial agents " with an evil eye, as obstructors of ministerial measures," and would be well pleased to get rid of them as " un-necessary " impediments in the transaction of business. " In truth," he adds, " the nominations, particularly of Dr. Lee and myself, have not been at all agreeable to his lordship." It soon appeared that his lordship had the Irish quickness for taking a keen point of law ; he broached the theory that no agent could lawfully be appointed by the mere resolution of an assembly, but that the appointment must be made by bill. The value of this theory is obvious when we reflect that a bill did not become law, and consequently an appointment could not be completed, save by the signature of the provincial governor. " This doctrine, if he could establish it," said Franklin, " would in a manner give to his lordship the power of appointing, or, at least, negativing any choice of the House of Representatives and Council, since it would be easy for him to instruct the governor not to assent to the appointment of such and such men, who are obnoxious to him ; so that if the appointment is annual, every agent that valued his post must consider himself as holding it by the favor of his lordship;" whereof the consequences were easy to be seen.

There was a lively brush between the noble secretary and Franklin, when the former first propounded this troublesome view. It was in January, 1771, that Franklin called upon his lordship —

"to pay my respects . . . and to acquaint him with my appointment by the House of Representatives of Massachusetts Bay to be their agent here." But his lordship interrupted : —

"I must set you right there, Mr. Franklin; you are not agent.

"Why, my lord?   .

"You are not appointed.

"I do not understand your lordship; I have the appointment in my pocket.

"You are mistaken; I have later and better advices. I have a letter from Governor Hutchinson; he would not give his assent to the bill.

"There was no bill, my lord ; it was a vote of the House.

"There was a bill presented to the governor for the purpose of appointing you and another, one Dr. Lee I think he is called, to which the governor refused his assent.

"I cannot understand this, my lord ; I think there must be some mistake in it. Is your lordship quite sure that you have such a letter ?

"I will convince you of it directly; Mr. Pownall will come in and satisfy you."

So Mr. Pownall, invoked by the official bell,

appeared upon the scene. But he could not play his part; he was obliged to say that there was no such letter. This was awkward; but Franklin was too civil or too prudent to triumph in the discomfiture of the other. He simply offered the "authentic copy of the vote of the House" appointing him, and asked if his lordship would "please to look at it." His lordship took the paper unwillingly, and then, without looking at it, said: —

"An information of this kind is not properly brought to me as secretary of state. The board of trade is the proper place.

"I will leave the paper then with Mr. Pownall to be —

"(*Hastily.*) To what end would you leave it with him?

"To be entered on the minutes of the board, as usual.

"(*Angrily.*) It shall not be entered there. No such paper shall be entered there while I have anything to do with the business of that board. The House of Representatives has no right to appoint an agent. We shall take no notice of any agents but such as are appointed by acts of Assembly, to which the governor gives his assent. We have had confusion enough already. Here is one agent appointed by the Council, another by the House of Representatives.[1] Which of these is agent for the Province? Who are we to hear in provincial affairs? An agent appointed by act of Assembly we can under-

[1] The agent for the Council, Mr. Bollan, acted in entire accord with Dr. Franklin; there was no inconsistency between the two offices, which were altogether distinct, neither any clashing between the incumbents, as might be inferred from Lord Hillsborough's language.

stand. No other will be attended to for the future, I can assure you.

"I cannot conceive, my lord, why the consent of the governor should be thought necessary to the appointment of an agent for the people. It seems to me that —

"(*With a mixed look of anger and contempt.*) I shall not enter into a dispute with *you*, Sir, upon this subject.

"I beg your lordship's pardon; I do not mean to dispute with your lordship. I would only say that it appears to me that every body of men who cannot appear in person, where business relating to them may be transacted, should have a right to appear by an agent. The concurrence of the governor does not seem to be necessary. It is the business of the people that is to be done; he is not one of them; he is himself an agent.

"(*Hastily.*) Whose agent is he?

"The king's, my lord.

"No such matter. He is one of the corporation by the Province charter. No agent can be appointed but by an act, nor any act pass without his assent. Besides, this proceeding is directly contrary to express instructions.

"I did not know there had been such instructions. I am not concerned in any offense against them, and —

"Yes, your offering such a paper to be entered is an offense against them. No such appointment shall be entered. When I came into the administration of American affairs I found them in great disorder. By *my firmness* they are now something mended; and while I have the honor to hold the seals I shall continue the same conduct, the same *firmness*. I think my duty to the master I serve, and to the government of this nation, requires it of me. If that conduct is not approved, *they* may take that office from me when they please : I shall make them a bow and thank them; I shall resign with pleasure. That gentleman [Mr. Pownall] knows it; but while I continue in it I shall resolutely persevere in the same *firmness.*"

Speaking thus, his lordship seemed warm, and grew pale, as if "angry at something or somebody besides the agent, and of more consequence to himself." Franklin thereupon, taking back his credentials, said, speaking with an innuendo aimed at that which had not been expressed, but which lay plainly visible behind his lordship's pallor and excitement : —

"I beg your lordship's pardon for taking up so much of your lordship's time. It is, I believe, of no great importance whether the appointment is acknowledged or not, for I have not the least conception that an agent can, *at present*, be of any use to any of the colonies. I shall therefore give your lordship no further trouble."

Therewith he made his exit, and went home to write the foregoing sketch of the scene. Certainly throughout so irritating an interview he had conducted himself with creditable self - restraint and moderation, yet with his closing sentence he had sent home a dart which rankled. He soon heard that his lordship "took great offense" at these last words, regarding them as "extremely rude and abusive," and as "equivalent to telling him to his face that the colonies could expect neither favor nor justice during his administration." " I find,"

adds Franklin, with placid satisfaction in the skill
with which he had shot his bolt, " I find he did not
mistake me."

So Franklin retained the gratification which lies
in having administered a stinging and appreciated
retort; a somewhat empty and entirely personal
gratification, it must be admitted. Hillsborough
kept the substance of victory, inasmuch as he persisted in refusing to recognize Franklin as the agent
of the Massachusetts Bay. Yet in this he did not
annihilate, indeed very slightly curtailed, Franklin's
usefulness. It merely signified that Franklin ceased
to be an official conduit for petitions and like communications. His weight and influence, based upon
his knowledge and prestige, remained unimpugned.
In a word, it was of little consequence that the
lord secretary would not acknowledge him as the
representative of one Province, so long as all England practically treated him as the representative
of all America.

From this time forth, of course, there was warfare
between the secretary and the unacknowledged
agent. Franklin began to entertain a " very mean
opinion " of Hillsborough's "abilities and fitness
for his station. His character is conceit, wrong-
headedness, obstinacy, and passion. Those who
speak most favorably of him allow all this; they
only add that he is an honest man and means well.
If that be true, as perhaps it may, I only wish him
a better place, where only honesty and well-mean-
ing are required, and where his other qualities can

do no harm. . . . I hope, however, that our affairs
will not much longer be perplexed and embarrassed
by his perverse and senseless management." But
for the present Franklin was of opinion that it
would be well " to leave this omniscient, infallible
minister to his own devices, and be no longer at the
expense of sending any agent, whom he can displace
by a repeal of the appointing act."

Hillsborough's theory was adopted by the board
of trade, and Franklin therefore remained practically stripped of the important agency for Massachusetts. He anticipated that this course would
soon put an end to all the colonial agencies; but
he said that the injury would be quite as great
to the English government as to the colonies, for
the agents had often saved the cabinet from introducing, through misinformation, " mistaken measures," which it would afterward have found to be
" very inconvenient." He expressed his own opinion that when the colonies " came to be considered
in the light of *distinct states*, as I conceive they
really are, possibly their agents may be treated
with more respect and considered more as public
ministers." But this was a day-dream; the current
was setting in quite the opposite direction.

In point of fact, Massachusetts seems to have
taken no detriment from this foolish and captious
bit of chicanery. All the papers and arguments
which she had occasion to have presented always
found their way to their destination as well as they
would have done if Franklin had been acknowl-

edged as the *quasi* public minister, which he conceived to be his proper character.

Franklin perfectly appreciated that Hillsborough
retained his position by precarious tenure. He
shrewdly suspected that if the war with Spain,
which then seemed imminent, were to break out,
Hillsborough would at once be removed. For in
that case it would be the policy of the government
to conciliate the colonies, at any cost, for the time
being. This crisis passed by, fortunately for the
secretary and unfortunately for the provinces.
Yet still the inefficient and ill-friended minister
remained very infirm in his seat. An excuse only
was needed to displace him, and by a singular and
unexpected chance Franklin furnished that excuse.
It was the humble and discredited colonial agent
who unwittingly but not unwillingly gave the jar
which toppled the great earl into retirement. His
fall when it came gave general satisfaction. His
unfitness for his position had become too obvious
to be denied; he had given offense in quarters
where he should have made friends; he had irritated the king and provoked the cabinet. Franklin, with his observant sagacity, quickly divined
that George III. was "tired" of Hillsborough and
"of his administration, which had weakened the
affection and respect of the colonies for a royal
government;" and accordingly he "used proper
means from time to time that his majesty should
have due information and convincing proofs" of
this effect of his lordship's colonial policy.

It was, however, upon a comparatively trifling matter that Hillsborough finally lost his place. It has been already mentioned that many years before this time Franklin had urged the establishment of one or two frontier, or " barrier," provinces in the interior. He had never abandoned this scheme, and of late had been pushing it with some prospect of success ; for among other encouraging features he astutely induced three privy councilors to become financially interested in the project. The original purpose of the petitioners had been to ask for only 2,500,000 acres of land ; but Hillsborough bade them ask for " enough to make a province." This advice was grossly disingenuous ; for Hillsborough himself afterward admitted that from the beginning he had intended to defeat the application, and had put the memorialists " upon asking so much with that very view, supposing it too much to be granted." But they, not suspecting, fell into the trap and increased their demand to 23,000,000 acres, certainly a sufficient quantity to call for serious consideration. When the petition came before the board of trade, Lord Hillsborough, who was president of the board, took upon himself the task of rendering a report. To the surprise of the petitioners, who had reason to suppose him well inclined, he replied adversely. The region was so far away, he said, that it would not "lie within the reach of the trade and commerce of this kingdom ; " so far, also, as not to admit of " the exercise of that authority and jurisdiction . . . necessary for the preservation of the colonies in due subordination to and dependence upon the mother country." The territory appeared, " upon the fullest evidence," to be " utterly inaccessible to shipping," and therefore the inhabitants would " probably be led to manufacture for themselves, . . . a consequence . . . to be carefully guarded against." Also part belonged to the Indians, who ought not to be disturbed, and settlements therein would of course lead to Indian wars and to " fighting for every inch of the ground." Further, the occupation of this tract " must draw and carry out a great number of people from Great Britain," who would soon become "a kind of separate and independent people, . . . and set up for themselves," meeting their own wants and taking no " supplies from the mother country nor from the provinces " along the seaboard. At so great a distance from " the seat of government, courts, magistrates, etc.," the territory would " become a receptacle and kind of asylum for offenders," full of crime itself, and encouraging crime elsewhere. This disorderly population would soon " become formidable enough to oppose his majesty's authority, disturb government, and even give law to the other or first-settled part of the country, and thus throw everything into confusion." Such arguments were as feeble as they were bodeful. The only point which his lordship really scored was in reply to Franklin's theory of the protection against the Indians which these colonies would afford to those on the seaboard. Hillsbor·

ough well said that the new settlements themselves would stand most in need of protection. It was only advancing, not eliminating, a hostile frontier.

Evidently it required no very able reasoning, coming from the president of the board, to persuade his subordinates; and this foolish report was readily adopted. But Franklin was not so easily beaten; the privy council furnished one more stage at which he could still make a fight. He drew up a reply to Lord Hillsborough's paper and submitted it to that body. It was a long and very carefully prepared document; it dealt in facts historical and statistical, in which the report was utterly deficient; it furnished evidence and illustration; in arguing upon probabilities it went far toward demolishing the theories advanced by the president of the board. The two briefs were laid before a tribunal in which three men sat who certainly ought not to have been sitting in this cause, since Franklin's interest was also their own; but probably this did not more than counterbalance the prestige of official position in the opposite scale. Certainly Franklin had followed his invariable custom of furnishing his friends with ample material to justify them in befriending him. In this respect he always gallantly stood by his own side. The allies whom at any time he sought he always abundantly supplied with plain facts and sound arguments, in which weapons he always placed his chief trust. So at present, whatever was the motive which induced privy councilors to open their ears to what Franklin had to say, after they had heard him they could not easily decide against him. Nor had those of them who were personally disinterested any great inducement to do so, since, though some of them may have disliked him, none of them had any great liking for his noble opponent. So they set aside the report of the board of trade.[1]

Upon this Lord Hillsborough fell into a hot rage, and sent in his resignation. It was generally understood that he had no notion that it would be accepted, or that he would be allowed to leave upon such a grievance. He fancied that he was establishing a dilemma which would impale Franklin. But he was in error; he himself was impaled. No one expostulated with him; he was left to exercise "the Christian virtue of resignation" without hindrance. Franklin said that the anticipation of precisely this result, so far from being an obstacle in the way of his own success, had been an additional incitement to the course taken by the council.

So the earl, the enemy of America, went out; and the colonial agent had shown him the door, with all England looking on. It was a mortification which Hillsborough could never forgive, and upon four occasions, when Franklin made the conventional call to pay his respects, he did not find his lordship at home. At his fifth call he received from a lackey a very plain intimation that there

[1] A very interesting statement of these proceedings may be found in Franklin's *Works*, x. 346.

was no chance that he ever would find the ex-secre-
tary at home, and thereafter he desisted from the
forms of civility. " I have never since," he said,
" been nigh him, and we have only abused one another at a distance." Franklin had fully balanced
one account at least.

So far as the special matter in hand was concerned, the worsting of Hillsborough, though a
gratification, did not result in the bettering of
Franklin and his co-petitioners. April 6, 1773, he
wrote : " The affair of the grant goes on but slowly.
I do not yet clearly see land. I begin to be a little
of the sailors' mind, when they were landing a cable
out of a store into a ship, and one of 'em said :
' 'T is a long heavy cable, I wish we could see the
end of it.' ' Damn me,' says another, ' if I believe it has any end ; somebody has cut it off.' "
A cable twisted of British red tape was indeed a
coil without an end. In this case, before the patent
was granted, Franklin had become so unpopular,
and the Revolution so imminent, that the matter
was dropped by a sort of universal consent.

Franklin rejoiced in this departure of Hillsborough as a good riddance of a man whom he
thought to be as " double and deceitful " as any
one he had ever met. It is possible that, as he had
been instrumental in creating the vacancy, he may
also have assisted in some small degree in disposing of the succession. One day he was complaining of Hillsborough to a " friend at court," when
the friend replied that Hillsborough was wont to

represent the Americans "as an unquiet people, not easily satisfied with any ministry; that, however, it was thought too much occasion had been given them to dislike the present;" and the question was asked whether, in case of Hillsborough's removal, Franklin "could name another likely to be more acceptable" to his countrymen. He at once suggested Lord Dartmouth. This was the appointment which* was now made, in August, 1772, and the news of which gave much satisfaction to all the "friends of America." For Dartmouth was of kindly disposition, and when previously president of the board of trade had shown a liberal temper in provincial affairs.

The relationship between Franklin and Lord Dartmouth opened auspiciously. Franklin waited upon him at his first levee, at the close of October, 1772, and was received "very obligingly." Further Franklin was at once recognized as agent for Massachusetts, with no renewal of the caviling as to the manner of his appointment, from which he hopefully augured that "business was getting into a better train." A month later he reported himself as being still "upon very good terms" with the new minister, who, he had "reason to think," meant well by the colonies." So Dartmouth did, undoubtedly, and if the best of intentions and of feelings could have availed much at this stage of affairs, Franklin and his lordship might have postponed the Revolution until the next generation. But it was too late to counteract the divergent movements of the two nations, and no better proof could be desired of the degree to which this divergence had arrived than the fact itself that the moderate Franklin and the well-disposed Dartmouth could not come into accord. Each people had declared its political faith, its fundamental theory; and the faith and theory of the one were fully and fairly adverse to those of the other; and the instant that the talk went deep enough, this irreconcilable difference was sure to be exposed.

During the winter of 1772–3, following Lord Dartmouth's appointment, a lively dispute arose in Massachusetts between the Assembly and Governor Hutchinson. It was the old question, whether the English Parliament had control in matters of colonial taxation. The governor made speeches and said Yea, while the Assembly passed resolutions and said Nay. The early ships, arriving in England in the spring of 1773, brought news of this dispute, which seemed to have been indeed a hot one. The English ministry were not pleased; they wanted to keep their relationship with the colonies tranquil for a while, because there was a renewal of the danger of a war with Spain. Therefore they were vexed at the over zeal of Hutchinson; and Lord Dartmouth frankly said so. Franklin called one day upon the secretary and found him much perplexed at the "difficulties" into which the governor had brought the ministers by his "imprudence." Parliament, his lordship said, could not "suffer such a declaration of the colonial

Assembly, asserting its independence, to pass un-
noticed." Franklin thought otherwise : " It is
words only," he said ; " acts of Parliament are
still submitted to there ; " and so long as such was
the case " Parliament would do well to turn a deaf
ear. . . . Force could do no good." Force, it was
replied, might not be thought of, but rather an act
to lay the colonies " under some inconveniences, till
they rescind that declaration." Could they by no
possibility be persuaded to withdraw it ? Franklin
was clearly of opinion that the resolve could only
be withdrawn after the withdrawal of the speech
which it answered, " an awkward operation, which
perhaps the governor would hardly be directed to
perform." As for an act establishing " inconveniences," probably it would only put the colonies, " as
heretofore, on some method of incommoding this
country till the act is repealed ; and so we shall go
on injuring and provoking each other instead of
cultivating that good-will and harmony so necessary
to the general welfare." Divisions, his lordship
admitted, " must weaken the whole ; for we are yet
one empire, whatever may be the opinions of the
Massachusetts Assembly." But how to escape
divisions was the conundrum. Could his lordship
withhold from Parliament the irritating documents,
though in fact they were already notorious, and
" hazard the being called to account in some future
session of Parliament for keeping back the communication of despatches of such importance ? "
He appealed to Franklin for advice ; but Franklin

would undertake to give none, save that, in his opinion, if the despatches should be laid before Parliament, it would be prudent to order them to lie on the table. For, he said, "were I as much an Englishman as I am an American, and ever so desirous of establishing the authority of Parliament, I protest to your lordship I cannot conceive of a single step the Parliament can take to increase it that will not tend to diminish it, and after abundance of mischief they must finally lose it." So whenever the crucial test was applied these two men found themselves utterly at variance, and the hopelessness of a peaceful conclusion would have been obvious, had not each shunned a prospect so painful.

It must be confessed that, if Lord Dartmouth was so pathetically desirous to undo an irrevocable past, Dr. Franklin was no less anxious for the performance of a like miracle. Both the statesman and the philosopher would have appreciated better the uselessness of their efforts, had their feelings been less deeply engaged. Franklin's vain wish at this time was to move the peoples of England and America back to the days before the passage of the Stamp Act. "I have constantly given it as my opinion," he wrote, early in 1771, "that, if the colonies were restored to the state they were in before the Stamp Act, they would be satisfied and contend no farther." Two and a half years later, following the fable of the sibylline books, he expressed the more extreme opinion that "the letter

of the two houses of the 29th of June, proposing
as a satisfactory measure the restoring things to
the state in which they were at the conclusion of
the late war, is a fair and generous offer on our
part, . . . and more than Britain has a right to expect from us. . . . If she has any wisdom left, she
will embrace it, and agree with us immediately."

But the insuperable trouble was that, at the close
of the last war and before the passage of the
Stamp Act, the controversy upon the question of
right had been unborn. Now, having come into
being, this controversy could not be laid at rest by
a mere waiver; it was of that nature that its resur-
rection would be sure and speedy. Anything else
would have been, of course, the practical victory of
the colonies and defeat of England; and the English could not admit that things had reached this
pass as yet. If England should not renounce her
right, the colonies would always remain uneasy beneath the unretracted assertion of it; if she should
never again seek to exercise it, she would be really
yielding. It was idle to talk of such a state of
affairs; it could not be brought about, even if it
were conceivable that each side could be induced to
repeal all its acts and resolves touching the subject,
— and even this preliminary step was what no
reasonable man could anticipate. In a word, when
Franklin longed for the restoration of the *status
quo ante* the Stamp Act, he longed for a chimera.
A question had been raised, which was of that kind
that it could not be compromised, or set aside, or

ignored, or forgotten; it must be *settled* by the recession or by the defeat of one contestant or the other. Nothing better than a brief period of restless and suspicious truce could be gained by an effort to restore the situation of a previous date, even were such restoration possible, since the intervening period and the memory of its undetermined dispute concerning a principle could not be annihilated.

Still Franklin persistently refused to despair, so long as peace was still unbroken. Until blood had been shed, war *might* be avoided. This was no lack of foresight; occasionally an expression escaped him which showed that he fully understood the drift of affairs and saw the final outcome of the opposing doctrines. In 1769 he said that matters were daily tending more and more "to a breach and final separation." In 1771 he thought that any one might "clearly see in the system of customs to be exacted in America by act of Parliament, the seeds sown of a total disunion of the countries, though as yet that event may be at a considerable distance." By 1774 he said, in an article written for an English newspaper, that certain "angry writers" on the English side were using "their utmost efforts to persuade us that this war with the colonies (for a war it will be) is a national cause, when in fact it is a ministerial one." But he very rarely spoke thus. It was at once his official duty as well as his strong personal wish to find some other exit from the public embarrassments than by this direful conclusion. Therefore, so long as war did not exist he refused to admit that it was inevitable, and he spared no effort to prevent it, leaving to fervid orators to declare the contrary and to welcome it; nor would he ever allow himself to be discouraged by any measure of apparent hopelessness.

His great dread was that the colonies might go so fast and so far as to make matters incurable before thinking people were ready to recognize such a crisis as unavoidable. He seldom wrote home without some words counseling moderation. He wanted to see " much patience and the utmost discretion in our general conduct." It must not, however, be supposed that such language was used to cover any lukewarmness, or irresolution, or tendency towards halfway or temporizing measures. On the contrary, he was wholly and consistently the opposite of all this. His moderation was not at all akin to the moderation of Dickinson and such men, who were always wanting to add another to the long procession of petitions and protests. He only desired that the leading should be done by the wise men, so as not to have a Braddock's defeat in so grave and perilous an undertaking. He feared that a mob might make an irrevocable blunder, and the mischievous rabble create a condition of affairs which the real statesmen of the provinces could neither mend nor excuse. Certainly his anxiety was not without cause. He warned his country people that there was nothing which their enemies

in England more wished than that, by insurrec-
tions, they would give a good pretense for establishing a large military force in the colonies. As
between friends, he said, every affront is not worth
a duel, so " between the governed and governing
every mistake in government, every encroachment
on right, is not worth a rebellion." So he thought
that an " immediate rupture " was not in accord-
ance with " general prudence," for by " a prema-
ture struggle " the colonies might " be crippled and
kept down another age." No one, however, was
more resolute than he that the mistakes and encroachments which had occurred should not be repeated. An assurance against such repetition, he
tried to think, might be effected within a reasonably short time by two peaceful influences. One
of these was a cessation of all colonial purchases of
English commodities; the other was the rapid increase of the visible strength and resources of the
colonies. He was urgent and frequent in reiterating his opinion of the great efficacy of the non-
purchasing agreements. It is a little odd to find
him actually declaring that, if the people would
honestly persist in these engagements, he " should
almost wish " the obnoxious act " never to be repealed ; " for, besides industry and frugality, such
a condition of things would promote a variety of
domestic manufactures. In a word, this British
oppression would bring about all those advantages
for the infant nation, which, through the medium
of the protective tariff, have since been purchased

by Americans at a vast expense. Moreover, the money which used to be sent to England in payment for superfluous luxuries would be kept at home, to be there laid out in domestic improvements. Gold and silver, the scarcity of which caused great inconvenience in the colonies, would remain in the country. All these advantages would accrue from a course which at the same time must give rise in England itself to a pressure so extreme that Parliament could not long resist it. " The trading part of the nation, with the manufacturers, are become sensible how necessary it is for their welfare to be on good terms with us. The petitioners of Middlesex and of London have numbered among their grievances the *unconstitutional* taxes on America; and similar petitions are expected from all quarters. So that I think we need only be quiet, and persevere in our schemes of frugality and industry, and the rest will do itself." But it was obvious that, if the measures were not now persisted in until they should have had their full effect, a like policy could never again be resorted to; and Franklin gave it as his belief that, " if we do persist another year, we shall never afterwards have occasion to use " the remedy.

To him it seemed incredible that the people of America should not loyally persist in a policy of non-importation of English goods. Not only was the doing without these a benefit to domestic industries, but buying them was a direct aid and maintenance to the oppressor. He said : " If our people will, by consuming such commodities, purchase and pay for their fetters, who that sees them so shackled will think they deserve either redress or pity? Methinks that in drinking tea, a true American, reflecting that by every cup he contributed to the salaries, pensions, and rewards of the enemies and persecutors of his country, would be half choked at the thought, and find no quantity of sugar sufficient to make the nauseous draught go down." [1]

In this connection he was much "diverted" and gratified by the results of the Stamp Act, and especially of the act laying the duty on tea. The gross proceeds of the former statute, gathered in the West Indies and Canada, since substantially nothing was got in the other provinces, was £1,500; while the expenditure had amounted to £12,000! The working of the Customs Act had been far worse. According to his statement, the unfortunate East India Company, in January, 1773, had at least £2,000,000, some said £4,000,000, worth of goods which had accumulated in their warehouses since the enactment, of which the chief part would, in the natural condition of business, have been absorbed by the colonies. The consequence was that the company's shares had fallen enormously in price, that it was hard pressed to make its payments, that its credit was so seriously impaired that the Bank of England would not help it, and that its dividends had been reduced below the point at and above which it was obliged to pay, and heretofore regularly had paid, £400,000 annually to the govern-

[1] See also letter to Marshall, April 22, 1771, *Works*, x. 315.

ment. Many investors were painfully straitened, and not a few bankruptcies ensued. Besides the loss of this annual stipend the treasury was further the sufferer by the great expense which had been incurred in endeavoring to guard the American coast against smugglers; with the added vexation that these costly attempts had, after all, been fruit-less. Fifteen hundred miles of shore line, occupied by people unanimously hostile to the king's revenue officers, presented a task much beyond the capabilities of the vessels which England could send thither. So the Dutch, the Danes, the Swedes, and the French soon established a thriving contra-band trade; the American housewives were hardly interrupted in dispensing the favorite beverage; the English merchant's heavy loss became the foreign smuggler's aggravating gain; and the costly sacri-fice of the East India Company fell short of effect-ing the punishment of the wicked Americans. Franklin could not " help smiling at these blun-ders." Englishmen would soon resent them, he said, would turn out the ministry that was respons-ible for them, and put in a very different set of men, who would undo the mischief. " If we con-tinue firm and united, and resolutely persist in the non-consumption agreement, this adverse ministry cannot possibly stand another year. And surely the great body of our people, the farmers and arti-ficers, will not find it hard to keep an agreement by which they both save and gain." Thus he contin-ued to write so late as February, 1775, believing to the last in the efficacy of this policy.

CHAPTER VII.

THE famous episode of the Hutchinson letters, occurring near the close of Franklin's stay in England, must be narrated with a brevity more in accord with its real historical value than with its interest as a dramatic story. In conversation one day with an English gentleman, Franklin spoke with resentment of the sending troops to Boston and the other severe measures of the government. The other in reply engaged to convince him that these steps were taken upon the suggestion and advice of Americans. A few days later he made good his promise by producing certain letters, signed by Hutchinson, Oliver, and others, all natives of, and residents and office-holders in, America. The addresses had been cut from the letters ; but in other respects they were unmutilated, and they were the original documents. They contained just such matter as the gentleman had described, — opinions and advice which would have commended themselves highly to a royalist, but which could have seemed to a patriot in the provinces only the most danger-

ous and abominable treason. Induced by obvious
motives, Franklin begged leave to send these letters to Massachusetts, and finally obtained permission to do so, subject to the stipulation that they
should not be printed nor copied, and should be
circulated only among a few leading men. His
purpose, he said, lay in his belief that when the
"principal people" in Boston "saw the measures
they complained of took their rise in a great degree from the representations and recommendations
of their own countrymen, their resentment against
Britain might abate, as mine has done, and a reconciliation be more easily obtained." [1] Franklin accordingly sent over the letters, together with strict
injunctions in pursuance of his engagement to the
giver of them : "In confidence of your following
inviolably my engagement," etc., he wrote. But
this solemn instruction was not complied with ; the
temptation was too great for the honor of some
among the patriots, who resolved that the letters

[1] The importance of establishing the fact that the government's
course was instigated by Hutchinson is liable at the present day
to be underrated. For his name has fallen into such extreme disrepute in America that to have been guided by his advice seems
only an additional offense. But such was not the case ; Hutchinson came of old and prominent Massachusetts stock ; he was a
descendant of Anne Hutchinson, of polemic fame, and when appointed to office he appeared a man of good standing and ability.
The English government had a perfect right to rely upon the
soundness of his statements and opinions. Thus it was really of
great moment for Franklin to be able to convince the people of
Massachusetts that the English measures were in strict conformity
with Hutchinson's suggestions. It was an excuse for the English,
as it also was the condemnation of Hutchinson, in colonial opinion.

should be made public despite any pledge to the contrary, and resorted to a shallow artifice for achieving their end. A story was started that authenticated copies of the same papers had been received from England by somebody. There was a prudent abstention from any inquiry into the truth of this statement. " I know," said Franklin, " that could not be. It was an expedient to disengage the House." Dishonest as it obviously was, it was successful ; members accepted it as a removal of the seal of secrecy; and the documents having thus found their way before the Assembly were ordered to be printed. That body, greatly incensed, immediately voted a petition to the king for the removal of the governor and lieutenant - governor, and sent it over to Franklin to be presented.

The publication of these letters made no little stir. The writers were furious, and of course brought vehement charges of bad faith and dishonorable behavior. But they were at a loss to know upon whom to visit their wrath. For the person to whom they had written the letters was dead, and they knew no one else who had been concerned in the matter. The secret of the channel of conveyance had been rigidly kept. No one had the slightest idea by whom the letters had been transmitted to Massachusetts, nor by whom they had been received there. To this day it is not known by whom the letters were given to Franklin. July 25, 1773, he wrote to Mr. Cushing, the speaker of the Assembly, to whom he had inclosed the let-

ters : " I observe that you mention that no person
besides Dr. Cooper and one member of the committee knew they came from me. I did not accompany them with any request of being myself concealed ; for, believing what I did to be in the way
of my duty as agent, though I had no doubt of
its giving offense, not only to the parties exposed
but to administration here, I was regardless of the
consequences. However, since the letters themselves are now copied and printed, contrary to the
promise I made, I am glad my name has not been
heard on the occasion ; and, as I do not see how it
could be of any use to the public, I now wish it
may continue unknown; though I hardly expect
it." Unfortunately it soon became of such use to
two individuals in England that Franklin himself
felt obliged to divulge it ; otherwise it might have
remained forever a mystery.

Though the addresses had been cut from the
letters, yet they had previously been shown to many
persons in England, and it soon became known
there that they had been written to Mr. William
Whately, now dead, but who, when the letters
were written, was a member of Parliament and
private secretary to George Grenville, who was
then in the cabinet. Amid the active surmises as
to the next link in the chain suspicion naturally
attached to Thomas Whately, brother and executor
of the dead man, and in possession of his papers.
This gentleman denied that he had ever, to his
knowledge, had these letters in his hands. Sus-

picion next attached to Mr. Temple, "our friend," as Franklin described him. He had had access to the letters of William Whately for the purpose of getting from among them certain letters written by himself and his brother; he had lived in America, had been governor of New Hampshire, and later in letters to his friends there had announced the coming of the letters before they had actually arrived. The expression of suspicion towards Temple found its way into a newspaper, bolstered with an intimation that the information came from Thomas Whately. Temple at once made a demand upon Whately to exculpate him. This of course Whately could not do, since he had not inspected the letters taken by Temple, and so could not say of his knowledge that these were not among them. But instead of taking this perfectly safe ground, he published a card stating that Temple had had access to the letters of the deceased for a special purpose, and that Temple had solemnly averred to him, Whately, that he had neither removed nor copied any letters save those written by himself and his brother. This exoneration was far from satisfying Temple, who conceived that it rather injured than improved his position. Accordingly he challenged Whately and the two fought in Hyde Park ring. The story of the duel, which was mingled of comedy and tragedy, is vividly told by Mr. Parton. Whately was wounded twice, and at his request the fight then ceased. Temple was accused, but unfairly, of having thrust at him when he was down. But it was no conventional duel, or result of temporary hot blood. The contestants were profoundly angry with each other, and were bent on more serious results than curable wounds. It was understood that so soon as Whately should be well, the fight would be renewed. Thus matters stood when Franklin came up to London from a visit in the country, to be astonished by the news of what had occurred, and annoyed at the prospect of what was likely to occur. At once he inserted this letter: —

To the Printer of the " Public Advertiser : "

Sir, — Finding that two gentlemen have been unfortunately engaged in a duel about a transaction and its circumstances of which both of them are totally ignorant and innocent, I think it incumbent upon me to declare (for the prevention of further mischief, as far as such a declaration may contribute to prevent it) that I alone am the person who obtained and transmitted to Boston the letters in question. Mr. Whately could not communicate them, because they were never in his possession; and for the same reason they could not be taken from him by Mr. Temple. They were not of the nature of *private* letters between friends. They were written by public officers to persons in public stations on public affairs, and intended to procure public measures; they were therefore handed to other public persons, who might be influenced by them to produce those measures. Their tendency was to incense the mother country against her colonies, and, by the steps recommended, to widen the breach which they effected. The chief caution expressed with regard to privacy was, to keep their contents from the colony agents, who, the writers apprehended, might return them, or copies of them, to America. That apprehension was, it seems, well founded, for the first agent who laid his hands on them thought it his duty to transmit them to his constituents.

B. FRANKLIN,
*Agent for the House of Representatives of
Massachusetts Bay.*

CRAVEN STREET, *December 25, 1773.*

The petition, forwarded by the House of Representatives of Massachusetts Bay, after they had read the famous letters, recited that the petitioners had " very lately had before them *certain papers*," and it was upon the strength of the contents of these papers that they humbly prayed that his majesty would be "pleased to remove from their posts in this government" Governor Hutchinson and Lieutenant - Governor Oliver. Immediately upon receipt of this petition Franklin transmitted it to Lord Dartmouth, with a very civil and conciliatory note, to which Lord Dartmouth replied in the same spirit. This took place in August, 1773; the duel followed in December, and in the interval Franklin had heard nothing from the petition. But when his foregoing letter was published and conned over it seemed that the auspicious moment for the ministry was now at hand, and that it had actually been furnished to them by the astute Franklin himself. There is no question that he had acted according to his conscience, and it seems now to be generally agreed that his conscience did

not mislead him. But he had been placed in a
difficult position, and it was easily possible to give
a very bad coloring to his conduct. There was in
this business an opportunity to bring into discredit
the character of the representative man of America,
the man foremost of Americans in the eyes of the
world, the man most formidable to the ministerial
party ; such an opportunity was not to be lost.[1]

Franklin had anticipated that the " king would
have considered this petition, as he had done the
preceding one, in his cabinet, and have given an
answer without a hearing." But on the afternoon
of Saturday, January 8, 1774, he was surprised to
receive notice of a hearing upon the petition before

---

[1] It must be confessed that the question whether Franklin
should have sent these letters to be seen by the leading men of
Massachusetts involves points of some delicacy. The very elab-
orateness and vehemence of the exculpations put forth by American writers indicate a lurking feeling that the opposite side is at
least plausible. I add my opinion decidedly upon Franklin's side,
though I certainly see force in the contrary view. Yet before one
feels fully satisfied he would wish to know from whom these letters came to Franklin's hands, the information then given him
concerning them, and the authority which the giver might be
supposed to have over them, in a word all the attendant and qual-
ifying circumstances and conversation upon which presumptions
might have been properly founded by Franklin. Upon these
essential matters there is absolutely no evidence. Franklin was
bound to secrecy concerning them, at whatever cost to himself.
But it is evident that Franklin never for an instant entertained
the slightest doubt of the entire propriety of his action, and even
in his own cause he was wont to be a fair-minded judge. One
gets a glimpse of the other side in the *Diary and Letters of his
Excellency Thomas Hutchinson, Esq.*, etc., by Thomas Orlando
Hutchinson, pp. 5, 82–93, 192, 356.

the Lords of the Committee for Plantation Affairs, at the Cockpit, on the Tuesday following, at noon. Late in the afternoon of Monday he got notice that Mr. Mauduit, agent for Hutchinson and Oliver, would be represented at the hearing on the following morning by counsel. A less sagacious man than Franklin would have scented trouble in the air. He tried to find Arthur Lee; but Lee was in Bath. He then sought advice from Mr. Bollan, a barrister, agent for the Council of Massachusetts Bay, and who also had been summoned. There was no time to instruct counsel, and Mr. Bollan advised to employ none; he had found "lawyers of little service in colony cases." "Those who are eminent and hope to rise in their profession are unwilling to offend the court, whose disposition on this occasion was well known." The next day at the hearing Mr. Bollan endeavored to speak; but, though he had been summoned, he was summarily silenced, on the ground that the colonial Council, whose agent he was, was not a party to the petition. Franklin then laid the petition and authenticated copies of the letters before the committee. Some objections to the receipt of copies instead of originals were raised by Mr. Wedderburn, solicitor-general and counsel for Hutchinson and Oliver. Franklin then spoke with admirable keenness and skill. He said that he had not conceived the matter to call for discussion by lawyers; but that it was a " question of civil or political prudence, whether, on the state of the fact that the governors had lost all trust and confidence with the people, and become universally obnoxious, it would be for the interest of his majesty's service to continue them in those stations in that Province." Of this he conceived their lordships to be " perfect judges," not requiring "assistance from the arguments of counsel." Yet if counsel was to be heard he asked an adjournment to enable him to engage and instruct lawyers. Time was accordingly granted, until January 29. Wedderburn waived his objection to the copies, but both he and Lord Chief Justice De Grey intimated that inquiry would be made as to " how the Assembly came into possession of them, through whose hands and by what means they were procured, . . . and to whom they were directed." This was all irrelevant to the real issue, which had been sharply defined by Franklin. The lord president, near whom Franklin stood, asked him whether he intended to answer such questions. " In that I shall take counsel," replied Franklin.

The interval which elapsed before the day nominated could not have been very lightsome for the unfortunate agent for the Massachusetts Bay. Not only had he the task of selecting and instructing competent counsel, but even his self-possessed and composed nature must have been severely harassed by the rumors of which the air was full. He heard from all quarters that the ministry and courtiers were highly enraged against him; he was called an incendiary, and the newspapers teemed with invectives against him. He heard that he was to be apprehended and sent to Newgate, and that his papers were to be seized; that after he had been sufficiently blackened by the hearing he would be deprived of his place; with disheartening news also that the disposition of the petition had already been determined.[1] At the same time a subpœna was served upon him at the private suit of Whately, who was under personal obligations to him, but was also a banker to the government. Certainly the heavens threatened a cloudburst with appalling thunder and dangerous lightning.

Upon reflection Franklin was disposed to do without counsel, but Mr. Bollan now became strongly of the contrary opinion. So Mr. Dunning and Mr. John Lee were retained. The former had been solicitor-general, and was a man of mark and ability in the profession. When the hearing came on, the Cockpit presented such a spectacle that Franklin felt assured that the whole affair had been "preconcerted." The hostile courtiers had been "invited, as to an entertainment, and there never was such an appearance of privy councilors on any occasion, not less than thirty-five, besides an immense crowd of other auditors." Every one save the privy councilors had to stand from beginning to end of the proceedings. Franklin occupied a position beside the fireplace, where he stood throughout immovable as a statue, his features carefully composed so that not one trace of emotion was apparent upon them, showing a degree

[1] Franklin's *Works*, v. 297, 298.

of self-control which was extraordinary even in one who was at once a man of the world and a philosopher, with sixty-eight years of experience in life. Mr. Dunning, with his voice unfortunately weakened by a cold, was not always audible and made little impression. Mr. Lee was uselessly feeble. Wedderburn, thus inefficiently opposed, and conscious of the full sympathy of the tribunal, poured forth a vile flood of personal invective. Throughout his life he approved himself a mean-spirited and ignoble man, despised by those who used and rewarded his able and debased services. On this occasion he eagerly took advantage of the protection afforded by his position and by Dr. Franklin's age to use language which, under such circumstances, was as cowardly as it was false. Nothing, he said, " will acquit Dr. Franklin of the charge of obtaining [the letters] by fraudulent or corrupt means, for the most malignant of purposes, unless he stole them from the person who stole them." " I hope, my lords, you will mark and brand the man, for the honor of this country, of Europe, and of mankind." " He has forfeited all the respect of societies and of men. Into what companies will he hereafter go with an unembarrassed face or the honest intrepidity of virtue ? Men will watch him with a jealous eye ; they will hide their papers from him, and lock up their escritoires. He will henceforth esteem it a libel to be called *a man of letters*, *homo* TRIUM [1] *literarum.*" " But he not

---

[1] A play upon the Latin word, FUR, a thief.

only took away the letters from one brother, but kept himself concealed till he nearly occasioned the murder of the other. It is impossible to read his account, expressive of the coolest and most deliberate malice, without horror. Amidst these tragical events, — of one person nearly murdered, of another answerable for the issue, of a worthy governor hurt in his dearest interests, the fate of America in suspense, — here is a man who, with the utmost insensibility of remorse, stands up and avows himself the author of all. I can compare it only to Zanga, in Dr. Young's ' Revenge.'

> ' Know then 't was — I;
> I forged the letter, I disposed the picture;
> I hated, I despised, and I destroy.'

I ask, my lords, whether the revengeful temper attributed, by poetic fiction only, to the bloody African, is not surpassed by the coolness and apathy of the wily American."

Such was the torrent of vilification which flowed from the lips of one of the meanest of England's lawyers, and the speaker was constantly encouraged by applause, and by various indications of gratification on the part of the tribunal before which he argued. Dr. Priestley, who was present, said that from the opening of the proceedings it was evident " that the real object of the court was to insult Dr. Franklin," an object in which their lordships were, of course, able to achieve a complete success. " No person belonging to the council behaved with decent gravity, except Lord North," who came late and remained standing behind a chair. It was a disgraceful scene, but not of long duration; apparently there was little else done save to hear the speeches of counsel. The report of the lords was dated on the same day, and was a severe censure upon the petition and the petitioners. More than this, their lordships went out of their way to inflict a wanton outrage upon Franklin. The question of who gave the letters to him was one which all concerned were extremely anxious to hear answered. But it was also a question which he could not lawfully be compelled to answer in these proceedings; it was wholly irrelevant; moreover it was involved in the cause then pending before the lord chancellor in which Franklin was respondent. Accordingly, by advice of counsel, advice unquestionably correct, he refused to divulge what their lordships were so curious to hear. Enraged, they said in their report that his " silence " was abundant support for the conclusion that the " charge of surreptitiously obtaining the letters was a true one," although they knew that in law and in fact his silence was wholly justifiable.

Resolutely as Franklin sought at the time to repress any expression of his natural indignation, there is evidence enough of how deeply he felt this indignity. For example, there is the familiar story of his dress. He wore, at the Cockpit, " a full dress suit of spotted Manchester velvet." Many years afterward, when it befell him, as one of the ambassadors of his country, to sign the treaty of alliance with France, the first treaty ever made by the United States of America, and which practically insured the defeat of Great Britain in the pending war, it was observed by Dr. Bancroft that he was attired in this same suit. The signing was to have taken place on February 5, but was unexpectedly postponed to the next day, when again Franklin appeared in the same old suit and set his hand to the treaty. Dr. Bancroft says : " I once intimated to Dr. Franklin the suspicion which his wearing these clothes on that occasion had excited in my mind, when he smiled, without telling me whether it was well or ill founded." Having done this service, the suit was again laid away until it was brought forth to be worn at Paris at the signing of the treaty of peace with England, a circumstance the more noteworthy since at that time the French court was in mourning.[1]

It appears that Franklin for a time entertained a purpose of drawing up an " answer to the abuses " cast at him upon this occasion. There was, however, no need for doing so, and his reason for not doing it is more eloquent on his behalf with posterity than any pamphlet could be. He said : " It was partly written, but the affairs of public importance I have been ever since engaged in prevented my finishing it. The injuries too that my country has suffered have absorbed private resentments, and made it appear trifling for an individual to trouble the world with his particular justifica-

[1] Parton's *Life of Franklin*, ii. 508.

tion, when all his compatriots were stigmatized by
the king and Parliament as being in every respect
the worst of mankind."

The proceedings at the Cockpit took place on a
Saturday. On the following Monday morning
Franklin got a " written notice from the secretary
of the general post-office, that his majesty's postmaster-general *found it necessary* to dismiss me
from my office of deputy postmaster-general in
North America." In other ways too the mischief
done him by this public assault could not be concealed. It published to all the world the feeling
of the court and the ministry toward him, and told
Englishmen that it was no longer worth while to
keep up appearances of courtesy and good will. It
put upon him a judicial stigma, which was ample
excuse for the enemies of America henceforth to
treat him as both dishonored and dishonorable.
Hitherto his tact and his high character had preserved him in a great measure from the social an-
noyances and curtailments which he would naturally
have suffered as the prominent representative of
an unpopular cause. But it seemed now as if his
judgment had once and fatally played him false,
and certainly his good name and his prestige were
given over to his enemies, who dealt cruelly with
them. He felt that it was the end of his usefulness, also that his own self-respect and dignity
must be carefully preserved ; and he wrote to the
Assembly of Massachusetts to say that it would be
impossible for him longer to act as its agent. From

that time he never attended the levee of a minister.
The portcullis had dropped ; the days of his service
in England were over.

The conclusion had come painfully, yet it was
not without satisfaction that he saw himself free
to return home. His affairs had suffered in his
absence, and needed his attention now more than
ever, since he was deprived of his income from the
post-office. Moreover his efforts could no longer be
cheered with hopes of success or even of achieving
any substantial advantage for his countrymen. He
was obliged to admit that the good disposition of
Lord Dartmouth had had no practical results.
" No single measure of his predecessor has since
been even attempted to be changed, and, on the
contrary, new ones have been continually added,
further to exasperate these people, render them desperate, and drive them, if possible, into open rebellion." It had been a vexatious circumstance, too,
that not long before this time he had received a
rebuke from the Massachusetts Assembly for having been lax, as they fancied, in notifying them of
some legislation of an injurious character, which
was in preparation. " This censure," he said,
" though grievous, does not so much surprise me,
as I apprehended all along from the beginning
that between the friends of an old agent, my predecessor, who thought himself hardly used in his
dismission, and those of a young man impatient for
the succession, my situation was not likely to be
a very comfortable one, as my faults could scarce

pass unobserved." This reference to the malicious
and untrustworthy backbiter, Arthur Lee, might
have been much more severe, and still amply deserved. The most important acts of his ignoble
life, by which alone his memory is preserved, were
the slanders which he set in circulation concerning
Franklin. Yet Franklin, little suspicious and very
magnanimous, praised him as a "gentleman of
parts and ability," likely to serve the Province with
zeal and activity. Probably from this impure Lee
fount, but possibly from some other source, there now
came a renewal of the rumors that Franklin was to
be gained over to the ministerial side by promotion
to some office superior to that which he had held.
The injurious story was told in Boston, where perhaps a few persons believed it to be true of a man
who in fact could hardly have set upon his fealty a
price so high that the British government would
not gladly have paid it, and who heretofore had
been, and at this very time again was, tempted by
repeated solicitations and the intimations of grand
rewards, only to change his mind — a matter so
very easy in politics.

Furthermore, beyond these assaults upon his
fidelity, these insults of the privy council, Franklin had to contemplate the possibility of personal
danger. He was a man of abundant courage, but
courage does not make a prison or a gallows an
agreeable object in one's horizon. The newspapers
alleged that in his correspondence "treason"
had been discovered. The ministry, as he was

directly informed, thought no better of him than did the editors, regarding him as "the great fomenter of the opposition in America," the "great adversary to any accommodation." "It is given out," he wrote, "that copies of several letters of mine to you are sent over here to the ministers, and that their contents are treasonable, for which I should be prosecuted if copies could be made evidence." He was not conscious of any treasonable intention, but treason was a word to make a man anxious in those days, when uttered by the ministry and echoed by the court. Franklin was quite aware that, though ministers might offer him a tempting place by way of bribe, they would far rather give him "a place in a cart to Tyburn." His friends warned him that his situation was hazardous; that, "if by some accident the troops and the people of New England should come to blows," he would doubtless be seized; and they advised him to withdraw while yet he could do so. Hutchinson frankly avowed that, if his advice were taken, the withdrawal would not be permitted. "But," said Franklin, "I venture to stay," upon the chance of still being of use, "and I confide on my innocence that the worst which can happen to me will be an imprisonment upon suspicion; though that is a thing I should much desire to avoid, as it may be expensive and vexatious, as well as dangerous to my health." So spoke this imperturbable man, and calmly stayed at his post.

He was still consulted by both sides in England.

In the August following the scene in the privy
council chamber, he called upon Lord Chatham
and had a long and interesting interview.   He
then said that he attributed the late " wrong politics " to the departure from the old and true British principle, " whereby every Province was well
governed, being trusted in a great measure with
the government of itself."   When it was sought
to take this privilege from the colonies, grave
blunders had inevitably ensued ; because, as he
admirably expressed it, Parliament insisted upon
being *omnipotent* when it was not *omniscient*.   In
other words, the affairs of the unrepresented colonies were mismanaged through sheer ignorance.
It is noteworthy that England has since recognized
the necessity of precisely the principle indicated by
Franklin for colonial government ; all her great
colonies are now " trusted in a great measure with
the government" of themselves, and are consequently " well governed."   Franklin further assured his lordship that in all his travels in the
provinces he had never once heard independence
hinted at as a desirable thing.   This gave Chatham much pleasure ; but perhaps neither of them
at the moment reflected how many eventful years
had elapsed since Franklin was last journeying in
America.   He further declared that the colonists
were " even not against regulations of the general
commerce by Parliament, provided such regulations
were *bonâ fide* for the benefit of the *whole empire*,
not to the small advantage of one part to the great

injury of another." This, by the way, was a good
point, which he found very serviceable when people talked to him about the unity of the empire.
A genuine unity was just the gospel which he liked
to preach. " An equal dispensation," he said, " of
protection, rights, privileges, and advantages is
what every part is entitled to, and ought to enjoy,
it being a matter of no moment to the state whether
a subject grows rich and flourishing on the Thames
or the Ohio, in Edinburgh or Dublin." But no
living Englishman could accept this broad and
liberal doctrine. The notion that the colonies were
a dependency and should be tributary to the greater
power was universal. It was admitted that they
should not be oppressed ; but it was believed that
between oppression and that perfect unity which
involved entire equality there was certainly a middle ground whereon the colonies might properly be
established.

Lord Chatham expressed in courteous compliments the gratification which this visit afforded
him. Not long afterward he came gallantly to the
defense of Franklin in the House of Lords. It was
one day in February, 1775 ; Franklin was standing in full view, leaning on a rail ; Lord Sandwich
was speaking against a measure of conciliation or
agreement just introduced by Chatham. He said
that it deserved " only contempt," and " ought to
be immediately rejected. I can never believe it
to be the production of any British peer. It appears to me rather the work of some American.

I fancy I have in my eye the person who drew it up, one of the bitterest and most mischievous enemies this country has ever known." Speaking thus, he looked full at Franklin, and drew upon him the general attention. But Chatham hastened to defend the defenseless one. "The plan is entirely my own," he said; "but if I were the first minister, and had the care of settling this momentous business, I should not be ashamed of calling to my assistance a person so perfectly acquainted with the whole of American affairs, one whom all Europe ranks with our Boyles and Newtons, as an honor not to the English nation only but to human nature." This was spirited and friendly; Franklin had a way of making warm and loyal friends. Most men would have rejoiced to be so abused by Sandwich in order to be so complimented by Chatham.[1]

Yet in spite of the high esteem in which so many Englishmen still held Franklin an incident occurred at this time which showed very plainly that the term of his full usefulness was indeed over, though not altogether for the reasons which had led him to think so. The fact was that the proverbial last feather which breaks the back had been laid upon him. His endurance had been overtaxed, and he was at last in that temper and frame of mind in which the wisest men are liable to make grave mistakes. He was one day present at a debate in the House of Commons, and found himself, as he says,

[1] Bancroft, *Hist. U. S.*, v. 220.

" much disgusted, from the ministerial side, by many base reflections on American courage, religion, understanding, etc., in which we were treated with the utmost contempt, as the lowest of mankind, and almost of a different species from the English of Britain ; but particularly the American honesty was abused by some of the lords, who asserted that we were all knaves, etc." Franklin went home " somewhat irritated and heated," and before he had cooled he wrote a paper which he hastened to show to his friend Mr. Thomas Walpole, a member of the House of Commons. Mr. Walpole " looked at it and at me several times alternately, as if he apprehended me a little out of my senses." Nor would Mr. Walpole have been altogether without reason, if in fact he entertained such a suspicion. The paper was the memorial of Benjamin Franklin to the Earl of Dartmouth, secretary of state. In its first clause it demanded " reparation " for the injury done by the blockade of the port of Boston. Conventional forms of speech were observed, yet there was an atmosphere almost of injurious insolence, entirely foreign to all other productions of Franklin's brain and pen. Its second paragraph recited that the conquests made in the northeast from France, which included all those extensive fisheries which still survive as a bone of contention between the two countries, had been *jointly* won by England and the American colonies, at their common cost, and by an army in which the provincial troops were nearly equal in

numbers to the British. "It follows," the audacious memorialist said, "that the colonies have an
equitable and just right to participate in the advantage of those fisheries," and the present English
attempt to deprive the Massachusetts people of
sharing in them was " an act highly unjust and injurious." He concluded : " I give notice that satisfaction will probably one day be demanded for all
the injury that may be done and suffered in the
execution of such act; and that the injustice of the
proceeding is likely to give such umbrage to *all the
colonies* that in no future war, wherein other conquests may be meditated, either a man or a shilling
will be obtained from any of them to aid such conquests, till full satisfaction be made as aforesaid."

Here was indeed a fulmination to strike an Englishman breathless and dumb with amazement. It
put the colonies in the position of a coequal or allied power, entitled to share with Britain the spoils
of victory ; even in the position of an independent
power which could refuse the military allegiance
of subjects. English judges would have found
abundant treason in this insubordinate document.
It may soothe common men to see the wise, the serene, the self-contained Dr. Franklin, the philosopher and diplomatist, for once lose his head in a
gust of uncontrollable passion. Walpole, though
a loyal Englishman, was fortunately his true friend,
and wrote him, with a brevity more impressive than
argument, that the memorial " might be attended
with dangerous consequences to your person and

contribute to exasperate the nation." He closed
with the significant sentence: " I heartily wish
you a prosperous voyage and long health." The
significant words remind one of the woodcock's
feather with which Wildrake warned the disguised
monarch that no time was to be lost in fleeing from
Woodstock. But if the hint was curt, it was no
less wise. There was no doubt that it was full
time for the sage to be exchanging his farewells,
when such a point had been reached. The next
day, as Franklin relates, Walpole called and said
that " it was thought my having no instructions
directing me to deliver such a protest would make
it appear still more unjustifiable, and be deemed a
national affront. I had no desire to make matters
worse, and, being grown cooler, took the advice so
kindly given me."

The last business which Franklin had to transact on the eve of his departure came in the shape of
one of those mysterious and obscure bits of negotiation which are at times undertaken by private persons who are very "near" to ministers, and who
conduct their affairs with impressive secrecy. Just
how much this approach amounted to it is difficult
to say; no less a person than Lord Howe was concerned in it, and he was undoubtedly in direct
communication with Lord North. But whether
that potentate really anticipated any substantial
good result may be doubted. Franklin himself has
told the story with much particularity, and since it
will neither bear curtailment nor admit of being

related at length, and since the whole palaver accomplished absolutely nothing, the relation will be
omitted here. In the course of it the efforts to
bribe Franklin were renewed, and briefly rejected
by him. Also he met, and established a very
friendly personal relation with, Lord Howe, who
afterward commanded the British fleet in American
waters.

Having discovered the emptiness of this business Franklin at last completed his arrangements
for his return home. He placed his agencies in the
hands of Arthur Lee. His last day in London he
passed with his staunch old friend, Dr. Priestley,
and a large part of the time, says the doctor, " he
was looking over a number of American news.
papers, directing me what to extract from them for
the English ones ; and in reading them he was frequently not able to proceed for the tears literally
running down his cheeks." Such was the depth of
feeling in one often accounted callous, indifferent,
or even untrustworthy in the matter of American
relations with England. He felt some anxiety as
to whether his departure might not be prevented
by an arrest, and made his journey to Portsmouth
with such speed and precautions as were possible.[1]
But he was not interrupted, and sailed on some day
near the middle of March, 1775. His departure
marked an era in the relations of Great Britain
with her American colonies. It signified that all
hope of agreement, all possibility of reconciliation

[1] Parton's *Life of Franklin*, ii. 70.

upon one side or of recession upon the other, were absolutely over. That Franklin gave up in despair the task of preventing a war meant that war was certain and imminent. He arrived in Philadelphia May 5, 1775. During his absence his wife had died, and his daughter had married a young man, Richard Bache, whom he had never yet seen.

CHAPTER VIII.

SERVICES IN THE STATES.

FROM the solitude of the ocean to the seething turmoil which Franklin found in the colonies must have been a startling transition. He had come home an old man, lacking but little of the allotted threescore years and ten. He had earned and desired repose, but never before had he encountered such exacting, important, and unremitting labor as immediately fell to his lot. Lexington and Concord fights had taken place a fortnight before he landed, and the news preceded him in Philadelphia by a few days only. Many feelings may be discerned in the brief note which he wrote on May 16th to Dr. Priestley : —

"DEAR FRIEND, — You will have heard, before this reaches you, of a march stolen by the regulars into the country by night, and of their *expedition* back again. They retreated twenty miles in six hours. The governor had called the Assembly to propose Lord North's pacific plan, but before the time of their meeting began the cutting of throats. You know it was said he carried the sword in one hand and the olive branch in the other, and it seems he chose to give them a taste of the sword first."

To another correspondent he said that "the feeble Americans, who pelted them all the way, could scarcely keep up with" the rapidly retreating redcoats. But the occurrence of bloodshed had an immense meaning for Franklin; it opened to his vision all the future: an irreconcilable struggle, and finally independence, with a bitter animosity long surviving. He could not address all those who had once been near and dear to him in England as he did the good Dr. Priestley. The letter to Strahan of July 5, 1775, is famous: —

"Mr. Strahan, — You are a member of Parliament, and one of that majority which has doomed my country to destruction. You have begun to burn our towns and murder our people. Look upon your hands; they are stained with the blood of your relations! You and I were long friends; you are now my enemy, and I am,
"Yours,   B. Franklin."

But strained as his relations with Strahan were for a while, it is agreeable to know that the estrangement between such old and close friends was not everlasting.

To write at length concerning Franklin's services during his brief stay at home would involve giving a history of the whole affairs of the colonies at this time. But space presses, and this ground is familiar and has been traversed in other volumes in this series. It seems sufficient therefore rather to enumerate than to narrate his various engagements, and thus to reserve more room for less well known matters.

On the very day after his return, when he had scarce caught the breath of land, he was unanimously elected by the Assembly a delegate to the Provincial Congress. It was an emergency when the utmost must be made of time, brains, and men. By subsequent reëlections he continued to sit in that body until his departure for France. There was business enough before it: the organization of a government, of the army, of the finances; most difficult of all, the arrangement of a national policy, and the harmonizing of conflicting opinions among men of influence at home. In all that came before the Congress Franklin was obliged to take his full share. He seems to have been upon all the busy and important committees. There were more ardent spirits, greater propelling forces, than he was; but his wisdom was transcendent. Dickinson and his followers were bent upon sending one more petition to the king, a scheme which was ridiculed almost with anger by the more advanced and resolute party. But Franklin's counsel was to give way to their wishes, as being the best policy for bringing them later into full accord with the party which was for war. He had no hopes of any other good result from the proceeding; but it also chimed with his desire to put the English as much as possible in the wrong. In the like direction was a clause in his draft of a declaration, intended to be issued by Washington in the summer of 1775. To counteract the charge that the colonies refused to contribute to the cost of their own protection, he proposed that, if Great Britain would abolish her monopoly of the colonial trade, allowing free commerce between the colonies and all the rest of the world, they would pay into the English sinking fund £100,000 annually for one hundred years; which would be more than sufficient, if "faithfully and inviolably applied for that purpose, . . . to extinguish all her present national debt."

At the close of this document he administered a telling fillip in his humorous style to that numerous class who seek to control practical affairs by sentiment, and who now would have had their prattle about the "mother country" outweigh the whole accumulation of her very unmaternal oppression and injustice. Concerning the allegation of an unfilial ingratitude, he said: "There is much more reason for retorting that charge on Britain, who not only never contributes any aid, nor affords, by an exclusive commerce, any advantages to Saxony, *her* mother country; but, no longer since than the last war, without the least provocation, subsidized the king of Prussia while he ravaged that *mother country*, and carried fire and sword into its capital. . . . An example we hope no provocation will induce us to imitate." Had this declaration ever been used, which it was not, the dignity of the grave general who commanded the American forces would have compelled him to cut off this closing snapper from the lash, amusing as it was. The witty notion had found a more appropriate place in the newspaper article which

had dumfounded the guests at the English country house. Commenting upon this, Mr. Parton
well says: "Here perhaps we have one of the reasons why Dr. Franklin, who was universally confessed to be the ablest pen in America, was not always asked to write the great documents of the
Revolution. He would have put a joke into the
Declaration of Independence, if it had fallen to him
to write it. . . . His jokes, the circulating medium
of Congress, were as helpful to the cause as Jay's
conscience, or Adams's fire; . . . but they were out
of place in formal, exact, and authoritative papers." [1]

A document which cost Dr. Franklin much more
labor than this declaration was a plan for a union
of the colonies, which he brought forward July
21, 1775. It was the "first sketch of a plan of
confederation which is known to have been presented to Congress." No final action was ever
taken upon it. It contained a provision that Ireland, the West India Islands, the Canadian possessions, and Florida might, upon application, be received into the confederation.

Franklin's duties in Congress were ample to
consume his time and strength; but they were far
from being all that he had to do. Almost immediately after his return he was made chairman of a
committee for organizing the postal service of the
country. In execution of this duty he established
in substance that system which has ever since prevailed; and he was then at once appointed post-

master-general, with a salary of £1,000 per annum. When franking letters he amused himself by changing the formula, "Free: B. Franklin" into "B. Free, Franklin."

He was next made chairman of the provincial committee of safety, a body which began its sittings at the comfortable, old-fashioned hour of six o'clock in the morning. Its duty was to call out and organize all the military resources of Pennsylvania, and generally to provide for the defenses of the Province. It worked with much efficiency in its novel and difficult department. Among other things, Franklin devised and constructed some ingenious "marine *chevaux de frise*" for closing the river approaches to Philadelphia.

In October, 1775, he was elected a member of the Assembly of the Province. But this did not add to his labors; for the oath of allegiance had not yet been dispensed with; he would not take it, and resigned his seat.

In September, 1775, Franklin, Lynch of South Carolina, and Harrison of Virginia, as a committee of Congress, were dispatched to Cambridge, Massachusetts, to confer with Washington concerning military affairs. They rode from Philadelphia to the leaguer around Boston in thirteen days. Their business was achieved with no great difficulty; but they lingered a few days more in that interesting camp, and were absent six weeks. General Greene has recorded how he gazed upon Franklin, "that very great man, with silent admiration;"

and Abigail Adams tells with what interest she met him whom "from infancy she had been taught to venerate," and how she read in his grave countenance "patriotism in its full lustre" and with it "blended every virtue of a Christian." The phrase was not well chosen to fall from the pen of Mrs. Adams, yet was literally true; Franklin had the virtues, though dissevered from the tenets which that worthy Puritan dame conceived essential to the make up of a genuine Christian. The time came when her husband would not have let her speak thus in praise of Benjamin Franklin.

In the spring of 1776 Congress was inconsiderate enough to impose upon Franklin a journey to Montreal, there to confer with General Arnold concerning affairs in Canada. It was a severe, even a cruel task to put upon a man of his age; but with his usual tranquil courage he accepted the mission. He met the ice in the rivers, and suffered much from fatigue and exposure; indeed, the carelessness of Congress was near depriving the country of a life which could not have been spared. On April 15th he wrote from Saratoga: "I begin to apprehend that I have undertaken a fatigue that at my time of life may prove too much for me; so I sit down to write to a few friends by way of farewell;" and still the real wilderness with all its hardships lay before him. After he had traversed it he had the poor reward of finding himself on a bootless errand. The Canadian enterprise had no possible future save failure and retreat. There was absolutely nothing which he could do in Canada; he was being wasted there, and resolved to get away as soon as he could. Accordingly he made his painful way homeward; but worn out as he was, he was given scant opportunity to recuperate from this perilous and mistaken journey. The times called upon every patriot to spend all he had of vigor, intellect, money, life itself, for the common cause, and Franklin was no niggard in the stress.

In the spring of 1776 the convention charged to prepare a constitution for the independent State of Pennsylvania was elected. Franklin was a member, and when the convention came together he was chosen to preside over its deliberations. It sat from July 16th to September 28th. The constitution which it presented to the people established a legis-lature of only one house, a feature which Franklin approved and defended. At the close of the delib-erations thanks were unanimously voted to him for his services as presiding officer, and for his " able and disinterested advice."

Yet in spite of abundant acts, like this, of real independence taking place upon all sides, profession of it inspired alarm in a large proportion of the people. Congress even declared formally that independence was not aimed at. Sam Adams, dis-gusted, talked of forming a New England confed-eracy, and Franklin approved the scheme and said that in such an event he would cast in his lot with the New Englanders. But the stream ran on in spite of some snags in the current. It was not much later that Franklin found himself one of the committee of five elected by ballot to frame a declaration of independence. Had he been called upon to write the document he would certainly have given something more terse and simple than that rotund and magniloquent instrument which Jefferson bequeathed to the unbounded admiration of American posterity. As it was, Franklin's recorded connection with the preparation of that famous paper is confined to the amusing tale about John Thompson, Hatter, wherewith he mitigated the miseries of Jefferson during the debate; and to his familiar bon-mot in reply to Harrison's appeal for unanimity: "Yes, we must indeed all hang together, or assuredly we shall all hang separately." With this rather grim jest upon his lip, he set his signature to one of the greatest documents in the world's history.

When it came to shaping the machinery of the confederation, the great difficulty, as is well known, lay in establishing a just proportion between the larger and the smaller states. Should they have equal weight in voting, or not? It was a question so vital and so hard to settle that the confederacy narrowly survived the strain. Franklin was decidedly in favor of making the voting value proportionate to the size, measured by population, of the several states. He said: Let the smaller colonies give equal money and men, and then let them have an equal vote. If they have an equal vote without bearing equal burdens, a confederation based on such iniquitous principles will not last long. To set out with an unequal representation is unreasonable. There is no danger that the larger states will absorb the smaller. The same apprehension was expressed when Scotland was united to England. It was then said that the whale had swallowed Jonah; but Lord Bute's administration came in, and then it was seen that Jonah had swallowed the whale. That Scotch favorite was the provocation for many witty sayings, but for none better than this.

In July, 1776, Lord Howe arrived, in command of the English fleet. He immediately sought to open a friendly correspondence with Franklin. He had played a prominent part in those efforts at conciliation which had come to naught just before Franklin's departure from England; and he now renewed his generous attempt to act as a mediator. There is no doubt that this nobleman, as kindly as brave, would far rather have reconciled the Americans than have fought them. By permission of Congress Franklin replied by a long letter, not deficient in courtesy of language, but full of argument upon the American side, and in a tone which there was no misconceiving. Its closing paragraph was : —

"I consider this war against us, therefore, as both unjust and unwise; and I am persuaded that cool, dispassionate posterity will condemn to infamy those who advised it; and that even success will not save from some degree of dishonor those who voluntarily engaged to conduct it. I know your great motive in coming hither was the hope of being instrumental in a reconciliation; and I believe, when you find *that* impossible on any terms given you to propose, you will relinquish so odious a command, and return to a more honorable private station."

If the Englishman had been hot-tempered, this would probably have ended the correspondence; as it was, he only delayed for a while before writing civilly again. The battle of Long Island next occurred, and Lord Howe fancied that that disaster might bring the Americans to their senses. He paroled General Sullivan and by him sent a message to Congress: That he and his brother had full powers to arrange an accommodation; that they could not at present treat with Congress as such, but would like to confer with some of its members as private gentlemen. After a long debate it was resolved to send a committee of Congress to meet the admiral and the general, and Franklin, John Adams, and Edward Rutledge were deputed. Lord Howe received them with much courtesy, and gave them a lunch before proceeding to business. But when luncheon was over and the substance of the errand was reached, it was very shortly disposed of. His lordship opened with a speech of elaborate civility, and concluded by saying that he felt for America as for a brother, and if America should fall he should feel and lament it like the loss of a brother. Franklin replied: " My lord, we will use our utmost endeavors to save your

lordship that mortification." But Lord Howe did
not relish this Yankee wit. He continued by a
long, explanatory, conciliatory address. At its
close there was necessarily brought up the question
of the character in which the envoys came. His
lordship thought that the idea of Congress might
"easily be thrown out at present." Franklin
adroitly settled it: "Your lordship may consider
us in any view you think proper. We on our part
are at liberty to consider ourselves in our real character. But there is really no necessity on this
occasion to distinguish between members of Congress and individuals. The conversation may be
held as among friends." Mr. Adams made one of
those blunt and pugnacious remarks which, whenever addressed to Englishmen, are sure to endear
the speaker to the American nation. Mr. Rutledge
laid over it the courtesy of a gentleman; and then
the conference came to the point.

Lord Howe expressed his majesty's earnest desire for a permanent peace and for the happiness
of his American subjects, his willingness for a reform and for a redress of grievances. But he admitted that the Declaration of Independence was
an awkward obstacle. He asked: "Is there no way
of treating *back* of this step of independency?"
Franklin replied at some length, closing with the
words: "Forces have been sent out, and towns
have been burnt. We cannot now expect happiness under the domination of Great Britain. All
former attachments are obliterated. America can-

not return to the domination of Great Britain, and I imagine that Great Britain means to rest it upon force." Adams said: " It is not in our power to treat otherwise than as independent states; and for my own part, I avow my determination never to depart from the idea of independency." Rutledge said: " With regard to the people consenting to come again under the English government, it is impossible. I can answer for South Carolina." Lord Howe replied: " If such are your sentiments, I can only regret that it is not in my power to bring about the accommodation I wish." Thus the fruitlessness of such efforts was made manifest; of all concerned it is probable that the most amiable of Englishmen was the only one who was disappointed at the result. The Americans were by no means displeased at having another and conclusive proof to convince the doubting ones that reconciliation was an impossibility.

Franklin's language was expressive of the way in which his mind had worked. Until it came to the " cutting of throats," he had never altogether and avowedly given up hopes that, from the reservoir of unknown things in the future, something might in time come forth that would bring about a reasonable accommodation. But the first bloodshed effected a change in his feelings as irrevocable as that which Hawthorne so subtly represents as having been worked in the nature of Donatello by a violent taking of life. " Bunker's Hill " excited him; the sack of Falmouth affected him with ter-

rible intensity. When the foolish petition of the
Dickinson party was sent to England, he wrote to
Dr. Priestley that the colonies had given Britain
one more chance of recovering their friendship,
" which, however, I think she has not sense enough
to embrace; and so I conclude she has lost them
forever. She has begun to burn our seaport towns,
secure, I suppose, that we shall never be able to
return the outrage in kind. . . . If she wishes to
have us subjects . . . she is now giving us such
miserable specimens of her government that we
shall ever detest and avoid it, as a combination of
robbery, murder, famine, fire, and pestilence." His
humor could not be altogether repressed, but there
was sternness and bitterness underlying it : " Tell
our dear, good friend, Dr. Price, who sometimes
has his doubts and despondencies about our firmness, that America is determined and unanimous ;
a very few Tories and placemen excepted, who will
probably soon export themselves. Britain, at the
expense of three millions, has killed one hundred
and fifty Yankees, this campaign, which is twenty
thousand pounds a head ; and at Bunker's Hill she
gained a mile of ground, half of which she lost
again by our taking post at Ploughed Hill. During
the same time 60,000 children have been born in
America. From these data his mathematical head
will easily calculate the time and expense necessary
to kill us all, and conquer our whole territory." It
was a comical way of expressing the real truth that
Britain neither would nor could give enough either

of men, or money, or time to accomplish the task she had undertaken. To another he wrote : " We hear that more ships and troops are coming out. We know that you may do us a great deal of mischief, and are determined to bear it patiently, as long as we can. But if you flatter yourselves with beating us into submission, you know neither the people nor the country." Other men wrote ardent words and indulged in the rhetorical extravagance of intense excitement in those days; Franklin sometimes cloaked the intensity of his feeling in humor, at other times spoke with a grave and self-contained moderation which was within rather than without the facts and the truth. Everything which he said was true with precision to the letter. But his careful statement and measured profession indicate rather than belie the earnestness of his feeling, the strength of his conviction, and the fixedness of his resolution.

Thus briefly must be dismissed the extensive and important toil of eighteen months, probably the busiest of Franklin's long and busy life. In September, 1776, he was elected envoy to France, and scant space is left for narrating the events of that interesting embassage.

CHAPTER IX.

IT is difficult to pass a satisfactory judgment upon the diplomacy of the American Revolution. If one takes its history in detail it presents a disagreeable picture of importunate knocking at the closed doors of foreign courts, of incessant and almost shameless begging for money and for any and every kind of assets that could be made useful in war, of public bickering and private slandering among the envoys and agents themselves. If, on the other hand, its achievements are considered, it appears crowned with the distinction of substantial, repeated, sometimes brilliant, successes. A like contrast is found in its *personnel*. Between Franklin and Arthur Lee a distance opens like that between the poles, in which stand such men as Jay and Adams near the one extreme, Izard, William Lee, and Thomas Morris near the other, with Deane, Laurens, Carmichael, Jonathan Williams, and a few more in the middle ground. Yet what could have been reasonably expected? Franklin had had some dealings with English statesmen upon what may be called international business, and had justly regarded himself in the light of a *quasi* foreign minister. But with this exception not one man in all the colonies had had the slightest experience in diplomatic affairs, or any personal knowledge of the requirements of a diplomatic office, or any opportunity to gain any ideas on the subject beyond such as a well-educated man could glean from reading the scant historical literature which existed in those days. It was difficult also for Congress to know how to judge and discriminate concerning the material which it found at its disposal. There had been nothing in the careers of the prominent patriots to indicate whether or not any especial one among them had a natural aptitude for diplomacy. The selection must be made with little knowledge of the duties of the position, and with no knowledge of the responsive characteristics of the man. It was only natural that many of the appointments thus blindly made should turn out ill. After they were made, and the appointees had successfully crossed the ocean through the dangerous gauntlet of the English cruisers, there arose to be answered in Europe the embarrassing question : What these self-styled representatives represented. Was it a nation, or only a parcel of rebels ? Here was an unusual and vexatious problem, concerning which most of the cautious royal governments were in no hurry to commit themselves ; and their reticence added greatly to the perplexities of the fledgling

diplomats. Nearly all cabinets felt it a great temptation to assist the colonies of the domineering
mistress of the seas to change themselves from her
dependencies into her naval rivals. But the attempt and not the deed might prove confounding;
neither could a wise monarch assume with entire
complacency the position of an aider and an abet-
tor of a rebellion on the part of subjects whose
grievances appeared chiefly an antipathy to taxation.

From the earliest moment France had been hopefully regarded by the colonists as probably their
friend and possibly their ally. To France, therefore, the first American envoy was dispatched with
promptitude, even before there was a declaration
of independence or an assumption of nationality.
Silas Deane was the man selected. He was the
true Yankee jack-at-all-trades; he had been gradu-
ated at Yale College, then taught school, then practiced law, then engaged in trade, had been all the
while advancing in prosperity and reputation, had
been a member of the first and second congresses,
had failed of reëlection to the third, and was now
without employment. Mr. Parton describes him
as "of somewhat striking manners and good appearance, accustomed to live and entertain in liberal style, and fond of showy equipage and appointment." Perhaps his simple-minded fellow-country-
men of the provinces fancied that such a man would
make an imposing figure at an European court. He
developed no other peculiar fitness for his position:

he could not even speak French; and it proved an ill hour for himself in which he received this trying and difficult honor. By dint of native shrewdness, good luck, and falling among friends he made a fair beginning; but soon he floundered beyond his depth, committed some vexatious blunders, and in the course of conducting some important business at last found himself in a position where he had really done right but appeared to have done wrong, without being free to explain the truth. The result was that he was recalled upon a pretext which poorly concealed his disgrace, that he found even his reputation for financial honesty clouded, and that his prospects for the future were of the worst. He was not a man of sufficient mental calibre or moral strength to endure his unmerited sufferings with constancy. After prolonged disappointments in his attempts to set himself right in the opinion of the country, he became embittered, lost all judgment and patriotism, turned a renegade to the cause of America, which had wronged him indeed, but rather in ignorance than from malice, and died unreconciled, a broken and miserable exile. Such were the perils of the diplomatic service of the colonies in those days.

Deane arrived in France in June, 1776. He had with him a little ready money for his immediate personal expenses, and some letters of introduction from Franklin. It was intended to keep him supplied with money by sending cargoes of tobacco, rice, and indigo consigned to him, the proceeds of

which would be at his disposal for the public service. He was instructed to seek an interview with
de Vergennes, the French minister for foreign affairs, and to endeavor with all possible prudence
and delicacy to find out what signs of promise the
disposition of the French government really held
for the insurgents. He was also to ask for equipment for 25,000 troops, ammunition, and 200 pieces
of field artillery, all to be paid for — when Congress should be able! In France he was to keep
his mission cloaked in secure secrecy, appearing
simply as a merchant conducting his own affairs ;
and he was to write home common business letters
under the very harmless and unsuggestive name of
Timothy Jones, adding the real despatch in invisible ink. But these commonplace precautions were
rendered of no avail through the treachery of Dr.
Edward Bancroft, an American resident abroad,
who had the confidence of Congress, but who " accepted the post of a paid American spy, to prepare
himself for the more lucrative office of a double
spy for the British ministers." [1] Deane, going somewhat beyond his instructions to correspond with
Bancroft, told him everything. Bancroft is supposed to have passed the information along to the
British ministry, and thus enabled them to interpose serious hindrances in the way of the ingenious
devices of the Frenchmen.

Before the arrival of Deane the interests of the
colonies had been already taken in hand and sub-

[1] Bancroft, *Hist. U. S.*, ix. 63.

stantially advanced in France by one of the most extraordinary characters in history. Caron de Beaumarchais was a man whom no race save the French could produce, and whose traits, career, and success lie hopelessly beyond the comprehension of the Anglo-Saxon. Bred a watchmaker, he had the skill, when a mere youth, to invent a clever escapement balance for regulating watches; had he been able to insert it into his own brain he might have held more securely his elusive good fortunes. From being an ingenious inventor he became an adventurer general, watchmaker to the king, the king's mistresses, and the king's daughters, the lover, or rather the beloved, of the wife of the controller of the king's kitchen, then himself the controller, thence a courtier, and a favorite of the royal princesses. Through a clever use of his opportunities he was able to do a great favor to a rich banker, who in return gave him chances to amass a fortune, and lent him money to buy a patent of nobility. This connection ended in litigation, which was near ruining him; but he discovered corruption on the part of the judge, and thereupon wrote his Memorials, of which the wit, keenness, and vivacity made him famous. He then rendered a private, personal, and important service to Louis XV., and soon afterwards another to the young Louis XVI. His capacity for secret usefulness gave him further occupation and carried him much to London. There he wrote the "Barber of Seville," and there also he fell in with Arthur Lee and became indoctrinated with grand notions of the resources and value of the colonies, and of the ruin which their separation must inflict upon England. Furthermore, as a Frenchman he naturally consorted with members of the opposition party who took views very favorable to America. With such corroboration of Lee's statements, Beaumarchais, never moderate in any sentiment, leaped to the conclusion that the colonies "must be invincible," and that England was "upon the brink of ruin, if her neighbors and rivals were but in a state to think seriously of it." At once the lively and ambitious fancy of the impetuous Frenchman spread an extravagant panorama of the possibilities thus opened to England's "natural enemy." He became frenzied in the American cause. In long and ardent letters he opened upon King Louis and his ministers a rattling fire of arguments sound and unsound, statements true and untrue, inducements reasonable and unreasonable, forecastings probable and improbable, policies wise and unwise, all designed to show that it was the bounden duty of France to adopt the colonial cause. The king, with no very able brain at any time, was very young and wholly inexperienced. He gazed bewildered at the brilliant pageantry of Beaumarchais's wonderful and audacious statecraft, and sensibly sought the advice of his ministers.

De Vergennes set out his views, in agreement with Beaumarchais. He declared that France now had her opportunity to reduce her dangerous rival

to the place of a second-rate power.   To this end it
was desirable that the rebellion should endure at
least one year.   The sufferings of the colonists in
that period would so embitter them that, even if
they should finally be subdued, they would ever
remain a restless, dangerous thorn in the side of
England, a bond with a heavy penalty effectually
binding her to keep the peace.   To make sure that
neither side should move for peace before this one
valuable year of warfare should have been secured,
it was the policy of France to maintain a pacific
front towards Great Britain, thus relieving her
from any fear that the colonies would obtain a
French alliance, but clandestinely to furnish the
insurgents with munitions of war and money sufficient to enable and encourage them to hold out.

The wise Turgot, in a state paper marked by
great ability, opposed French intervention, and
proved his case.   Colonial independence was sure
to come, a little sooner or later.   Yet the reduction
of the colonies would be the best possible assurance
that England would not break the peace with
France, since the colonists, being mutinous and dis-
contented, would give her concern enough.   On the
other hand, should England fail, as he anticipated
that she would, in this war, she would hardly emerge
from it in condition to undertake another with
France.   As for the colonies themselves, should
they win, the character of the Americans gave
augury of their wishing a solid government and
therefore cultivating peace.   He uttered an admi-

rable dissertation upon the relations between colonies and a parent country, and upon the value of colonies in its bearing upon the present question. In conclusion he gravely referred to the alarming deficit in the French exchequer as the strongest of all arguments against incurring the heavy charge of a war not absolutely unavoidable. "For a necessary war resources could be found; but war ought to be shunned as the greatest of misfortunes, since it would render impossible, perhaps forever, a reform absolutely necessary to the prosperity of the state and the solace of the people." The king, to whom these wise words were addressed, lived to receive terrible proof of their truth.

This good advice fell in well with the bent of Louis's mind. For, though no statesman, he had in this matter a sound instinct that an absolute monarch aiding rebels to erect a free republic was an anomaly, and a hazardous contradiction in the natural order of things. But de Vergennes was the coming man in France, and Turgot no longer had the influence or the popularity to which his ability entitled him. In May, 1776, on an ill day for the French monarchy, but a fair one for the American provinces, this able statesman was ousted from the cabinet. De Vergennes remained to wield entire control of the policy of the kingdom in this business, and his triumph was the great good fortune of the·colonies. Yet his design was sufficiently cautious, and strictly limited to the advantage of his own country. France was not to be compromised, and an ingenious scheme was arranged.

The firm of Roderigue Hortalez & Co. made sudden appearance in Paris. Beaumarchais alone conducted its affairs, the most extraordinary merchant surely who ever engaged in extensive commerce! The capital was secretly furnished by the Spanish and French governments; about $400,000 the firm had to start with, and later the French government contributed $200,000 more. De Vergennes was explicit in his language to Beaumarchais : to Englishmen and Americans alike the affair must be an "individual speculation." With the capital given him Beaumarchais must "found a great commercial establishment," and "at his own risk and peril" sell to the colonies military supplies. These would be sold to him from the French arsenals; but he "must pay for them." From the colonies he must "ask return in their staple products." Except that his silent partners might be lenient in demanding repayment Beaumarchais really was to be a merchant, engaged in an exceptionally hazardous trade. If he regarded himself in any other light he was soon painfully undeceived; for de Vergennes was in earnest. But for the immediate present, upon the moment when he had arranged these preliminaries, doubtless fancying the government at his back, this most energetic of men plunged into his work with all the ardor of his excitable nature. He flew hither and thither; got arms and munitions from the government; bought and loaded ships, and was soon conducting an enormous business.

But it was by no means all smooth sailing for
the vessels of Hortalez & Co. ; for Deane arrived,
not altogether opportunely, just as Beaumarchais
was getting well under weigh. The two were
soon brought together, and Deane was told all that
was going on save only the original connection
of the French government, which it seems that
he never knew. He in turn told all to Dr. Bancroft, and so unwittingly to the English government. Thereupon the watchful English cruisers
effectually locked up the ships of Hortalez in the
French harbors. Also Lord Stormont, the English ambassador, harassed the French government
with ceaseless representations and complaints concerning these betrayed shipments of contraband
cargoes. At the same time the news from America, coming chiefly through English channels, took
on a very gloomy coloring, and lent a certain
emphasis to these protests of the English minister.
De Vergennes felt compelled to play out his neutral part even more in earnest than had been intended. He sent to the ports at which Hortalez
& Co. had ships very stringent instructions to
check unlawful trade, and the officials obeyed in
good faith to the letter. Beaumarchais was seriously embarrassed at finding himself bearing in
fact the mercantile character which he had supposed that he was only dramatically assuming.
He had to load his cargoes and clear his ships as
best he could, precisely like any ordinary dealer in
contraband wares; there was no favoritism, no

winking at his breaches of the law. The result was that it was a long while before he got any arms, ammunition, and clothing into an American port. Moreover the ships from America which were to have brought him payment in the shape of tobacco and other American commodities failed to arrive; his royal co-partners declined to make further advances; the ready money was gone, credit had been strained to the breaking point, and a real bankruptcy impended over the sham firm. Thus in the autumn and early winter of 1776 prospects in France wore no cheerful aspect for the colonies. It was at this juncture that Franklin arrived, and he came like a reviving breeze from the sea.

Long and anxiously did Congress wait to get news from France; not many trustworthy ships were sent on so perilous a voyage, and of those that ventured it only a few got across an ocean " porcupined " with English war-ships. At last in September, 1776, Franklin received from Dr. Dubourg of Paris, a gentleman with whom his friendship dated back to his French trip in 1767, a long and cheering letter full of gratifying intelligence concerning the disposition of the court, and throwing out a number of such suggestions that the mere reading them was a stimulus to action. Congress was not backward to respond; it resolved at once to send a formal embassage. Franklin was chosen unanimously by the first ballot. " I am old and good for nothing," he whispered to Dr. Rush, " but, as the storekeepers say of their remnants of cloth, ' I am but a fag end and you may have me for what you please.' " [1] Thomas Jefferson and Deane were elected as colleagues; but Jefferson declined the service and Arthur Lee was put in his stead. The Reprisal, sloop of war, of sixteen guns, took Dr. Franklin and his grandson on board for the dangerous voyage. It was a very different risk from that which Messrs. Slidell and Mason took nearly a century later. They embarked on a British mail steamship, and were subject, as was proved, only to the ordinary perils of navigation. But had Franklin been caught in this little rebel craft, which had actually been captured from English owners and condemned as prize by rebel tribunals, and which now added the aggravating circumstance that she carried an armament sufficient to destroy a merchantman but not to encounter a frigate, he would have had before him at best a long imprisonment, at worst a trial for high treason and a halter. Horace Walpole gave the news that " Dr. Franklin, at the age of seventy-two or seventy-four, and at the risk of his head, had bravely embarked on board an American frigate." Several times he must have contemplated these pleasing prospects, for several times the small sloop was chased by English cruisers; but she was a swift sailer and escaped them all. Just before making port she captured two English brigs and carried them in as prizes.

[1] Parton's *Life of Franklin*, ii. 166.

The reference to Slidell and Mason, by the way, calls to mind the humorous but accurate manner in which Franklin described the difference between revolution and rebellion. Soon after landing from this hazardous voyage he wrote merrily to a lady friend: "You are too early, *hussy*, as well as too saucy, in calling me a *rebel*. You should wait for the event, which will determine whether it is a *rebellion* or only a *revolution*. Here the ladies are more civil; they call us *les insurgens*, a character which usually pleases them."

The voyage, though quick, was very rough, and Franklin, confined in a small cabin and "poorly nourished," since much of the meat was too tough for his old teeth, had a hard time of it; so that upon coming on shore he found himself "much fatigued and weakened," indeed, "almost demolished." He therefore rested several days at Nantes before going to Paris, where he arrived just before the close of the year.

The excitement which his arrival in the French capital created was unmistakable evidence of the estimate set by Europe upon his abilities. Some persons in England endeavored to give to his voyage the color of a desertion from a cause of which he despaired. "The arch ——, Dr. Franklin, has lately eloped under a cloak of plenipotentiary to Versailles," wrote Sir Grey Cooper. But Edmund Burke refused to believe that the man whom he had seen examined before the privy council was "going to conclude a long life, which has brightened

every hour it has continued, with so foul and dishonorable a flight." Lord Rockingham said that
the presence of Franklin in Paris much more than
offset the victory of the English on Long Island,
and their capture of New York. Lord Stormont,
it is said, threatened to leave *sans prendre congé*,
if the " chief of the American rebels " were allowed
to come to Paris. The adroit de Vergennes replied
that the government had already dispatched a
courier to direct Franklin to remain at Nantes;
but since they knew neither the time of his departure nor his route, the message might not reach him.
Should he thus innocently arrive in Paris it would
be scandalous, inhospitable, and contrary to the
laws of nations to send him away.[1]

But while the English were angry, the French
indulged in a *furore* of welcome. They made
feasts and hailed the American as the friend of
human kind, as the " ideal of a patriarchal republic and of idyllic simplicity," as a sage of anti-
quity; and the exuberant classicism of the nation
exhausted itself in glorifying him by comparisons
with those great names of Greece and Rome which
have become symbols for all private and public
virtues. They admired him because he did not
wear a wig; they lauded his spectacles; they were
overcome with enthusiasm as they contemplated
his great cap of martin fur, his scrupulously white
linen, and the quaint simplicity of his brown
Quaker raiment of colonial make. They noted

[1] Hale's *Franklin in France*, i. 73.

with amazement that his " only defense" was a
" walking-stick in his hand." The print-shops were
soon full of countless representations of his noble
face and venerable figure, set off by all these pleasing adjuncts. The people thronged the streets to
see him pass, and respectfully made way for him.
He seemed, as John Adams said later, to enjoy a
reputation " more universal than that of Leibnitz
or Newton, Frederick or Voltaire."

So soon as all this uproar gave him time to look
about him, he established himself at Passy, in a
part of the Hôtel de Valentinois, which was kindly
placed at his disposal by its owner, M. Ray de Chaumont. In this at that time retired suburb he hoped
to be able to keep the inevitable but useless inter-
ruptions within endurable limits. Not improbably
also he was further influenced, in accepting M.
Chaumont's hospitality, by a motive of diplomatic
prudence. His shrewdness and experience must
soon have shown him that his presence in Paris, if
not precisely distasteful to the French government,
must at least in some degree compromise it, and
might by any indiscretion on his part easily be made
to annoy and vex the ministers. It therefore behoved him to make himself as little as possible conspicuous in any official or public way. A rebuke, a
cold reception, might do serious harm; nor was it
politic to bring perplexities to those whose friendship he sought. He could not avoid, nor had he any
reason to do so, the social *éclat* with which he was
greeted; but he must shun the ostentation of

any relationship with men in office. This would be more easily accomplished by living in a quarter somewhat remote and suburban. His retirement, therefore, while little curtailing his intercourse with private society, evinced his good tact, and doubtless helped his good standing with the ministers. The police record reports that, if he saw them at all, it was secretly and under cover of night. He lived in comfortable style, but not showily, keeping a moderate retinue of servants for appearance as much as for use, and a carriage, which was indispensable to him. John Adams charged him with undue luxury and extravagance, but the accusation was ridiculous.

Very exacting did the business of the American envoys soon become. On December 23, 1776, they wrote to acquaint the Count de Vergennes that they were " appointed and fully empowered by the Congress of the United States of America to propose and negotiate a treaty of amity and commerce between France and the United States ; " and they requested an audience for the purpose of presenting their credentials to his excellency. Five days later the audience was given them. They explained the desire of the American colonies to enter into a treaty of alliance and of commerce. They said that the colonists were anxious to get their ships, now lying at the home wharves laden with tobacco and other products, out of the American harbors, and to give them a chance to run for France. But the English vessels hovered thick up and down the

coasts, and the Americans, though able to take
care of frigates, could not encounter ships of the
line. Would not France lend eight ships of the
line, equipped and manned, to let loose all this
blockaded commerce which was ready to seek her
ports and to fill the coffers of her merchants?
Under all the circumstances this was certainly asking too much ; and in due time the envoys were
courteously told so, but were also offered a strictly
secret loan of $400,000, to be repaid after the war,
without interest.

It appears that Franklin had substantially no
concern in the *quasi* commercial transactions pending at the time of his arrival between Deane and
Beaumarchais. Deane himself did not know and
could not disclose the details of the relationship
between Beaumarchais and the government, which
indeed were not explored and made public until
more than half a century had elapsed after their
occurrence. Therefore Franklin saw nothing more
than mercantile dealings in various stages of for-
wardness, whose extensive intricacies it did not
seem worth while for him to unravel at a cost of
much time and labor, which could be better expended in other occupations.[1] Deane held all the
threads, and it seemed natural and proper to
leave this business as his department. So Franklin never had more than a general knowledge concerning this imbroglio.

[1] Franklin's *Works*, vi. 199, 205 ; viii. 153, 183 ; Hale's *Franklin in France*, i. 53.

This leaving all to Deane might have been
well enough had not Deane had an implacable
enemy in Arthur Lee, who, for that matter,
resembled the devil in at least one particular,
inasmuch as he was the foe of all mankind.
Beaumarchais early in the proceedings had summarily dropped Lee from his confidence and instated Deane in the vacancy. This was sufficient
to set Lee at once at traducing, an art in which
long experience had cultivated natural aptitude.
He saw great sums of money being used, and he
was not told whence they came. But he guessed,
and upon his guess he built up a theory of financial knavery. Deane had repeatedly assured
Beaumarchais that he should receive the cargoes
of American produce with promptitude,[1] and he did
his best to make these promises good, writing urgent letters to Congress to hasten forward the colonial merchandise. But Arthur Lee mischievously
and maliciously blocked these perfectly straightforward and absolutely necessary arrangements. For
he had conceived the notion that Beaumarchais was
an agent of the French court, that the supplies
were free gifts from the French government, and
that any payments for them to Hortalez & Co. would
only go to fill the rascal purses of Deane and Beaumarchais, confederates in a scheme for swindling.
He had no particle of evidence to sustain this notion, which was simply the subtle conception of his
own bad mind ; but he was not the less positive

---

[1] Hale's *Franklin in France,* i. 45.

and persistent in asserting it in his letters to members of Congress. Such accounts sadly puzzled that body; and it may be imagined to what a further hopeless degree of bewilderment this gathering of American lawyers and tradesmen, planters and farmers, must have been reduced by the extraordinary letters of the wild and fanciful Beaumarchais. The natural consequence was that the easier course was pursued, and no merchandise was sent to Hortalez. If affairs had not soon taken a new turn in France this error might have had disastrous consequences for the colonies. In fact, it only ruined poor Deane.

After this unfortunate man had been recalled, and while he was in great affliction at home because he could not get his reputation cleared from these Lee slanders, being utterly unable in America to produce even such accounts and evidence as might have been had in France, Franklin more than once volunteered to express kindly and emphatically his entire belief in Deane's integrity. So late as October, 1779, though admitting his lack of knowledge concerning an affair in which he had "never meddled," he still thought Deane "innocent." Finally in 1782, when Deane had become thoroughly demoralized by his hard fate, Franklin spoke of his fall not without a note of sympathy: "He resides at Ghent, is distressed both in mind and circumstances, raves and writes abundance, and I imagine it will end in his going over to join his friend Arnold

in England. I had an exceedingly good opinion
of him when he acted with me, and I believe he
was then sincere and hearty in our cause. But he
is changed, and his character ruined in his own
country and in this, so that I see no other but England to which he can now retire. He says we owe
him about £12,000 sterling." [1] But of this Franklin
knew nothing, and proposed getting experts to examine the accounts. He did know very well, however, what it was to be accused by Arthur Lee, and
would condemn no man upon that basis !

Yet the matter annoyed him greatly. On June
12, 1781, he wrote acknowledging that he was absolutely in the dark about the whole business : —

" In 1776, being then in Congress, I received a letter
from Mr. Lee, acquainting me that M. Beaumarchais
had applied to him in London, informing him that
200,000 guineas had been put into his hands, and was at
the disposal of the Congress; Mr. Lee added that it was
agreed between them that he, M. Beaumarchais, should
remit the same in arms, ammunition, etc., under the
name of Hortalez & Co. Several cargoes were accordingly sent. Mr. Lee understood this to be a private aid
from the government of France; but M. Beaumarchais
has since demanded from Congress payment of a gross
sum, as due to him, and has received a considerable part,
but has rendered no particular account. I have, by
order of Congress, desired him to produce his account,

---

[1] See also letter to Morris, March 30, 1782, *Works*, vii. 419 ;
also viii. 225. In 1835 sufficient evidence was discovered to induce Congress to pay to the heirs of this unfortunate man a part
of the sum due to him. Parton's *Life of Franklin*, ii. 362.

that we might know exactly what we owed, and for what ; and he has several times promised it, but has not yet done it; and in his conversation he often mentions, as I am told, that we are greatly in his debt. These accounts in the air are unpleasant, and one is neither safe nor easy under them. I wish, therefore, you could help me to obtain a settlement of them. It has been said that Mr. Deane, unknown to his colleagues, wrote to Congress in favor of M. Beaumarchais's demand; on which Mr. Lee accuses him of having, to the prejudice of his constituents, negotiated a gift into a debt. At present all that transaction is in darkness ;[1] and we know not whether the whole, or a part, or no part, of the supplies he furnished were at the expense of government, the reports we have had being so inconsistent and contradictory ; nor, if we are in debt for them, or any part of them, whether it is the king or M. de Beaumarchais who is our creditor."[2]

What chiefly irritated Congress against Deane and led to his recall was neither his dealings with Beaumarchais nor the slanders of Lee, but quite another matter, in which he certainly showed much lack of discretion. Cargoes of arms and munitions of war were very welcome in the States, but cargoes of French and other European officers were by no means so. Yet the inconsiderate Deane sent over these enthusiasts and adventurers in throngs. The

---

[1] Light was first let in upon this darkness by Louis de Loménie, in his *Beaumarchais et Son Temps* ; and the story as told by him may be read, in a spirited version, in Parton's *Life of Franklin*, chapters vii., viii.

[2] Hale's *Franklin in France*, i. 53.

outbreak of the rebellion seemed to arouse a spirit of martial pilgrimage in Europe, a sort of crusading ardor, which seized the Frenchmen especially, but also some few officers in other continental armies. These all flocked to Paris and told Deane that they were burning to give the insurgent States the invaluable assistance of their distinguished services. Deane was little accustomed to the highly appreciative rhetoric with which the true Frenchman frankly describes his own merit, and apparently accepted as correct the appraisal which these warriors made of themselves. Soon they alighted in swarms upon the American coast, besieged the doors of Congress, and mingled their importunities with all the other harassments of Washington. Each one of them had his letter from Deane, reciting the exaggerated estimate of his capacity, and worse still each one was armed with Deane's promise that he should hold in the American army a rank one grade higher than he had held in his home service. To keep these unauthorized pledges would have resulted in the resignation of all the good American officers, and in the utter disorganization of the army. So the inevitable outcome was that the disappointed adventurers became furious ; that Congress, greatly annoyed, went to heavy expenses in sending them back again to Europe, and in giving some *douceurs,* which could be ill afforded by the giver and were quite insufficient to prevent the recipients from spreading at home their bitter grudge against the young republic. Altogether it was a bad business.

No sooner was Franklin's foot on French soil than the same eager horde assailed him. But they found a respondent very different from Deane. Franklin had experience. He knew the world and men; and now his tranquil judgment and firmness saved him and the applicants alike from further blunders. His appreciation of these fiery and priceless gallants, who so dazzled the simple-minded Deane, is shown with charming humor in his effort to say a kindly word for his unfortunate colleague. He did not wonder, he said, that Deane, —

"being then a stranger to the people, and unacquainted with the language, was at first prevailed on to make some such agreements, when all were recommended, as they always are, as *officiers expérimentés, braves comme leurs épées, pleins de courage, de talent, et de zèle pour notre cause,* etc., etc.; in short, mere Cæsars, each of whom would have been an invaluable acquisition to America. You can have no conception how we are still besieged and worried on this head, our time cut to pieces by personal applications, besides those contained in dozens of letters by every post. . . . I hope therefore that favorable allowance will be made to my worthy colleague on account of his situation at the time, as he has long since corrected that mistake, and daily approves himself, to my certain knowledge, an able, faithful, active, and extremely useful servant of the public; a testimony I think it my duty of taking this occasion to make to his merit, unasked, as, considering my great age, I may probably not live to give it personally in Congress, and I perceive he has enemies."

But however firmly and wisely Franklin stood

out against the storm of importunities he could not for a long time moderate it. He continued to be "besieged and worried," and to have his time "cut to pieces;" till at last he wrote to a friend: "You can have no conception how I am harassed. All my friends are sought out and teased to tease me. Great officers of all ranks, in all departments, ladies great and small, besides professed solicitors, worry me from morning to night. The noise of every coach now that enters my court terrifies me. I am afraid to accept an invitation to dine abroad. . . . Luckily I do not often in my sleep dream of these vexatious situations, or I should be afraid of what are now my only hours of comfort. . . . For God's sake, my dear friend, let this, your twenty-third application, be your last."

His plain-spoken replies, however harshly they may have struck upon Gallic sensitiveness, at least left no room for any one to misunderstand him. "I know that officers, going to America for employment, will probably be disappointed," he wrote; "that our armies are full; that there are a number of expectants unemployed and starving for want of subsistence; that my recommendation will not make vacancies, nor can it fill them to the prejudice of those who have a better claim." He also wrote to Washington, to whom the letter must have brought joyous relief, that he dissuaded every one from incurring the great expense and hazard of the long voyage, since there was already an oversupply of officers and the chance of employment was extremely slight.[1]

The severest dose which he administered must have made some of those excitable swords quiver in their scabbards. He drew up and used this

"MODEL OF A LETTER OF RECOMMENDATION OF A PERSON YOU ARE UNACQUAINTED WITH."

"SIR, — The bearer of this, who is going to America, presses me to give him a letter of recommendation, though I know nothing of him, not even his name. This may seem extraordinary, but I assure you it is not uncommon here. Sometimes, indeed, one unknown person brings another equally unknown to recommend him; and sometimes they recommend one another! As to this gentleman, I must refer you to himself for his character and merits, with which he is certainly better acquainted than I can possibly be. I recommend him however to those civilities, which every stranger, of whom one knows no harm, has a right to; and I request you will do him all the good offices and show him all the favor, that, on further acquaintance, you shall find him to deserve. I have the honor to be, &c."

It would be entertaining to know how many of these letters were delivered, and in what phrases of

[1] As an example of the manner in which Franklin sometimes was driven to express himself, his letter to M. Lith is admirable. This gentleman had evidently irritated him somewhat, and Franklin demolished him with a reply in that plain, straightforward style of which he was a master, in which appeared no anger, but sarcasm of that severest kind which lies in a simple statement of facts. I regret that there is not space to transcribe it, but it may be read in his *Works*, vi. 85.

French courtesy gratitude was expressed for them. Sometimes, if any one persisted, in spite of discouragement, in making the journey at his own cost, and, being forewarned, also at his own risk of disappointment, Franklin gave him a letter strictly confined to the scope of a civil personal introduction. Possibly, now and again, some useful officer may have been thus deterred from crossing the water ; but any such loss was compensated several hundredfold by shutting off the intolerable inundation of useless foreigners. Nor was Franklin wanting in discretion in the matter; for he commended Lafayette and Steuben by letters, which had real value from the fact of the extreme rarity of such a warranty from this source.

Franklin was little given to political prophecy, but it is interesting to read a passage written shortly after his arrival, May 1, 1777: —

"All Europe is on our side of the question, as far as applause and good wishes can carry them. Those who live under arbitrary power do nevertheless approve of liberty, and wish for it ; they almost despair of recovering it in Europe ; they read the translations of our separate colony constitutions with rapture ; and there are such numbers everywhere who talk of removing to America, with their families and fortunes, as soon as peace and our independence shall be established, that it is generally believed that we shall have a prodigious addition of strength, wealth, and arts from the emigration of Europe ; and it is thought that to lessen or prevent such emigrations, the tyrannies established there must relax, and allow more liberty to their people. Hence it is a common observation here that our cause is the *cause of all mankind*, and that we are fighting for their liberty in defending our own. It is a glorious task assigned us by Providence, which has, I trust, given us spirit and virtue equal to it, and will at last crown it with success."

The statesmanship of the time-honored European school, ably practiced by de Vergennes, was short-sighted and blundering in comparison with this broad appreciation of the real vastness and far-reaching importance of that great struggle betwixt the Old and the New.

CHAPTER X.

No sooner had the war taken on an assured character than many quick-eyed and adventurous Americans, and Franklin among the first, saw irresistible temptation and great opportunity in that enormous British commerce which whitened all the seas. The colonists of that day, being a seafaring people with mercantile instincts, were soon industriously engaged in the lucrative field of maritime captures. Franklin recommended the fortifying of three or four harbors into which prizes could be safely carried. Nothing else, he said, would give the new nation " greater weight and importance in the eyes of the commercial states." Privateering is not always described by such complimentary and dignified language, but the practical-minded rebel spoke well of that which it was so greatly to the advantage of his countrymen to do. After arriving in France he found himself in a position to advance this business very greatly. Conyngham, Wickes, with others only less famous, all active and gallant men as ever trod a deck, took the neighboring waters as their chosen scene of action, and very soon were stirring up a commotion such as Englishmen had never experienced before. They harried the high, and more especially the narrow, seas with a success at least equal to that of the Alabama, while some of them differed from Semmes and his compeers in being as anxious to fight as the Southern captains were to avoid fighting. Prize after prize they took and carried into port, or burned and sank ; prisoners they had more than they knew what to do with ; they frightened the underwriters so that in London the insurance against capture ran up to the ruinous premium of sixty per cent. The Lisbon and the Dutch packets fell victims, and insurance of boats plying between Dover and Calais went to ten per cent. Englishmen began to feel that England was blockaded ! We are not so familiar as we ought to be with the interesting record of all these audacious and brilliant enterprises, conducted with dare-devil recklessness by men who would not improbably have been hanged both as pirates and as traitors, had fortune led to their capture at this moment of British rage and anxiety.[1]

All this cruising was conducted under the auspices of Franklin. To him these gallant rovers looked for instructions and suggestions, for money and supplies. He had to issue commissions, to settle personal misunderstandings, to attend to questions of prize money, to soothe unpaid mutineers, to advise as to the purchase of ships, and as to the

[1] In fact, Conyngham, being at last captured, narrowly escaped this fate.

enterprises to be undertaken; in a word, he was the only *American government* which these independent sailors knew. The tax thus laid upon him was severe, for he was absolutely without experience in such matters.

There was one labor, however, in this connection, which properly fell within his department, and in this his privateersmen gave him abundant occupation. It was to stand between them and the just wrath and fatal interference of the French government. Crude as international law was in those days, it was far from being crude enough for the strictly illegitimate purposes of these vikings. What they expected was to buy, equip, man, and supply their vessels in French ports, to sail out on their prize-taking excursions, and, having captured their fill, to return to these same ports, and there to have their prizes condemned, to sell their booty, to refit and re-supply, and then to sally forth again. In short, an Englishman would have been puzzled to distinguish a difference between the warlike ports of America and the neutral ports of France, save as he saw that the latter, being nearer, were much the more injurious. But de Vergennes had no notion of being used for American purposes in this jeopardizing style. He did not mean to have a war with England, if he could avoid it; so he gave to the harbor masters orders which greatly annoyed and surprised the American captains, "extraordinary" orders, as these somewhat uninstructed sea-dogs described them in their complaining letters to Franklin. They thought it an outrage that the French minister should refuse to have English prizes condemned within French jurisdiction, and that he should not allow them to refit and to take on board cannon and ammunition at Nantes or Rochelle. They called upon Franklin to check these intolerable proceedings. Their audacious and boundless insolence is very entertaining to read, with the memory of " Alabama outrages " fresh in mind.

Franklin knew, just as well as de Vergennes did, that the French ministry was all the time favoring the privateersmen and cruisers far beyond the law, and that it was ready to resort to as many devices as ingenuity could concoct for that purpose; also that the Americans by their behavior persistently violated all reason and neutral toleration. Nevertheless he stood gallantly by his own, and in one case after another he kept corresponding with de Vergennes under pretense of correcting misrepresentations, presenting requests, and arguing points, until, by the time thus gained, the end was achieved. The truth was that Franklin's duty was to get from France just as much aid, direct and indirect, as could be either begged or filched from her. Such orders could not be written down in plain words in his instructions, but none the less they lurked there not illegible to him among the lines. He obeyed them diligently. France was willing to go fully as far as she could with safety; his function was to push, to pull, to entice, even to mislead, in order to make her go farther. Perhaps it was a fair game ; France had her interest to see Great Britain dismembered and weakened, but not herself to fight other people's battles ; the colonies had their interest to get France into the fight if they possibly could. It was a strictly selfish interest, and was pursued almost shamelessly. The colonial policy and the details of its execution are defensible simply on the basis that all nations in their dealings with each other are always utterly selfish and generally utterly unscrupulous. By and by, when it comes to the treating for peace between England and the colonies, we shall find de Vergennes much reviled because he pursued exclusively French interests ; but it will be only fair to reflect that little more can be charged against him than that he was playing the game with cards drawn from the same pack which the Americans had used in these earlier days of the war.

A matter which grew out of privateering gave Franklin much trouble. The American captains, who were cruising on the European side of the Atlantic prior to the treaty of alliance with France, had no place in which to deposit their prisoners. They could not often send them to the States, neither of course could they accumulate them on board their ships, nor yet store them, so to speak, in France and Spain ; for undeveloped as were the rules of neutrality they at least forbade the use of neutral prisons for the keeping of English prisoners of war in time of peace.   Meanwhile the colonial captives, in confinement just across the Channel, in the prisons at Plymouth and Portsmouth, were subjected to very harsh treatment; and others were even being sent to the fort of Senegal on the coast of Africa, and to the East Indies, whence they could not hope ever to regain their homes.   Franklin immediately resolved, if possible, to utilize these assets in the shape of English sailors in the usual course of exchange.   A letter was accordingly addressed by him to Lord Stormont, asking whether it would be worth while to approach the British court with an offer to exchange one hundred English prisoners in the hands of the captain of the Reprisal for a like number of American sailors from the English prisons.   The note was a simple interrogatory in proper form of civility.   No answer was received. After a while a second letter was prepared, less formal, more forcible in statement and argument, and in the appeal to good sense and decent good feeling.   This elicited from his lordship a brief response : " The king's ambassador receives no applications from rebels, unless they come to implore his majesty's mercy."   The commissioners indignantly rejoined : " In answer to a letter which concerns some of the most material interests of humanity, and of the two nations, Great Britain and the United States of America, now at war, we received the inclosed indecent paper, as coming from your lordship, which we return for your lordship's more mature consideration."

The technical position of the English in this business was that the captured Americans were not prisoners of war, but traitors. Their practical position was that captains of American privateers, not finding it a physical possibility to keep their prisoners, would erelong be obliged to let them go without exchange. This anticipation turned out to be correct, and so far justified their refusal; for soon some five hundred English sailors got their freedom as a necessity, without any compensatory freeing of Americans. Each of them gave a solemn promise in writing to obtain the release of an American prisoner in return; but he had as much authority to hand over the Tower of London, and the British government was not so romantically chivalrous as to recognize pledges entered into by foremast hands.

All sorts of stories continued to reach Franklin's ears as to the cruelty which his imprisoned countrymen had to endure. He heard that they were penniless and could get no petty comforts; that they suffered from cold and hunger, and were subjected to personal indignities; that they were not allowed to read a newspaper or to write a letter; that they were all committed by a magistrate on a charge of high treason, and were never allowed to forget their probable fate on the gibbet; that some of them, as has been said, were deported to distant and unwholesome English possessions. For the truth of these accounts it is not necessary to believe that the English government was intentionally brutal; but it was neglectful and indifferent, and those who had prisoners in charge felt assured that no sympathy for rebels would induce an investigation into peculations or unfeeling behavior. Moreover there was a deliberate design, by terror and discouragement, to break the spirit of the so-called traitors and persuade them to become real traitors by entering the English service.

By all these tales Franklin's zeal in the matter of exchange was greatly stimulated. His humane soul revolted at keeping men who were not criminals locked up in wasting misery, when they might be set free upon terms of perfect equality between the contending parties. Throughout his correspondence on this subject there is a magnanimity, a humanity, a spirit of honesty and even of honor so extraordinary, or actually unique, in dealings between diplomats and nations, that the temptation is irresistible to give a fuller narrative than the intrinsic importance of the subject would warrant. For after all there were never many English prisoners in France to be exchanged; after a while they might be counted by hundreds, but perhaps they never rose to a total of one thousand.

There was at this time in England a man to whose memory Americans ought to erect statues. This was David Hartley. He was a gentleman of the most liberal and generous sentiments, an old and valued friend of Franklin, member of Parliament for Hull, allied with the opposition in this matter of the American war, but personally on

good terms with Lord North. He had not very
great ability; he wrote long letters, somewhat sur-
charged with morality and good-feeling. One would
expect to hear that he was on terms of admiring
intimacy with his contemporary, the good Mrs.
Barbauld. But he had those opportunities which
come only to men whose excellence of character
and purity of motive place them above suspicion, —
opportunities which might have been shut off from
an abler man, and which he now used with untiring zeal and much efficiency in behalf of the
American prisoners. Lord North did not hesitate
to permit him to correspond with Franklin, and he
long acted as a medium of communication more
serviceable than Lord Stormont had been. Furthermore Hartley served as almoner to the poor fellows,
and pushed a private subscription in England to
raise funds for securing to them reasonable comforts. There were responsive hearts and purses,
even for rebels, among his majesty's subjects, and
a considerable sum was collected.

Franklin's first letter to Hartley on this subject,
October 14, 1777, has something of bitterness in
its tone, with much deep feeling for his countrymen, whose reputed woes he narrates. " I can assure you," he adds, " from my certain knowledge,
that your people, prisoners in America, have been
treated with great kindness, having had the same
rations of wholesome provisions as our own troops,"
" comfortable lodgings" in healthy villages, with
liberty " to walk and amuse themselves on their

parole." "Where you have thought fit to employ contractors to supply your people, these contractors have been protected and aided in their operations. Some considerable act of kindness towards our people would take off the reproach of inhumanity in that respect from the nation and leave it where it ought with more certainty to lie, on the conductors of your war in America. This I hint to you out of some remaining good will to a nation I once loved sincerely. But as things are, and in my present temper of mind, not being over-fond of receiving obligations, I shall content myself with proposing that your government should allow us to send or employ a commissary to take some care of those unfortunate people. Perhaps on your representations this might be obtained in England, though it was refused most inhumanly at New York."

In December following he had arranged with Major Thornton, "who appears a man of humanity," to visit the prisons and give relief to the prisoners, and he hopes that Thornton "may obtain permission for that purpose." "I have wished," he added, "that some voluntary act of compassion on the part of your government towards those in your power had appeared in abating the rigors of their confinement, and relieving their pressing necessities, as such generosity towards enemies has naturally an effect in softening and abating animosity in their compatriots, and disposing to reconciliation." Of such unconventional humanity was he!

Hartley met Franklin's ardent appeals with responsive ardor. May 29, 1778, he writes that he will press the point of exchange as much as he can, "which in truth," he says, "I have done many times since I saw you; but official departments move slowly here. A promise of five months is yet unperformed." But a few days later, June 5, he is "authorized" to propose that Franklin should send to him "the number and rank of the prisoners, upon which an equal number shall be prepared upon this side for the exchange." Franklin at once demanded lists from his captains, and replied to Hartley: "We desire and expect that the number of ours shall be taken from Forton and Plymouth, in proportion to the number in each place, and to consist of those who have been longest in confinement." He then made this extraordinary suggestion: "If you think proper to clear all your prisoners at once, and give us all our people, we give you our solemn engagement, which we are sure will be punctually executed, to deliver to Lord Howe in America, or to his order, a number of your sailors equal to the surplus, as soon as the agreement arrives there." It is easy to fancy a British minister thrusting his tongue into his cheek as this simple-minded proposal of the plain-dealing colonist was read to him. The only occasion on which Franklin showed ignorance of diplomacy was in assuming, in this matter of the prisoners, that honesty and honor were bases of dealing between public officials in international matters.

He suggested also retaining a distinction between sailors of the navy and of the commercial marine. After repeated applications to the Board of Admiralty, Hartley was only able to reply to all Franklin's proposals that no distinction could be made between the naval and merchant services, because all the Americans were "detained under commitments from some magistrate, as for high treason."

July 13, 1778, Franklin remitted to Hartley the lists of English prisoners. September 14 he recurs again to the general release: "You have not mentioned whether the proposition of sending us the whole of those in your prisons was agreed to. If it is, you may rely on our sending immediately all that come to our hands for the future; or we will give you, [at] your option, an order for the balance to be delivered to your fleet in America. By putting a little confidence in one another, we may thus diminish the miseries of war." Five days later he took a still more romantic position: heretofore, he said, the American commissioners had encouraged and aided the American prisoners to try to escape; "but if the British government should honorably keep their agreement to make regular exchanges, we shall not think it consistent with the honor of the United States to encourage such escapes, or to give any assistance to such as shall escape."

Yet at the same time he showed himself fully able to conduct business according to the usual commonplace method. This same letter closes with a threat under the *lex talionis:* " We have now obtained permission of this government to put all British prisoners, whether taken by continental ¶ frigates or by privateers, into the king's prisons; and we are determined to treat such prisoners precisely as our countrymen are treated in England, to give them the same allowance of provisions and accommodations, and no other." He was long obliged to reiterate the like menaces.[1]

October 20, 1778, he reverts to his favorite project: " I wish their lordships could have seen it well to exchange upon account; but though they may not think it safe trusting to us, we shall make no difficulty in trusting to them; " and he proposes that, if the English will " send us over 250 of our people, we will deliver all we have in France; " if these be less than two hundred and fifty, the English may take back the surplus Americans; but if these be more than two hundred and fifty, Franklin says that he will nevertheless deliver them all in expectation that he will receive back an equivalent for the surplus. " We would thus wish to commence, by this first advance, that mutual confidence which it would be for the good of mankind that nations should maintain honorably with each other, tho' engaged in war."

November 19, 1778, nothing has been achieved, and he gets impatient: " I have heard nothing from you lately concerning the exchange of the

[1] Hale's *Franklin in France*, i. 352.

prisoners. Is that affair dropt? Winter is coming on apace." January 25, 1779: "I a long time believed that your government were in earnest in agreeing to an exchange of prisoners. I begin now to think I was mistaken. It seems they cannot give up the pleasing idea of having at the end of the war 1,000 Americans to hang for high treason." Poor Hartley had been working with all the energy of a good man in a good cause; but he was in the painful position of having no excuse to offer for the backwardness of his government.

February 22, 1779, brought more reproaches from Franklin. Months had elapsed since he had heard that the cartel ship was prepared to cross the Channel, but she had never come. He feared that he had been "deceived or trifled with," and proposed sending Edward Bancroft on a special mission to England, if a safe conduct could be procured. At last, on March 30, Hartley had the pleasure of announcing that the exchange ship had "sailed the 25th instant from Plymouth." Franklin soon replied that the transaction was completed, and gave well-earned thanks to Hartley for his "unwearied pains in that affair."

Thus after infinite difficulty the English government had been pushed into conformity with the ordinary customs of war among civilized nations. Yet subsequent exchanges seem to have been effected only after every possible obstacle had been contumaciously thrown in the way by the English and patiently removed by Franklin. The Americans were driven to various devices. The captains sometimes released their prisoners at sea upon the written parole of each either to secure the return of an American, or to surrender himself to Franklin in France. In November, 1781, Franklin had about five hundred of these documents, "not one of which," he says, "has been regarded, so little faith and honor remain in that corrupted nation." At last, after France and Spain had joined in the war, Franklin arranged that the American captors might lodge their prisoners in French and Spanish prisons.

Under flags of truce two cargoes of English sailors were dispatched from Boston to England; but the English refused to reciprocate. "There is no getting anything from these barbarians," said Franklin, "by advances of civility or humanity." Then much trouble arose because the French borrowed from Franklin some English prisoners for exchange in Holland, and returned to him a like number a little too late for delivery on board the cartel ship, which had brought over one hundred Americans. Thereupon the Englishmen charged Franklin with "breach of faith," and with "deceiving the Board," and put a stop to further exchanging. This matter was, of course, set right in time. But the next point made by the admiralty was that they would make no exchanges with Franklin except for English sailors taken by American cruisers, thus excluding captives taken by the privateersmen. Franklin, much angered at the thwarting of his humane and reasonable scheme, said that they

had "given up all pretensions to equity and honor."
In his disappointment he went a little too far; if
he had said "liberality and humanity" instead of
"equity and honor" he would have kept within
literal truth. To meet this last action on the part
of England he suggested to Congress: "Whether
it may not be well to set apart 500 or 600 English
prisoners, and refuse them all exchange in America,
but for our countrymen now confined in England?"

Another thing which vexed him later was that
the English government would not give the Americans an "equal allowance" with the French and
Spanish prisoners. He suggested retaliation upon
a certain number of English prisoners in America.
He himself was constantly remitting money to be
distributed to the American prisoners, at the rate
of one shilling apiece each week. But he had
the pain to hear that the wretched fellow, one
Digges, to whom he sent the funds, embezzled
much of them. "If such a fellow is not damned,"
he said, "it is not worth while to keep a devil."
One prisoner of distinction, Colonel Laurens, captured on his way to France, complained that Franklin did not show sufficient zeal in his behalf. But
he made the assertion in ignorance of Franklin's
efforts, which for a long while Franklin had reason
to believe had been successful in securing kind and
liberal treatment for this captive.

In all this business Franklin ought to have received efficient assistance from Thomas Morris,
who held the position of commercial agent for the

States at Nantes, and who might properly have extended his functions to include so much of the naval business as required personal attention at that port. But he turned out to be a drunken rascal, active only in mischief. Thereupon, early in 1777, Franklin employed a nephew of his own from Boston, Jonathan Williams, not to supersede Morris in the commercial department, but to take charge of the strictly naval affairs, which were construed to include all matters pertaining to warships, privateers, and prizes. This action became the source of much trouble. It was a case of nepotism, of course, which was unfortunate; yet there was an absolute necessity to engage some one for these duties, and there was scant opportunity for choice. During the year that Williams held the office there is no reason to believe that he did not prove himself both efficient and honest. Robert Morris, however, whose brother Thomas was, and who had obtained for him the commercial office, was much offended, and it was not until in the course of time he received masses of indisputable evidence of his brother's worthlessness, that he was placated. Then at length he wrote a frank, pathetic letter, in which he acknowledged that he had been misled by natural affection, and that his resentment had been a mistake.

Arthur Lee also poured the destructive torrent of his malignant wrath over the ill-starred Williams. For William Lee pretended to find his province and his profits also trenched upon. The facts were that he was appointed to the commercial agency jointly with Thomas Morris; but shortly afterward he was promoted to the diplomatic service, and left Nantes for a permanent stay in Paris. He did not formally vacate his agency, but practically he abandoned it by rendering himself unable to attend to its duties. So even if by any construction he could have established a show of right to conduct the naval business, at least he never was on hand to do so. These considerations, however, did not in the least mitigate the rage of the Lee brethren, who now brought a great variety of charges. Franklin, they said, had no authority to make the appointment, and Williams was a knave engaged in a scandalous partnership with Deane to make money dishonestly out of the public business, especially the prizes. The quarrel continued unabated when John Adams arrived, in 1778, as joint commissioner with Franklin and Arthur Lee. At once the active Lee besieged the ear of the new-comer with all his criminations; and he must have found a ready listener, for so soon as the fourth day after his arrival Adams felt himself sufficiently informed to take what was practically judicial action in the matter. He declared upon Lee's side. The two then signed an order for Williams's dismissal, and presented it to Franklin. It was discourteous if not insulting behavior to an old man and the senior commissioner; but Franklin wisely said not a word, and added his signature to those of his colleagues. The rest of the story is the familiar one of many cases: the agent made repeated demands for the appointment of an accountant to examine his accounts, and Franklin often and very urgently preferred the same request. But the busy Congress would not bother itself ever so little with a matter no longer of any practical moment. Lee's charges remained unrefuted, though not a shadow of justifiable suspicion rested upon Franklin's unfortunate nephew.

CHAPTER XI.

THE enthusiastic reception of Franklin in France was responded to by him with a bearing so cheerful and words so encouraging that all the auguries for America seemed for a while of the best. For he was sanguine by nature, by resolution, and by policy; and his way of alluring good fortune was to welcome it in advance. But in fact there were clouds enough floating in the sky, and soon they expanded and obscured the transitory brightness. Communication between the two continents was extremely slow; throughout the war intervals occurred when for long and weary months no more trustworthy news reached Paris than the rumors which got their coloring by filtration through Great Britain. Thus in the dread year of 1777, there traveled across the Channel tales that Washington was conducting the remnant of his forces in a demoralized retreat; that Philadelphia had fallen before Howe; that Burgoyne, with a fine army, was moving to bisect the insurgent colonies from the north. It was very well for Franklin, when told that Howe had taken Philadelphia, to reply: " No,

sir: Philadelphia has taken Howe." The jest
may have relieved the stress of his mind, as President Lincoln used often to relieve his own overtaxed endurance in the same way. But the unde-
niable truth was that it looked much as if the affair,
to use Franklin's words, would prove to be a "rebellion" and not a "revolution." Still, any mis-
givings which he may have inwardly felt found no
expression, and to no one would he admit the possibility of such an ultimate outcome. Late in the
autumn of this dismal year he wrote: —

"You desire to know my opinion of what will probably be the end of this war, and whether our new estab-
lishments will not be thereby again reduced to deserts. I
do not, for my part, apprehend much danger of so great
an evil to us. I think we shall be able, with a little
help, to defend ourselves, our possessions, and our liberties so long that England will be ruined by persisting in
the wicked attempt to destroy them. . . . And I sometimes flatter myself that, old as I am, I may possibly
live to see my country settled in peace, when Britain
shall make no more a formidable figure among the
powers of Europe."

But though Franklin might thus refuse to despair for his country, the French ministry were not
to be blamed if they betrayed an increased reserve
in their communications with men who might soon
prove to be traitors instead of ambassadors, and if
they were careful to stop short of actually bringing
on a war with England. It was an anxious period
for Franklin when the days wore slowly into

months and the months lengthened almost into a year, during which he had no trustworthy information as to all the ominous news which the English papers and letters brought.

In this crisis of military affairs the anxious envoys felt that the awful burden of their country's salvation not improbably rested upon them. If they could induce France to come to the rescue, all would be well; if they could not, the worst might be feared. Yet in this mortal jeopardy they saw France growing more guarded in her conduct, while in vain they asked themselves, in an agony, what influence it was possible for them to exert. At the close of November, 1777, they conferred upon the matter. Mr. Deane was in favor of demanding from the French court a direct answer to the question, whether or not France would come openly to the aid of the colonies; and he advised that de Vergennes should be distinctly told that, if France should decline, the colonies would be obliged to seek an accommodation with Great Britain. But Dr. Franklin strenuously opposed this course. The effect of such a declaration seemed to him too uncertain; France might take it as a menace; she might be induced by it to throw over the colonies altogether, in despair or anger. Neither would he admit that the case was in fact so desperate; the colonies might yet work out their own safety, with the advantage in that event of remaining more free from any European influence. The soundness of this latter argument was afterward abundantly shown by the history of the country during the first three administrations. Fortunately upon this occasion Lee sided with Franklin, and the untimely trial of French friendship was not made. Had it been, it would have been more likely to jeopardize forever than to precipit~~e the good fortune which, though still invisible, was close at hand.

It was not until December 4, 1777, that there broke a great and sudden rift in the solid cloudiness. First there came a vague rumor of good news, no one at all knew what; then a post-chaise drove into Dr. Franklin's court-yard, and from it hastily alighted the young messenger, Jonathan Loring Austin, whom Congress had sent express from Philadelphia, and who had accomplished an extraordinarily rapid journey. The American group of envoys and agents were all there, gathered by the mysterious report which had reached them, and at the sound of the wheels they ran out into the court-yard and eagerly surrounded the chaise. " Sir," exclaimed Franklin, " is Philadelphia taken?" " Yes, sir," replied Austin; and Franklin clasped his hands and turned to reënter the house. But Austin cried that he bore greater news: that General Burgoyne and his whole army were prisoners of war! At the words the glorious sunshine burst forth. Beaumarchais, the ecstatic, sprang into his carriage and drove madly for the city to spread the story; but he upset his vehicle and dislocated his arm. The envoys hastily read and wrote; in a few hours Austin was again on the road, this time bound to de Vergennes at Versailles, to tell the great tidings. Soon all Paris got the news and burst into triumphant rejoicing over the disaster to England.

Austin's next errand was a secret and singular one. Franklin managed throughout his residence in France to maintain a constant communication with the opposition party in England. He now thought it wise to enable them to obtain full information from an intelligent man who was not many weeks absent from the States. Accordingly he dispatched Austin, using extreme precautions of secrecy, making him "burn every letter which he had brought from his friends in America," but giving him in exchange two other letters, which certainly introduced him to strange society for an American "rebel" to frequent. During his visit he was "domesticated in the family of the Earl of Shelburne ; placed under the particular protection of his chaplain, the celebrated Dr. Priestley ; introduced" to George IV., then Prince of Wales, with whom was Charles Fox, and was "present at all the coteries of the opposition." Almost every evening he was invited to dinner-parties, at which the company was chiefly composed of members of Parliament, and they plied him with interrogations about his country and its affairs, so that, as he reported, "no question which you can conceive is omitted." [1] He answered well, and rendered service as good as it was singular, for which Franklin

[1] Parton's *Life of Franklin,* ii. 307.

was probably the only American who could have furnished the opening. The adventure brings to mind some of the Jacobite tales of Sir Walter Scott's novels.

One half of the advantages accruing from " General Burgoyne's capitulation to Mr. Gates " — such was the Tory euphemism, somewhat ill-considered, since it implied that the gallant British commander had capitulated to a civilian — was to be reaped in Europe. The excellent Hartley was already benevolently dreaming of effecting an accommodation between the two contestants; and seeing clearly that an alliance with France must be fatal to any such project, he closed a letter on February 3, 1778, to Franklin, by " subjoining one earnest caution and request: Let nothing ever persuade America to throw themselves into the arms of France. Times may mend. I hope they will. An American must always be a stranger in France; Great Britain may for ages to come be their home." This was as kindly in intention as it was bad in grammatical construction; but it was written from a point of view very different from that which an American could adopt. Franklin promptly replied: " When your nation is hiring all the cut-throats it can collect, of all countries and colors, to destroy us, it is hard to persuade us not to ask or accept aid from any power that may be prevailed with to grant it; and this only from the hope that, though you now thirst for our blood, and pursue us with fire and sword, you may in some future time treat us kindly. This is too much patience to be expected of us; indeed, I think it is not in human nature."

A few days later he transposed Hartley's advice, not without irony: "Let nothing induce [the English Whigs] to join with the Tories in supporting and continuing this wicked war against the Whigs of America, whose assistance they may hereafter want to secure their own liberties, or whose country they may be glad to retire to for the enjoyment of them." Hartley must have had a marvelous good temper, if he read without resentment the very blunt and severe replies which Franklin a little mercilessly made to the other's ever temperate and amiable letters.

Hartley's advice, if not acceptable, was at least timely. At the very moment when he warned America against taking refuge in the arms of France, the colonists were joyously springing into that international embrace. The victory at Saratoga had at last settled that matter. On December 6, 1777, two days after the news was received, M. Gérard called upon the envoys and said that the capacity of the colonies to maintain their independence could no longer be doubted, and that the French court would be pleased by a renewal of their proposals for an alliance. On December 8th a request for an alliance was placed by young Temple Franklin in the hands of de Vergennes. On December 12th the cabinet met; also Arthur Lee reports that the envoys went out to Versailles and concealed themselves at an appointed spot in the wood, whither soon came to them de Vergennes. In the talk that ensued he said to them everything which a liberal spirit of friendship could suggest, but nothing which was actually positive and binding. For it was necessary, as he explained, first to consult with Spain, whose concurrence was desired; this, however, could be safely counted upon, and a courier was to be dispatched at once to Madrid. But the return of this messenger was not awaited; for on December 17 the commissioners were formally notified that France would acknowledge the independence of the colonies, and would execute with them treaties of commerce and alliance immediately upon getting the Spanish reply. In return for her engagements France only asked that, in the probable event of a war ensuing between herself and England, the colonies would pledge themselves never to make peace save upon the terms of independence.

On January 8, 1778, M. Gérard met the envoys after dark at Mr. Deane's quarters. He informed them that the government had resolved immediately to conclude with the colonies a treaty of amity and commerce; also another treaty, offensive and defensive, and guarantying independence, upon the conditions that the colonies would neither make a separate peace, nor one relinquishing their independence. The independence of the thirteen colonies being the king's sole purpose, no assistance would be extended for subduing Canada or the

English West Indies. As it would probably not
be agreeable to the colonies to have foreign troops
in their country, the design was to furnish only
naval aid. It would be left open for Spain to
accede to the treaties at any time. Nothing could
have been more agreeable and encouraging than
these arrangements, by which France did all the
giving and America all the receiving. A few days
later Gérard said that the king would not only
acknowledge, but would support American independence, and that the condition precluding the Americans from making a separate peace, if France
should be drawn into the war, would be waived.

On January 18th Gérard came to the envoys with
drafts which he had prepared for the two treaties,
and which he left for them to consider at their
leisure. It took them much longer to consider than
it had taken him to devise these documents. Lee
said that the delay was all Franklin's fault; but
at least Franklin illumined it by one of his *mots*.
There was sent to the envoys a large cake inscribed:
"Le digne Franklin." Deane said that, with
thanks, they would appropriate it to their joint use;
Franklin pleasantly replied that it was obviously
intended for all three, only the French donor did
not know how to spell "Lee, Deane, Franklin" correctly. But the uneasy jealousy of Lee suggested
a counter-argument: "When they remember us,"
i. e., himself and Deane, he said, "they always put
you first." Lee, who in his lifetime could never
endure being second to Franklin, must be astounded

indeed if, in another existence, he sees the place
which judicial posterity has assigned to him!

In their discussions concerning the treaty the
commissioners fell into a contention over one article.
Their secret instructions directed them to "press"
for a stipulation that no export duties should be
imposed by France upon molasses taken from the
French West Indies into the States; but they were
not to let the "fate of the treaty depend upon obtaining it." Of all merchandise imported into the
States molasses was the most important to their
general trade; it was the "basis on which a very
great part of the American commerce rested."[1]
In exchange for it they sent to the islands considerable quantities of pretty much all their products,
and they distilled it in enormous quantities into
rum. Every man who drank a glass of rum seemed
to be advancing *pro tanto* the national prosperity,
and the zeal with which those godly forefathers of
ours thus promoted the general welfare is feebly
appreciated by their descendants. All this rum,
said John Adams, has "injured our health and our
morals;" but "the taste for rum will continue;"
and upon this conviction the commissioners felt
obliged to act. Accordingly they proposed that it
should be "agreed and concluded that there shall
never be any duty imposed on the exportation of
molasses that may be taken by the subjects of the
United States from the islands of America which
belong or may hereafter appertain to his most

[1] *Diplomatic Correspondence of the Amer. Rev.*, i. 156.

Christian majesty." But Gérard said that this was "unequal," since the States made no balancing concession. It was not easy to suggest any "concession of equal importance on the part of the United States," and so "after long consideration Dr. Franklin proposed" this: "In compensation of the exemption stipulated in the preceding article, it is agreed and concluded that there shall never be any duties imposed on the exportation of any kind of merchandise, which the subjects of his most Christian majesty may take from the countries and possessions, present or future, of any of the thirteen United States, for the use of the islands which shall furnish molasses."

This pleased Lee as little as the other article had pleased Gérard; for it was "too extensive, and more than equivalent for molasses only." He was answered that "it was in reality nothing more than giving up what we could never make use of but to our own prejudice; for nothing was more evident than the bad policy of laying duties on our own exports." Franklin was of opinion that export duties were "a knavish attempt to get something for nothing;" that the inventor of them had the "genius of a pickpocket." Britain had lost her colonies by an export duty on tea. Moreover since the States produced no commodity which could not be procured elsewhere, to discourage consumption of their own and encourage the rivalship of others would be an "absolute folly" against which he would protest even if practiced by way of reprisal. Gérard finally said that he regarded these articles as "reciprocal and equal," that his majesty was "indifferent" about them, and that they might be retained or rejected together, but that one could not be kept without the other. Lee then yielded, and Gérard was notified that both articles would be inserted. He assented. Soon, however, William Lee and Izard, being informed of the arrangement, took Arthur Lee's original view and protested against it. Lee reports that this interference put Franklin "much out of humor," and that he said it would "appear an act of levity to renew the discussion of a thing we had agreed to." None the less, Lee now resumed his first position so firmly that Franklin and Deane in their turn agreed to omit both articles. But they stipulated that Lee should arrange the matter with Gérard, since, as they had just agreed in writing to retain both, they "could not with any consistency make a point of their being expunged," and they felt that the business of a change at this stage might be disagreeable. In fact Lee found it so. When he called on Gérard and requested the omission of both, Gérard replied that the king had already approved the treaty, that it was now engrossed on parchment, and that a new arrangement would entail "inconvenience and considerable delay." But finally, not without showing some irritation at the fickleness of the commissioners, he was brought to agree that Congress might ratify the treaty either with or without these articles, as it should see fit. This business cost Franklin, as an annoying incident, an encounter with Mr. Izard, and a tart correspondence ensued.

On February 6th all was at length ready and the parties came together, M. Gérard for France and the envoys for the States, to execute these most important documents. Franklin wore the spotted velvet suit of privy council fame. They signed a treaty of amity and commerce, a treaty of alliance, and a secret article belonging with the latter providing that Spain might become a party to it — on the Spanish *mañana*. There was an express stipulation on the part of France that the whole should be kept secret until after ratification by Congress; for there was a singular apprehension that in the interval some accommodation might be brought about between the insurgent States and the mother country, which would leave France in a very embarrassing position if she should not be free to deny the existence of such treaties. It was undoubtedly a dread of some such occurrence which had induced the promptitude and the ever-increasing liberality in terms which France had shown from the moment when the news of Saratoga arrived. Nor perhaps was her anxiety so utterly absurd as it now seems. There was some foundation for Gibbon's epigrammatic statement that "the two greatest nations in Europe were fairly running a race for the favor of America." For the disaster to the army on the Hudson had had an effect in England even greater than it had had in France, and Burgoyne's capitulation

to "Mr. Gates" had very nearly brought on a
capitulation of Lord North's cabinet to the insurgent Congress. On February 17 that minister
rose, and in a speech of two hours introduced two
conciliatory bills. The one declared that Parliament had no intention of exercising the right of
taxing the colonies in America. The other authorized sending to the States commissioners empowered to "treat with Congress, with provincial assemblies, or with Washington; to order a truce;
to suspend all laws; to grant pardons and rewards;
to restore the form of constitution as it stood before the troubles." [1] The prime minister substantially acknowledged that England's course toward
her colonies had been one prolonged blunder, and
now she was willing to concede every demand save
actual independence. The war might be continued,
as it was; but such a confession could never be
retracted. "A dull melancholy silence for some
time succeeded to this speech. . . . Astonishment,
dejection, and fear overclouded the assembly."

But a fresh sensation was at hand. Horace and
Thomas Walpole had obtained private information
of what had taken place in France; but had cau-
tiously held it in reserve, and arranged that only
two hours before the meeting of the House of Commons on that eventful day the Duke of Grafton
should tell it to Charles Fox. So now when North
sat down Fox rose, indulged in a little sarcasm on
the conversion of the ministry to the views of the

[1] Bancroft, *Hist. U. S.*, ix. 484.

opposition, and then asked his lordship "Whether a commercial treaty with France had not been signed by the American agents at Paris within the last ten days? 'If so,' he said, 'the administration is beaten by ten days, a situation so threatening that in such a time of danger the House must concur with the propositions, though probably now they would have no effect.' Lord North was thunderstruck and would not rise." But at last, warned that it would be "criminal and a matter of impeachment to withhold an answer," he admitted that he had heard a rumor of the signature of such a treaty.[1] So the bills were passed too late.

So soon as their passage was assured, Hartley, "acting on an understanding with Lord North,"[2] dispatched copies to Franklin. Franklin upon his part, also first having an understanding with de Vergennes, replied that, if peace with the States upon equal terms were really desired, the commissioners need not journey to America for it, for "if wise and honest men, such as Sir George Saville, the Bishop of St. Asaph, and yourself were to come over here immediately with powers to treat, you might not only obtain peace with America but prevent a war with France." About the same time also Hartley visited Franklin in person; but nothing came of their interview, of which no record is preserved. The two bills were passed, almost

[1] Parton's *Life of Franklin*, ii. 309.

[2] Bancroft, *Hist. U. S.*, ix. 485; Hale's *Franklin in France*, i. 223.

unanimously. But every one felt that their usefulness had been taken out of them by the other consequences of that event which had induced their introduction. News of them, however, was dispatched
to America by a ship which followed close upon the
frigate which carried the tidings of the French
treaties. If the English ship should arrive first,
something might be effected. But it did not, and
probably nothing would have been gained if it had.
Franklin truly said to Hartley: "All acts that
suppose your future government of the colonies
can be no longer significant;" and he described
the acts as "two frivolous bills, which the present
ministry, in their consternation, have thought fit
to propose, with a view to support their public
credit a little longer at home, and to amuse and
divide, if possible, our people in America." But
even for this purpose they came too late, and stirred
no other response than a ripple of sarcastic triumph over such an act of humiliation, which was
aggravated by being rejected almost without consideration by Congress.

So there was an end of conciliation. On March
23d the American envoys had the significant distinction of a presentation to the king, who is said
to have addressed to them this gracious and royal
sentence: "Gentlemen, I wish the Congress to be
assured of my friendship. I beg leave also to observe that I am exceedingly satisfied, in particular,
with your own conduct during your residence in my
kingdom." [1] This personal compliment, if paid,

[1] Parton's *Life of Franklin*, ii. 312.

was gratifying; for the anomalous and difficult position of the envoys had compelled them to govern themselves wholly by their own tact and judgment, with no aid from experience or precedents.

The presentation had been delayed by reason of Franklin having an attack of the gout, and the effort, when made, laid him up for some time afterward. It was on this occasion, especially, that he made himself conspicuous by wearing only the simple dress of a gentleman of the day instead of the costume of etiquette. Bancroft says that again he donned the suit of spotted Manchester velvet. He did not wear a sword, but made up for it by keeping on his spectacles; he had a round white hat under his arm, and no wig concealed his scanty gray hair. America has always rejoiced at this republican simplicity; but the fact seems to be that it was largely due to chance. Parton says that the doctor had ordered a wig, but when it came home it proved much too small for his great head, and there was no time to make another. Hawthorne also repeats the story that Franklin's court suit did not get home in time, and so he had to go in ordinary apparel; but it "took" so well that the shrewd doctor never explained the real reason.

On March 13th the Marquis de Noailles, French ambassador at St. James's, formally announced to the English secretary of state the execution of the treaty of amity and commerce; and impudently added a hope that the English court would see therein "new proofs" of King Louis's "sincere disposition for peace;" and that his Britannic majesty, animated by the same sentiments, would equally avoid everything that might alter their good harmony; also that he would particularly take effective measures to prevent the commerce between his French majesty's subjects and the United States of North America from being interrupted. When this was communicated to Parliament Conway asked: "What else have we to do but to take up the idea that Franklin has thrown out with fairness and manliness?"[1] But Franklin's ideas had not now, any more than heretofore, the good fortune to be acceptable to English ministers. Indeed, the mere fact that a suggestion came from him was in itself unfortunate; for the king, whose influence was preponderant in this American business, had singled out Franklin among all the "rebels" as the object of extreme personal hatred.[2] Franklin certainly reciprocated the feeling with an intensity which John Adams soon afterward noted, apparently with some surprise. The only real reply to Noailles's message which commended itself to government was the instant recall of Lord Stormont, who left Paris on March 23d, *sans prendre congé*, just as he had once before threatened to do. On the same day the French ambassador left London, accompanied, as Gibbon said, by "some slight

---

[1] The reference was to the suggestion made to Hartley for sending commissioners to Paris to treat for peace.

[2] Franklin's *Works*, vi. 39, note.

expression of ill humor from John Bull." At the
end of the month M. Gérard sailed for America,
the first accredited minister to the new member of
the sisterhood of civilized nations. A fortnight
later the squadron of D'Estaing sailed from Toulon
for American waters, and two weeks later the English fleet followed.

Thus far the course of France throughout her relationship with the States had been that of a generous friend. She undoubtedly had been primarily
instigated by enmity to England; and she had been
for a while guarded and cautious; yet not unreasonably so; on the contrary, she had in many
instances been sufficiently remiss in regarding her
neutral obligations to give abundant cause for war,
though England had not felt ready to declare it.
At the first interview concerning the treaty of commerce de Vergennes had said that the French
court desired to take no advantage of the condition
of the States, and to exact no terms which they
would afterward regret, but rather to make an arrangement so based upon the interest of both parties that it should last as long as human institu-
tions should endure, so that mutual amity should
subsist forever. M. Gérard reiterated the same
sentiments. That this language was not mere
French courtesy was proved by the fact that the
treaties, when completed, were "founded on principles of equality and reciprocity, and for the most
part were in conformity to the proposals of Congress."[1] Each party, under the customs laws of

[1] Bancroft, *Hist. U. S*, ix. 481.

the other, was to be upon the footing of the most favored nation. The transfer of the valuable and growing trade of the States from England to France had been assiduously held out as a temptation to France to enter into these treaties; but no effort was made by France to gain from the needs of the Americans any exclusive privileges for herself. She was content to stipulate only that no other people should be granted preferences over her, leaving the States entirely unhampered for making subsequent arrangements with other nations. The light in which these dealings about the treaties made the French minister and the French court appear to Franklin should be remembered in the discussions which arose later concerning the treaty of peace.[1]

It may further be mentioned, by the way, that Franklin had the pleasure of seeing inserted his favorite principle: that free ships should make free goods, and free persons also, save only soldiers in actual service of an enemy. In passing, it is pleasant to preserve this, amid the abundant other testimony to Franklin's humane and advanced ideas as to the conduct of war between civilized nations.[2] The doctrine of free ships making free

[1] See Franklin's *Works*, vi. 133. At this time John Adams strongly entertained the same sentiments, though he afterward felt very differently about the sincerity of France. *Diplomatic Correspondence of American Revolution*, iv. 262, 292.

[2] He was able to give a practical proof of his liberality by furnishing a passport to the packets carrying goods to the Moravian brethren in Labrador. Hale's *Franklin in France*, i. 245.

goods, though promulgated early in the century, was still making slow and difficult progress. Franklin accepted it with eagerness. He wrote that he was "not only for respecting the ships as the house of a friend, though containing the goods of an enemy, but I even wish that . . . all those kinds of people who are employed in procuring subsistence for the species, or in exchanging the necessaries or conveniences of life, which are for the common benefit of mankind, such as husbandmen on their lands, fishermen in their barques, and traders in unarmed vessels, shall be permitted to prosecute their several innocent and useful employments without interruption or molestation, and nothing taken from them, even when wanted by an enemy, but on paying a fair price for the same." Also to the president of Congress he spoke of Russia's famous proposal for an "armed neutrality for protecting the liberty of commerce" as "the great public event" of the year in Europe. He proposed that Congress should order their cruisers "not to molest foreign ships, but to conform to the spirit of that treaty of neutrality." Congress promptly voted to request the admission of the States to the league, and John Adams took charge of this business during his mission to Holland.

Events having thus established the indefinite continuance of the war, the good Hartley, profoundly disappointed, wrote a brief note invoking blessings on his "dear friend," and closing with the ominous words, "If tempestuous times should

come, take care of your own safety; events are uncertain and men may be capricious." Franklin,
however, declined to be alarmed. "I thank you,"
he said, "for your kind caution, but having nearly
finished a long life, I set but little value on what
remains of it. Like a draper, when one chaffers
with him for a remnant, I am ready to say: ' As it
is only the fag end, I will not differ with you about
it; take it for what you please.' Perhaps the best
use such an old fellow can be put to is to make a
martyr of him."

A few weeks after the conclusion of this diplomatic bond of friendship between the two peoples,
Franklin, in the words of Mr. Bancroft, "placed
the public opinion of philosophical France con-
spicuously on the side of America." Voltaire came
back to Paris, after twenty-seven years of voluntary
exile, and received such adoration that it almost
seemed as if, for Frenchmen, he was taking the
place of that God whom he had been declaring
non-existent, but whom he believed it necessary for
mankind to invent. Franklin had an interview
with him, which presented a curious scene. The
aged French philosopher, shriveled, bright - eyed,
destructive - minded, received the aged American
philosopher, portly, serene, the humanest of men,
in theatrical French fashion, quoting a passage of
English poetry, and uttering over the head of
young Temple the appropriate benediction, "God
and Liberty." This drama was enacted in private,
but on April 29th occurred that public spectacle

made familiar by countless engravings, decorating the walls of so many old-fashioned American "sitting-rooms" and "best parlors," when, upon the stage of the Academy of Sciences, before a numerous and distinguished audience, the two venerable sages met and saluted each other. "*Il faut s'embrasser à la Française*," shouted the enthusiastic crowd ; so they fell into each other's arms, and kissed, after the continental mode. Great was the fervor aroused in the breasts of the classic people of France as they proudly saw upon their soil a new "Solon and Sophocles" in embrace. Who shall say that Franklin's personal prestige in Europe had not practical value for America?

Silas Deane, recalled, accompanied Gérard to America. He carried with him a brief but generous letter from Franklin to the president of Congress.[1] At the same time Izard was writing home that Deane's misbehavior had long delayed the alliance with France, and he repeated what he had said in former letters, that "whatever good dispositions were shown by Mr. Lee, they were always opposed and overruled by the two oldest commissioners." The departure of the two gentlemen was kept a close secret at Paris, and at the request of de Vergennes especially a secret from Arthur Lee. For the French ministry were well assured that Lee's private secretary was a spy in British pay, and had he got possession of this important bit of news, it would not only have been untimely in a

[1] Franklin's *Works*, vi. 153.

diplomatic way, but it might have given opportunity for British cruisers to waylay a vessel carrying such distinguished passengers. The precaution was justifiable, but it had ill consequences for Franklin, since it naturally incensed Lee to an extreme degree, and led to a very sharp correspondence, which still further aggravated the discomfort of the situation. The legitimate trials to which the aged doctor was subjected were numerous and severe enough, but the untiring and malicious enmity of Arthur Lee was an altogether illegitimate vexation.

Mr. Hale in his recent volumes upon Franklin truly says that " it is unnecessary to place vituperative adjectives to the credit [discredit?] of Arthur Lee ; " and in fact to do so seems a work of supererogation, since there probably remain few such epithets in the English language which have not already been applied to him by one writer or another. Yet it is hard to hold one's hand, although humanity would perhaps induce us to pity rather than to revile a man cursed with so unhappy a temperament. But whatever may be said or left unsaid about him personally, the infinite disturbance which he caused cannot be wholly ignored. It was great enough to constitute an important element in history. Covered by the powerful authority of his influential and patriotic family at home, and screened by the profound ignorance of Congress concerning men and affairs abroad, Lee was able for a long time to run his mis-

chievous career without discovery or interruption.
He buzzed about Europe like an angry hornet,
thrusting his venomous sting into every respectable and useful servant of his country, and irritating exceedingly the foreigners whom it was of
the first importance to conciliate. Incredible as
it seems, it is undoubtedly true that he did not
hesitate to express in Paris his deep antipathy to
France and Frenchmen; and it was only the low
esteem in which he was held that prevented his
singular behavior from doing irreparable injury to
the colonial cause. The English newspapers taunt-
ingly ridiculed his insignificance and incapacity;
de Vergennes could not endure him, and scarcely
treated him with civility. But his intense egotism
prevented him from gathering wisdom from such
harsh instruction, which only added gall to his native bitterness. He wreaked his revenge upon his
colleagues, and towards Franklin he cherished an
envious hatred which developed into a monoma-
nia. Perhaps Franklin was correct in charitably
saying that at times he was "insane." He began
by asserting that Franklin was old, idle, and useless, fit only to be shelved in some respectable sine-
cure mission; but he rapidly advanced from such
moderate condemnation until he charged Franklin
with being a party to the abstraction of his despatches from a sealed parcel, which was rifled in
some unexplained way on its passage home;[1] and
finally he even reached the extremity of alleging

[1] Parton's *Franklin*, ii. 354.

financial dishonesty in the public business, and insinuated an opinion that the doctor's great rascality
indicated an intention never again to revisit his
native land. In all this malevolence he found an
earnest colleague in the hot-blooded Izard, whose
charges against Franklin were unmeasured. "His
abilities," wrote this angry gentleman, "are great
and his reputation high. Removed as he is at so
considerable a distance from the observation of his
constituents, if he is not guided by principles of
virtue and honor, those abilities and that reputation may produce the most mischievous effects.
In my conscience I declare to you that I believe
him under no such restraint, and God knows that
I speak the real, unprejudiced sentiments of my
heart." Such fulminations, reaching the States
out of what was then for them the obscurity of
Europe, greatly perplexed the members of Congress; for they had very insufficient means for de-
termining the value of the testimony given by these
absent witnesses.

It would serve no useful purpose to devote valuable space to narrating at length all the slander
and malice of these restless men, all the correspondence, the quarrels, the explanations, and
general trouble to which they gave rise. But the
reader must exercise his imagination liberally in
fancying these things, in order to appreciate to
what incessant annoyance Franklin was subjected
at a time when the inevitable anxieties and severe
labors of his position were far beyond the strength

of a man of his years. He showed wonderful patience and dignity, and though he sometimes let some asperity find expression in his replies, he never let them degenerate into retorts. Moreover, he replied as little as possible, for he truly said that he hated altercation; whereas Lee, who reveled in it, took as an aggravation of all his other injuries that his opponent was inclined to curtail the full luxury to be expected from a quarrel. Franklin also magnanimously refrained from arraigning Lee and Izard to Congress, either publicly or privately, a forbearance which these chivalrous gentlemen did not emulate. The memorial [1] of Arthur Lee, of May, 1779, addressed to Congress, contains criminations enough to furnish forth many impeachments. But Franklin would not condescend to allow his serenity to be disturbed by the news of these assaults. He felt "very easy," he said, about these efforts to injure him, trusting in the justice of the Congress to listen to no accusations without giving him an opportunity to reply.[2] Yet his position was not so absolutely secure and exalted but that he suffered some little injury at home.

John Adams, going out to replace Silas Deane, crossed him on the passage, arriving at Bordeaux on March 31, 1778. This ardent New Englander, orderly, business-like, endowed with an insatiate industry, plunged headlong into the midst of af-

[1] Franklin's *Works*, vi. 363.
[2] To Richard Bache, Franklin's *Works*, vi. 414.

fairs. With that happy self-confidence characteristic of our people, which leads every American to
believe that he can at once and without training do
anything whatsoever better than it can be done by
any other living man no matter how well trained,
Adams began immediately to act and to criticise.
In a few hours he knew all about the discussions
between the various envoys, *quasi* envoys, and
agents, who were squabbling with each other to
the scandal of Paris ; in a few days he was ready
to turn out Jonathan Williams, unseen and un-
heard. He was shocked at the confusion in which
he saw all the papers of the embassy, and set vig-
orously about the task of sorting, labeling, dock-
eting, and tying up letters and accounts ; it was a
task which Franklin unquestionably had neglected,
and which required to be done. He was appalled
at the "prodigious sums of money" which had
been expended, at the further great sums which
were still to be paid, and at the lack of any proper
books of accounts, so that he could not learn " what
the United States have received as an equivalent."
He did not in direct words charge the other commissioners with culpable negligence ; but it was an
unavoidable inference from what he did say. Undoubtedly the fact was that the accounts were dis-
gracefully muddled and insufficient ; but the fault
really lay with Congress, which had never permitted
proper clerical assistance to be employed. Adams
soon found this out, and appreciated that besides
all the diplomatic affairs, which were their only

proper concern, the commissioners were also trans-
acting an enormous business, financial and commercial, involving innumerable payments great and
small, loans, purchases, and correspondence, and
that all was being conducted with scarcely any aid
of clerks or accountants; whereas a mercantile
firm engaged in affairs of like extent and moment
would have had an extensive establishment with a
numerous force of skilled employees.   When
Adams had been a little longer in Paris, he also
began to see where and how " the prodigious sums "
went,[1] and just what was the full scope of the functions of the commissioners ; then the censoriousness
evaporated out of his language.   He admitted that
the neglects of subordinate agents were such that
it was impossible for the commissioners to learn
the true state of their finances ; and he joined in
the demand, so often reiterated by Franklin, for
the establishment of the usual and proper commercial agencies.   The business of accepting and keeping the run of the bills drawn by Congress, and of
teasing the French government for money to meet
them at maturity, would still remain to be attended
to by the ministers in person ; but these things long
experience might enable them to manage.

No sooner had Adams scented the first whiff
of the quarrel-laden atmosphere of the embassy
than he expressed in his usual self-satisfied, impetuous, and defiant way his purpose to be rigidly im-
partial.   But he was a natural fault-finder, and by

[1] *Diplomatic Corresp. of Amer. Rev.*, iv. 249, 251.

no means a natural peacemaker; and his impartiality had no effect in assuaging the animosities which he found. However, amid all the discords of the embassy there was one note of harmony; and the bewildered Congress must have felt much satisfaction in finding that all the envoys were agreed that one representative at the French court would be vastly better as well as cheaper than the sort of caucus which now held its angry sessions there. At worst one man could not be forever at odds with himself. Adams, when he had finished the task of arranging the archives, found no other occupation; and he was scandalized at the extravagance of keeping three envoys. Lee, by the way, had constantly insinuated that Franklin was blamably lax, if not actually untrustworthy, in money matters, though all the while he and his friend Izard had been quite shameless in extorting from the doctor very large sums for their own expenses. When the figures came to be made up it appeared that Franklin had drawn less than either of his colleagues, and much less than the sum soon afterward established by Congress as the proper salary for the position.[1] The frugal-minded New Englander himself now acknowledged that he could "not find any article of expense which could be retrenched,"[2] and he honestly begged Congress to stop the triple outlay.

Franklin, upon his part, wrote that in many ways the public business and the national prestige

[1] *Diplomatic Corresp. of Amer. Rev.*, iv. 246.
[2] Ibid., 245.

suffered much from the lack of unanimity among
the envoys, and said: "In consideration of the
whole, I wish Congress would separate us." Neither
Adams nor Franklin wrote one word which either
directly or indirectly had a personal bearing.
Arthur Lee was more frank; in the days of Deane
he had begun to write that to continue himself
at Paris would "disconcert effectually the wicked
measures" of Franklin, Deane, and Williams, and
that it was "the one way of redressing" the "neglect, dissipation, and private schemes" prevalent
in the department, and of "remedying the public
evil." He said that the French court was the
place of chief importance, calling for the ablest and
most efficient man, to wit, himself. He suggested
that Franklin might be sent to Vienna, a dignified
retreat without labor. Izard and William Lee
wrote letters of like purport; it was true that it
was none of their affair, but they were wont to interfere in the business of the commissioners, as if the
French mission were common property. Congress
took so much of this advice as all their advisers
were agreed upon; that is to say, it broke up the
commission to France. But it did not appoint
Arthur Lee to remain there; on the contrary, it
nominated Franklin to be minister plenipotentiary
at the French court, left Lee still accredited to
Madrid, as he had been before, and gave Adams
neither any place nor any instructions, so that he
soon returned home. Gérard, at Philadelphia,
claimed the credit of having defeated the machina-

tions of the " dangerous and bad man," Lee, and congratulated de Vergennes on his relief from the burden.[1] Franklin's commission was brought over by Lafayette in February, 1779. Thus ended the Lee-Izard cabal against Franklin ; it was not unlike the Gates-Conway cabal against Washington, save that it lasted longer and was more exasperating. The success of either would have been almost equally perilous to the popular cause; for the instatement of Lee as minister plenipotentiary at the French court would inevitably have led to a breach with France. The result was very gratifying to Franklin, since it showed that all the ill tales about him which had gone home had not ruined, though certainly they had seriously injured, his good repute among his countrymen. Moreover, he could truly say that the office " was not obtained by any solicitation or intrigue," or by " magnifying his own services, or diminishing those of others." But apart from the gratification and a slight access of personal dignity, the change made no difference in his duties; he still combined the functions of loan-agent, consul, naval director, and minister, as before. Nor was he even yet wholly rid of Arthur Lee. He had, however, the satisfaction of absolutely refusing to honor any more of Lee's or Izard's exorbitant drafts for their personal expenses.

Shortly after his appointment Franklin sent his grandson to Lee, with a note requesting Lee to send to him such papers belonging to the embassy

[1] Parton's *Life of Franklin*, ii. 383.

as were in his possession. Lee insolently replied
that he had "no papers belonging to the department of minister plenipotentiary at the court of
Versailles;" that if Franklin referred to papers
relating to transactions of the late joint commission, he had "yet to learn and could not conceive"
by what reason or authority one commissioner was
entitled to demand custody of them. Franklin replied temperately enough that many of them were
essential to him for reference in conducting the
public business, but said that he should be perfectly content to have copies. The captious Lee
was still further irritated by this scheme for avoid-
ing a quarrel, but had to accede to it.

To John Paul Jones Franklin stood in the relation of a navy department. The daring exploits of
that gallant mariner form a chapter too fascinat-
ing to be passed by without reluctance, but limitations of space are inexorable. His success and
his immunity in his reckless feats seem marvelous.
His chosen field was the narrow seas which sur-
round Britain, which swarmed with British shipping, and were dominated by the redoubtable British navy as the streets of a city are kept in order
by police. But the rover Jones, though always
close to his majesty's coasts, was too much for all
his majesty's admirals and captains. He harried
these home waters and captured prizes till he became embarrassed by the extent of his own success;

he landed at Whitehaven, spiked the guns of the fort, and fired the ships of the fleet in the harbor beneath the eyes of the astounded Englishmen, who thronged the shore and gazed bewildered upon the spectacle which American audacity displayed for them; he made incursions on the land; he threatened the port of Leith, and would undoubtedly have bombarded it, had not obstinate counter winds thwarted his plans; he kept the whole British shores in a state of feverish alarm; he was always ready to fight, and challenged the English warship, the Serapis, to come out and meet him; she came, and he captured her after fighting so desperately that his own ship, the famous Bon Homme Richard, named after Poor Richard, sank a few hours after the combat was over.

All these glorious feats were rendered possible by Franklin, who found the money, consulted as to the operations, issued commissions, attended to purchases and repairs, to supplies and equipment, who composed quarrels, settled questions of authority, and interposed to protect vessels and commanders from the perils of the laws of neutrality. Jones had a great respect and admiration for him, and said to him once that his letters would make a coward brave. The projects of Jones were generally devised in consultations with Franklin, and were in the direct line of enterprises already suggested by Franklin, who had urged Congress to send out three frigates, disguised as merchantmen, which could make sudden descents upon the English coast,

destroy, burn, gather plunder, and levy contributions, and be off before molestation was possible.
"The burning or plundering of Liverpool or Glas-
gow," he wrote, "would do us more essential service than a million of treasure, and much blood
spent on the continent; " and he was confident that
it was "practicable with very little danger." This
was not altogether in accord with his humane theory for the conduct of war; but so long as that
theory was not adopted by one side, it could not of
course be allowed to handicap the other.

As if Franklin had not enough legitimate trouble
in furthering these naval enterprises, an entirely
undeserved vexation grew out of them for him.
There was a French captain Landais, who entered
the service of the States and was given the command of a ship in what was dignified by the name
of Jones's "squadron." Of all the excitable
Frenchmen who have ever lived none can have been
more hot-headed than this remarkable man. During the engagement between the Bon Homme Richard and the Serapis, he sailed up and down beside
the former and delivered broadsides into her until
he was near disabling and sinking the ship of his
own commander. The incomprehensible proceeding meant only that he was so wildly excited that
he did not know at whom he was firing. Soon he
quarreled with Jones; Franklin had to intervene;
then Landais advanced all sorts of preposterous demands, which Franklin refused ; thereupon he quarreled with Franklin ; a very disagreeable corre-

spondence ensued; Franklin finally had to displace Landais from command of his ship; Landais defied him and refused to surrender command. Then Lee decided to go home to the States in Landais's ship. When the two got together they stirred up a mutiny on board, and more trouble was made for Franklin. At last they got away, and Landais went crazy during the voyage, was deposed by his officers, and placed in confinement. If the ship had been lost, it would have been a more tolerable loss than many for which the ocean is accountable; but she was not, and Lee got safe ashore to continue his machinations at Philadelphia, and to publish an elaborate pamphlet against Franklin. All this story and the correspondence may be read at length in Mr. Hale's "Franklin in France." It is entertaining and shows vividly the misery to which Franklin was subjected in attending to affairs which were entirely outside of the proper scope of his office. "It is hard," said he, "that I, who give others no trouble with my quarrels, should be plagued with all the perversities of those who think fit to wrangle with one another."

CHAPTER XII.

WHETHER the financiering of the American Revolution is to be looked upon in a pathetic or in a comical light must depend upon the mood of the observer. The spectacle of a young people, with no accumulated capital, engaged in supporting the charge of a mortal struggle against all the vast resources of Britain, has in it something of pathos. But the methods to which this people resorted to raise funds were certainly of amusing simplicity. It was not until the appointment of Robert Morris, in 1781, that a treasury department came into existence and some slight pretense of system was introduced into the financial affairs of the confederation. During the years prior to that time Congress managed the business matters. But Congress neither had funds nor the power to obtain any. It had an unlimited power for contracting debts: absolutely no power for collecting money. It used the former power freely. When creditors wanted payment, requisitions were made upon the states for their respective quotas. But the states were found to be sadly irresponsive; probably the citizens really had not much ready money; certainly they had not enough to pay in taxes the cost of the war; no civilized state has been able to conduct a war, even a small one, in modern times without using the national credit. But the United States had absolutely no credit at all. It was well enough to exclaim "Millions for defense; but not one cent for tribute!" This was rhetoric, not business; and Congress soon found that the driblets which trickled tardily to them in response to their demands on the several states would hardly moisten the bottom of the great exchequer tank, which needed to be filled to the brim.

Two methods of relief were then adopted, crude, simple, but likely for a time to be efficient; and provided only that within that time the war could be finished, all might go well. One of these methods was to issue irredeemable paper "money;" the other was to borrow real money abroad. The droll part was that both these transactions were audaciously entered upon by a body which had absolutely no revenues at all to pledge as security, which had not a dollar of property, nor authority to compel any living man to pay it a dollar. A more utterly irresponsible debtor than Congress never asked for a loan or offered a promissory note. For the security of a creditor there was only the moral probability that in case of success the people would be honest enough to pay their debts; and there was much danger that the jealousies between the states as to their proportionate quotas might stimulate reluctance and furnish excuses

which might easily become serious in so unpleasant
a matter as paying out hard cash. At home Congress could manage to make its paper money percolate among the people, and could pay a good
many American creditors with it; but there were
some who would not be thus satisfied, and few
European creditors, of course, would meddle with
such currency. So to pay these people who would
have real money Congress solicited loans from
other nations. It was like the financiering of a
schoolboy, who issues his I O U's among his mates,
and refers the exacting and business-like tradesman to his father. France was cast for the *rôle*
of father to the Congressional schoolboy for many
wearisome years.

The arrangement bore hard upon the American
representatives, who, at European courts and upon
European exchanges, had the embarrassing task of
raising money. It was all very well to talk about
negotiating a loan; the phrase had a Micawberlike sound as of real business; but in point of plain
fact the thing to be done was to beg. Congress
had a comparatively easy time of it; such burden
and anxiety as lay upon that body were shared
among many ; and after all, the whole scope of its
duty was little else than to vote requisitions upon
the states, to order the printing of a fresh batch of
bills, and to " resolve that the Treasury Board be
directed to prepare bills of exchange of suitable denominations upon the Honorable Benjamin Franklin [or sometimes Jay, or Adams, or another], min-

ister plenipotentiary at the court of Versailles, for ——thousand dollars *in specie.*" Having done this, Congress had fulfilled its simple part, and serenely waited for something to turn up.

The plan which seemed most effective was to send a representative accredited to some foreign government, and instructed to raise money at once. Without wasting time by waiting to see whether he arrived safely, or was received, or was successful in his negotiations, the next ship which followed him brought drafts and bills which he was expected to accept, and at maturity to pay. Having thus skillfully shifted the laboring oar into his hands Congress bestirred itself no further. Poor Jay, in Spain, had a terrible time of it in this way, and if ever a man was placed by his country in a painful and humiliating position, it was he. He faced it gallantly, but had to be carried through by Franklin. From first to last it was upon Franklin that the brunt fell; he had to keep the country from financial failure as Washington had to save it from military failure; he was the real financier of the Revolution; without him Robert Morris would have been helpless. Spain yielded but trifling sums in response to Jay's solicitations; Holland, which was tried by Adams, was even more tardy and unwilling, though towards the end some money was got there. Franklin alone, at Paris, could tap the rock and make the waters flow. So upon him Congress sent in an endless procession of drafts, and compelled him to pay all their foreign bills and indebtedness; he gathered and he disbursed; to him were referred all the drafts upon Jay and others, which they themselves could not pay, and he discharged them one and all. A heavier task never fell upon any man, nor one bringing less recognition; for money matters usually seem so dry and unintelligible that every one shirks informing himself about them. We read about the horrors of the winter camp at Valley Forge, and we shudder at all the details of the vivid picture. The anxiety, the toil, the humiliation, which Franklin endured for many winters and many summers in Paris, in sustaining the national credit, do not make a picture, do not furnish material for a readable chapter in history. Yet many a man would far rather have faced Washington's lot than Franklin's.

I do not intend to tell this tale at length or minutely, for I could trust no reader to follow me in so tedious an enterprise; yet I must try to convey some notion of what this financiering really meant for Franklin, of how ably he performed it, of what it cost him in wear and tear of mind, of what toil it put upon him, and of what measure of gratitude was due to him for it. It may be worth mentioning by the way that he not only spent himself in efforts to induce others to lend, but he himself lent. Before he embarked for Philadelphia on his French mission, he gathered together all that he could raise in money, some £3,000 to £4,000, and paid it over as an unsecured loan for an indefinite period to the Continental Congress.

It is not probable that from any records now existing the most patient accountant could elicit any statement, even approximating to accuracy, of the sums which Franklin received and paid out. But if such an account could be drawn up, it would only indicate some results in figures which would have little meaning for persons not familiar with the national debts, revenues, and outlays of those times, and certainly would not at all answer the purpose of showing what he really did. The only satisfactory method of giving any passably clear idea on the subject seems to be to furnish some extracts from his papers.

The ship which brought Franklin also brought indigo to the value of £3,000, which was to serve as long as it could for the expenses of the commissioners. For keeping them supplied with money later on, it was the intention of Congress to purchase cargoes of American products, such as tobacco, rice, indigo, etc., etc., and consign these to the commissioners, who, besides paying their personal bills, were sure to have abundant other means for using the proceeds. Unfortunately, however, it so happened that the resources presented by this scheme were already exhausted. In January, 1777, a loan of one million livres had been advanced on a pledge of fifty-six thousand hogsheads of tobacco to the Farmers General of the French revenue; and the rice and indigo had been in like manner mortgaged to Beaumarchais. Congressional jugglery could not quite compass the payment of different creditors with the same money, even supposing that the money came to hand. But it did not; for a long while no cargoes arrived; of those that were dispatched, some were run away with by dishonest ship-masters, some were lost at sea, others were captured by the English, so that Franklin sadly remarked that the chief result was that the enemy had been supplied with these articles for nothing. But he preserved his resolute cheerfulness. "The destroying of our ships by the English," he said, "is only like shaving our beards, that will grow again. Their loss of provinces is like the loss of a limb, which can never again be united to their body." When at last a cargo did arrive, Beaumarchais demanded it as his own, and Franklin at last yielded to his importunities and tears, though having no really sufficient knowledge of his right to it. Later a second vessel arrived, and Beaumarchais endeavored to pounce upon it by process of law. That one also Franklin let him have. Then no more came, and this promising resource seems never to have yielded one dollar for Franklin's use.

Already so early as January 26, 1777, it was necessary to appeal to Thomas Morris, from whom remittances had been expected on account of sales made at Nantes: "You must be sensible how very unbecoming it is of the situation we are in to be dependent on the credit of others. We therefore desire that you will remit with all possible expedition the sum allotted by the Congress for our expenses." But the commissioners appealed in vain to this worthless drunkard.

Strange to say, the instructions given by Congress to the commissioners at the time of Franklin's appointment said nothing about borrowing money. In view of what he had to do in this way it was a singular omission; but it was soon repaired by letters. In March, 1777, Franklin writes to Lee: "We are ordered to borrow £2,000,000 on interest;" also to "build six ships of war," presumably on credit. In this same month Franklin wrote a paper, which was widely circulated in Europe, in which he endeavored to show that the honesty, the industry, the resources, and the prospects of the United States were so excellent that it would really be safer to lend to them than to England. It was a skillful piece of work, and its arguments had evidently persuaded the writer himself; but they did not induce the money-lenders of the old countries to accept moral qualities and probabilities as collateral security.

Fair success, however, was soon met with at the court of France, so that the commissioners had the pleasure of assuring Congress that they could safely be depended upon to meet the interest on a loan of $5,000,000, which by this aid Congress probably would be able to contract for. But that body had no idea of being content with this! March 17, 1778, Franklin writes to Lee that they have been drawn upon for 180,000 livres, to pay old indebtedness of the army in Canada; also that other bills have been drawn. The number and gross amount of these were not stated in the advices; but the commissioners were ordered to " accept them when they should appear." " I cannot conceive," said Franklin, " what encouragement the Congress could have had from any of us to draw on us for anything but that interest. I suppose their difficulties have compelled them to it. I see we shall be distressed here by these proceedings," etc., etc. Congress was composed of men far too shrewd to await " encouragement " to draw for money!

July 22, 1778, he wrote to Lovell: " When we engaged to Congress to pay their bills for the interest of the sums they could borrow, we did not dream of their drawing on us for other occasions. We have already paid of Congress's drafts, to returned officers, 82,211 livres ; and we know not how much more of that kind we have to pay, because the committee have never let us know the amount of those drafts, or their account of them never reached us, and they still continue coming in. And we are now surprised with drafts from Mr. B. for 100,000 more. If you reduce us to bankruptcy here by a non-payment of your drafts, consider the consequences. In my humble opinion no drafts should be made on us without first learning from us that we shall be able to answer them."

Congress could not fairly exact great accuracy from the drawees of its bills, when it never took pains to give notice of the facts of the drawing, of the number of bills drawn, of dates, or amounts ; in a word, really gave no basis for account-keeping or identification. No more helter-skelter way of conducting business has ever been seen since modern business methods were invented. The system, if system it may be called, would have been aggravating and confusing enough under any condition of attendant circumstances; but it so happened that all attendant circumstances tended to increase rather than to mitigate the difficulties created by the carelessness of Congress. One naturally fancies that a nation deals in few and large transactions, that these drafts may have been for inconveniently large sums, but that at least they probably were not numerous. The precise contrary was the case. The drafts were countless, and often were for very petty amounts, much as if a prosperous merchant were drawing cheques to pay his ordinary expenses. Further, the uncertainty of the passage across the Atlantic led to these bills appearing at all sorts of irregular times; seconds often came to hand before firsts, and thirds before either; the bills were often very old when presented. Knaves took advantage of these facts fraudulently to alter seconds and thirds into firsts, so that extreme care had to be taken to prevent constant duplication and even triplication of payments. It would have taken much of the time of an experienced banker's clerk to keep the bill and draft department in correct shape. It is not improbable that Congress lost a good deal of money by undetected rascalities, but if so the fault lay with that body itself, not with Franklin.

Amid the harassments of these demands, Frank-

lin was much vexed by the conduct of Arthur Lee
and Izard in drawing money for their own expenses. In February, 1778, each insisted that he
should be allowed a credit with the banker, M.
Grand, to an amount of £2,000, as each then expected to depart on a mission. Franklin reluctantly assented, and was then astonished and indignant to find that each at once drew out the full
sum from the national account; yet neither went
upon his journey. In January, 1779, Izard applied
for more. Franklin's anger was stirred; Izard was
a man of handsome private property, and was rendering no service in Paris; and his requirements
seemed to Franklin eminently unpatriotic and exorbitant. He therefore refused the request, writing to Izard a letter which is worth quoting, both
from the tone of its patriotic appeal and as a vivid
sketch of the situation: —

" Your intimation that you expect more money from
us obliges us to expose to you our circumstances. Upon
the supposition that Congress had borrowed in America
but $5,000,000, and relying on the remittances intended
to be sent to us for answering other demands, we gave
expectations that we should be able to pay here the interest of that sum as a means of supporting the credit of
the currency. The Congress have borrowed near twice
that sum, and are now actually drawing on us for the
interest, the bills appearing here daily for acceptance.
Their distress for money in America has been so great
from the enormous expense of the war that they have
also been induced to draw on us for very large sums to

stop other pressing demands ; and they have not been able to purchase remittances for us to the extent they proposed ; and of what they have sent, much has been taken, or treacherously carried into England, only two small cargoes of tobacco having arrived, and they are long since mortgaged to the Farmers General, so that they produce us nothing, but leave us expenses to pay.

" The continental vessels of war which come to France have likewise required great sums of us to furnish and refit them and supply the men with necessaries. The prisoners, too, who escape from England claim a very expensive assistance from us, and are much dissatisfied with the scanty allowance we are able to afford them. The interest bills above mentioned, of the drawing of which we have received notice, amount to $2,500,000, and we have not a fifth part of the sum in our banker's hands to answer them ; and large orders to us from Congress for supplies of clothing, arms, and ammunition remain uncomplied with for want of money.

" In this situation of our affairs, we hope you will not insist on our giving you a farther credit with our banker, with whom we are daily in danger of having no farther credit ourselves. It is not a year since you received from us the sum of 2,000 guineas, which you thought necessary on account of your being to set out immediately for Florence. You have not incurred the expense of that journey. You are a gentleman of fortune. You did not come to France with any dependence on being maintained here with your family at the expense of the United States, in the time of their distress, and without rendering them the equivalent service they expected.

" On all these considerations we should rather hope that you would be willing to reimburse us the sum we have advanced to you, if it may be done with any possible convenience to your affairs. Such a supply would at least enable us to relieve more liberally our unfortunate countrymen, who have long been prisoners, stripped of everything, of whom we daily expect to have nearly three hundred upon our hands by the exchange."

At this same time Franklin wrote to Congress to explain how it had happened that so large a sum as £4,000 had been allowed to these gentlemen; for he feared that this liberality might "subject the commissioners to censure." The explanation was so discreditable to Lee and Izard that it is charitable to think that there was some misunderstanding between the parties.[1] The matter naturally rankled, and in May Franklin wrote that there was much anger against him, that he was charged with "disobeying an order of Congress, and with cruelly attempting to distress gentlemen who were in the service of their country."

"They have indeed," he said, "produced to me a resolve of Congress empowering them to draw . . . for their expenses at foreign courts; and doubtless Congress, when that resolve was made, intended to enable us to pay those drafts; but as that has not been done, and the gentlemen (except Mr. Lee for a few weeks) have not incurred any expense at foreign courts, and, if they had, the 5,500 guineas received by them in about nine months seemed an ample provision for it, . . . I do not conceive that I disobeyed an order of Congress, and that if I did the circumstances will excuse it. . . . In

[1] See Franklin's *Works*, vi. 294.

short, the dreadful consequences of ruin to our public credit, both in America and Europe, that must attend the protesting a single Congress draft for interest, after our funds were out, would have weighed with me against the payment of more money to those gentlemen, if the demand had otherwise been well founded. I am, however, in the judgment of Congress, and if I have done amiss, must submit dutifully to their censure."

Burgoyne's surrender had a market value; it was worth ready money in France and Spain. Upon the strength of it the former lent the States 3,000,000 livres; and the like amount was engaged for by Spain. But, says Bancroft, " when Arthur Lee, who was equally disesteemed in Versailles and Madrid, heard of the money expected of Spain, he talked and wrote so much about it that the Spanish government, who wished to avoid a rupture with England, took alarm, and receded from its intention." [1]

In February and March, 1779, came demands from the officers of the frigate Alliance for their pay; but Franklin was "neither furnished with money nor authority for such purposes." It seemed, however, too hard to tell these gallant fellows, whose perilous and useful service was in European waters, that they could not have a dollar until they should get safely back to the States; so Franklin agreed to pay for one suit of clothes for each of them. But he begged them to be as " frugal as possible," and not make themselves

[1] Bancroft, *Hist. U. S.*, ix. 480.

" expensively fine " from a notion that it was for the honor of the States, which could be better promoted in more sensible ways.

May 26, 1779, he complains to the committee of foreign affairs that, whereas the commissioners had agreed to find in Paris means of paying interest on a loan of $5,000,000, that loan had been doubled, while, on the other hand, they had been " drained by a number of unforeseen expenses," including " orders and drafts " of Congress. " And now," he says, " the drafts of the treasurer of the loans coming very fast upon me, the anxiety I have suffered and the distress of mind lest I should not be able to pay them, have for a long time been very great indeed. To apply again to this court for money for a particular purpose, which they had already over and over again provided for and furnished us, was extremely awkward." One would think so, indeed! So he fell back on a " *general* application " made some time before, and received naturally the general answer that France herself was being put to enormous expenses, which were aiding the States as efficiently as a direct loan of money could do. The most he could extort was the king's guaranty for the payment of the interest on $3,000,000, provided that sum could be raised in Holland. The embarrassing fact was that the plea of poverty advanced by the French government was perfectly valid. Turgot said so, and no man knew better than Turgot. He had lately told the king that even on a peace footing the annual expenditures exceeded the annual receipts of the exchequer by 20,000,000 livres; and he even talked seriously of an avowal of national bankruptcy. The events preceding the French Revolution soon proved that this great statesman did not exaggerate the ill condition of affairs. Yet instead of practicing rigid prudence and economy, France had actually gone into a costly war for the benefit of America. It was peculiarly disagreeable to be ceaselessly appealing for money to an impoverished friend.

Another vexation was found in the way in which the agents of the various individual states soon began to scour Europe in quest of money. First they applied to Franklin, and " seemed to think it his duty as minister for the United States to support and enforce their particular demands." But the foreigners, probably not understanding these separate autonomies, did not relish these requisitions, and Franklin found that he could no nothing. On the contrary, he was hampered in effecting loans on the national credit; for these state agents, hurrying clamorously hither and thither, gave an impression of poverty and injured the reputation of the country, which, indeed, was already low enough upon the exchanges without any such gratuitous impairment.

February 19, 1780, there was an application from John Paul Jones for money for repairs on his ships. Franklin approved keeping the vessels in serviceable condition, but added : " Let me repeat, for God's sake be sparing, unless you mean to make me a bankrupt, or have your drafts dishonored for want of money in my hands to pay them."

May 31, 1780, he complains that he has been reproached by one of the congressional agents whose unauthorized drafts he had refused. He has been drawn upon by Congress, he says, for much more than the interest, which only he had agreed to furnish, and he has answered every demand, and supported their credit in Europe. "But if every agent of Congress in different parts of the world is permitted to run in debt, and draw upon me at pleasure to support his credit, under the idea of its being necessary to do so for the honor of Congress, the difficulty upon me will be too great, and I may in fine be obliged to protest the interest bills. I therefore beg that a stop may be put to such irregular proceedings." It was a reasonable prayer, but had no effect. Franklin continued to be regarded as paymaster-general for the States in Europe.

We next hear of his troubles in paying the bills which Congress, according to its usual custom, was drawing upon Jay. They sent Jay to Spain, and told him to borrow money there; and as soon as they had got him fairly at sea, they began drawing drafts upon him. He soon found himself, as he said, in a "cruel situation," and the torture of mind which he endured and the responsibility which he assumed are well known. He courageously accepted the bills, trusting to Providence and to Franklin, who seemed the agent of Providence, to arrange for their payment. Franklin did not fail him. One of Jay's earliest letters to Franklin said: " I have no reason as yet to think a loan here will be practicable. Bills on me arrive daily. Be pleased to send me a credit for the residue of our salaries." Five days later : " Bills to the amount of $100,000 have arrived. A loan cannot be effected here." And so on. In April, 1781, his appeal became pathetic : " Our situation here is daily becoming more disagreeable from the want of our salaries ; to be obliged to contract debts and live on credit is terrible. I have not to this day received a shilling from America, and we should indeed have been greatly distressed, had it not been for your good offices." An American minister without resources to pay his butcher and his grocer, his servant and his tailor, presented a spectacle which moved Franklin to great efforts ! In plain truth, Jay and his secretary, Carmichael, were dependent upon Franklin for everything ; they not only drew on him for their salaries to pay daily household expenses, but they sent him lists of the bills accepted by them for the " honor of Congress," and which they had no means of paying. It was fortunate that these two men were willing to incur such peril and anxiety in behalf of this same " honor of Congress," which otherwise would soon have been basely discredited ; for that body itself was superbly indifferent on the subject, and did not pretend to keep faith even with its own agents.

Thus matters continued to the end. Congress pledged itself not to draw bills, and immediately drew them in batches. Jay could report to Franklin only scant and reluctant promises won from the Spanish court; and small as these engagements were, they were ill kept. Perhaps they could not be kept; for, as Jay wrote, there was "little coin in Egypt," the country was really poor. So the end of it always was that Franklin remained as the only resource for payments, to be made week after week, of all sorts of sums ranging from little bills upon vessels up to great totals of $150,000 or $230,000 upon bankers' demands. Such was the burden of a song which had many more woful stanzas than can be repeated here.

By way of affording some sort of encouragement to the French court, Franklin now proposed that the United States government should furnish the French fleet and forces in the States with provisions, of which the cost could be offset, to the small extent that it would go, against French loans. It seemed a satisfactory arrangement, and France assented to it.

At the same time he wrote to Adams that he had "long been humiliated with the idea of our running about from court to court begging for money and friendship, which are the more withheld the more eagerly they are solicited, and would perhaps have been offered if they had not been asked. The proverb says, God helps them that help themselves; and the world too, in this sense, is very godly." This was an idea to which he more than once recurred. In March, 1782, in the course of a long letter to Livingston, he said : " A small increase of industry in every American, male and female, with a small diminution of luxury, would produce a sum far superior to all we can hope to beg or borrow from all our friends in Europe." He reiterated the same views again in March, and again in December, and doubtless much oftener.[1] No man was more earnest in the doctrine that every individual American owed his strenuous and unremitting personal assistance to the cause. It was a practical as well as a noble patriotism which he felt, preached, and exemplified; and it was thoroughly characteristic of the man.

What was then the real financial capacity of the people, and whether they did their utmost in the way of raising money to support the Revolution, is a question about which it is easy to express an opinion, but difficult to prove its accuracy by convincing evidence. On the one hand, it is true that the strain was extreme and that much was done to meet it; on the other hand, it is no less true that even beneath this stress the national prosperity actually made a considerable advance during the war. The people as a whole gathered money rather than impoverished themselves. In the country at large the commercial instinct fully held its own in competition with the spirit of inde-

[1] Franklin's *Works*, vii. 404 ; viii. 236.

pendence. There was not much forswearing of little luxuries. Franklin said that he learned by inquiry that of the interest money which was disbursed in Paris most was laid out for "superfluities, and more than half of it for tea." He computed that £500,000 were annually expended in the States for tea alone. This sum, "annually laid out in defending ourselves or annoying our enemies, would have great effect. With what face can we ask aids and subsidies from our friends, while we are wasting our own wealth in such prodigality?"

Henry Laurens, dispatched as minister to the Hague in 1780, was captured on the voyage and carried into England. But this little incident mattered not at all to the Congress, which for a long while cheerfully drew a great number of bills upon the poor gentleman, who, held in the Tower of London as a traitor, was hardly in a position to negotiate large loans for his fellow "rebels." In October, 1780, these bills began to flutter down upon Franklin's desk, drawn by a sort of natural gravitation. He felt "obliged to accept them," and said that he should "with some difficulty be able to pay them, though these extra demands often embarrass me exceedingly."

November 19, 1780, he wrote to de Vergennes announcing that Congress had notified him of drafts to the amount of about 1,400,000 livres, (about $280,000). The reply was: "You can easily imagine my astonishment at your request of the necessary funds to meet these drafts, since you perfectly well know the extraordinary efforts which I have made thus far to assist you and support your credit, and especially since you cannot have forgotten the demands you lately made upon me. Nevertheless, sir, I am very desirous of assisting you out of the embarrassed situation in which these repeated drafts of Congress have placed you; and for this purpose I shall endeavor to procure for you, for the next year, the same aid that I have been able to furnish in the course of the present. I cannot but believe, sir, that Congress will faithfully abide by what it now promises you, that in future no drafts shall be made upon you unless the necessary funds are sent to meet them."

Such a letter, though only gratitude could be felt for it, must have stung the sensitiveness of Franklin, who had already a great national pride. Nor was the pain likely to be assuaged by the conduct of Congress ; for that body had not the slightest idea of keeping the promises upon which de Vergennes expressed a reliance perhaps greater than he really felt. It is not without annoyance, even now, that one reads that only two days after the French minister wrote this letter, Congress instructed Franklin to do some more begging for clothes, and for the aid of a fleet, and said : " With respect to the loan, we foresee that the sum which we ask will be greatly inadequate to our wants."

December 2, 1780, Franklin acknowledges " favors," a conventional phrase which seems sarcastic.

These tell him that Congress has resolved to draw on him " bills extraordinary, to the amount of near $300,000." These were doubtless what led to the foregoing correspondence with de Vergennes. In reply he says that he has already engaged himself for the bills drawn on Mr. Laurens, and adds: " You cannot conceive how much these things perplex and distress me ; for the practice of this government being yearly to apportion the revenue to the several expected services, any after demands made, which the treasury is not furnished to supply, meet with great difficulty, and are very disagreeable to the ministers."

A short fragment of a diary kept in 1781 gives a painful vision of the swarm of bills : —

" Jan, 6. Accepted a number of loan office bills this day, and every day of the past week.

" Sunday, Jan. 7. Accepted a vast number of loan office bills. Some of the new drafts begin to appear.

" Jan. 8. Accepted many bills.

" Jan. 10th. Informed that my recall is to be moved for in Congress.

" Jan. 12th. Sign acceptation [qu. " of " ? mutilated] many bills. They come thick.

" Jan. 15th. Accepted above 200 bills, some of the new.

" Jan. 17th. Accepted many bills.

" Jan. 22d. M. Grand informs me that Mr. Williams has drawn on me for 25,000 livres ; . . . I order payment of his drafts.

" Jan. 24th. A great number of bills.

" Jan. 26th. Accept bills."

February 13th he writes a general begging and stimulating letter to de Vergennes. He says that the plain truth is that the present situation in the States " makes one of two things essential to us — a peace, or the most vigorous aid of our allies, particularly in the article of *money*. . . . The present conjuncture is critical; there is some danger lest the Congress should lose its influence over the people, if it is found unable to procure the aids that are wanted; " and in that case the opportunity for separation is gone, " perhaps for ages." A few days later he was " under the necessity of being importunate for an answer to the application lately made for stores and money." De Vergennes replied, in an interview, that Franklin must know that for France to lend the 25,000,000 livres asked for was " at present impracticable." Also his excellency mentioned other uncomfortable and distasteful facts, but concluded by saying that the king, as a " signal proof of his friendship," would make a free gift of 6,000,000 livres, in addition to 3,000,000 recently furnished for interest drafts. But the French court had at last so far lost confidence in Congress that in order to make sure that this money should be applied in aid of the army, and not be vaguely absorbed by committees, a stipulation was inserted that it should be paid only upon the order of General Washington. This was a trifle insulting to Congress, and made trouble; and it seems that ultimately the sum was intrusted to Franklin.

Almost immediately afterward he extorted from Necker an agreement that the king of France would guaranty a loan of 10,000,000 livres, if it could be raised in Holland ; and upon these terms he was able to raise this sum. Trouble enough the possession of it soon gave him ; for the demands for it were numerous. Franklin needed it to keep himself solvent in Europe ; Congress greedily sought it for America ; William Jackson, who was buying supplies in Holland, required much of it there. Franklin was expected to repeat with it the miracle of the loaves and fishes. 2,500,000 livres he sent to the States in the same ship which carried John Laurens. 2,200,000 Laurens disposed of in purchasing goods ; 1,500,000 were sent to Holland to be thence sent to the States in another ship, so as to divide the risk. But while he thus took care of others, he himself was drawn upon by Jackson for £50,000 ; and at the same time he was expected to provide for all the bills accepted by Laurens, Jay, and Adams, and now rapidly maturing. He sent in haste to Holland to detain the 1,500,000 livres *in transitu.* "I am sorry," he said, "that this operation is necessary ; but it must be done, or the consequences will be terrible."

Laurens and Jackson, however, in Holland had been actually spending this sum, and more. "I applaud the zeal you have both shown in the affair," said the harassed doctor, "but I see that nobody cares how much I am distressed, provided they can carry their own points." Fortunately the money still lay in the hands of the banker, and there Franklin stopped it; whereupon Jackson fell into extreme rage, and threatened some sort of a "proceeding," which Franklin said would only be exceedingly imprudent, useless, and scandalous. "The noise rashly made about this matter" by Jackson naturally injured American credit in Holland, and especially rendered unmarketable his own drafts upon Franklin. In these straits he journeyed to Paris to see Franklin, represented that his goods were on board ship; that they were articles much needed in America; that they must be paid for, or else relanded and returned, or sold, which would be a public disgrace. So Franklin was prevailed upon to engage for the payment, and was " obliged to go with this afterclap to the ministers," a proceeding especially disagreeable because, as he said, " the money was to be paid for the manufactures of other countries and not laid out in those of this kingdom, by whose friendship it was furnished." He was at first " absolutely refused," but in time prevailed, and " hoped the difficulty was over." Not at all! After all this exertion and annoyance, the officers of the ship said she was overloaded, and turned out a large part of the goods, which were accordingly put into two other ships; and then Franklin was offered the option of buying these two vessels, of hiring them at a freight scarcely less than their value, or of having the goods again set on shore. He was now "ashamed to show his face to the minister," and was casting about for resources, when suddenly he was surprised by new demands to pay for the goods which he had every reason to believe had already been paid for. This produced such a dispute and complication that the goods remained long in Holland before affairs could be arranged, and the final settlement is not clearly to be made out.

In the spring of 1781 John Adams was in Holland, and of course Congress was drawing bills upon him, and equally of course he had not a stiver with which to meet them. He had "opened a loan," but so little had fallen into the opening that he was barely able to pay expenses; so, still of course, he turned to Franklin: "When they [the bills] arrive and are presented I must write to you concerning them, and desire you to enable me to discharge them." He added that it was a "grievous mortification to find that America has no credit here, while England certainly still has so much." Apparently the pamphlet in which Franklin had so convincingly shown that the reverse of this should be the case had not satisfied the minds of the Dutch bankers.

In July, 1781, came a broad hint from Robert Morris: "I will not doubt a moment that, at your instance, his majesty will make pressing representations in support of Mr. Jay's application, and I hope that the authority of so great a sovereign and the arguments of his able ministry will shed auspicious influence on our negotiations at Madrid." This fulsome language, intended of course to be read to de Vergennes, imposed the gratifying duty of begging the French minister to second American begging in Spain.

In the same month Franklin wrote to Morris that the French were vexed at the purchasing of goods in Holland, and would not furnish the money to pay for them, and he actually suggested a remittance from America! "Otherwise I shall be ruined, with the American credit in Europe." He might have had some motive besides patriotism in thus uniting himself with the credit of his country; for he had been warned that the consul's court in Paris had power even over the persons of foreign ministers in the case of bills of exchange.

September 12, 1781, he announces triumphantly that "the remittances . . . which I requested are now unnecessary, and I shall finish the year with honor," notwithstanding "drafts on Mr. Jay and on Mr. Adams much exceeding what I had been made to expect."

He was now informed that Congress would not draw upon *other* ministers without providing funds, but that they would continue to draw on *him* "funds or no funds," an invidious distinction which "terrified" him; for he had been obliged to promise de Vergennes not to accept any drafts drawn later than March, 1781, unless he should have in hand or in view funds sufficient to pay them. But before long he began to suspect that Congress could outwit the French minister. For so late as January, 1782, bills dated prior to the

preceding April were still coming; and he said:
"I begin to suspect that the drawing continues, and
that the bills are antedated. It is impossible for
me to go on with demands after demands." The
next month also found these old bills on Laurens
still coming in. Congress never let the ministers
know how many bills it was drawing, perhaps fear-
ing to discourage them by so appalling a disclosure.
Franklin now wrote to Adams: "Perhaps from
the series of numbers and the deficiencies one may
be able to divine the sum that has been issued."
Moreover, he reflects that he has never had any instructions to pay the acceptances of Jay and Adams,
nor has had any ratification of his payments;
neither had he "ever received a syllable of approbation for having done so. Thus I stand charged
with vast sums which I have disbursed for the public service without authority." The thought might
cause some anxiety, in view of the moral obliquity
manifested by Congress in all its financial dealings.

In November, 1781, came a long letter from Livingston; everything was wanted; but especially the
States must have *money!* December 31, a day
that often brings reflection on matters financial,
de Vergennes sent a brief warning; 1,000,000
livres, which had been promised, Franklin should
have, but not one livre more under any circumstances; if he had accepted, or should accept, Morris's drafts in excess of this sum, he must trust to
his own resources to meet his obligations. Accordingly on January 9, 1782, he wrote to Morris:

" Bills are still coming in quantities. . . . You will see by the inclosed letter the situation I am at at last brought into. . . . I shall be able to pay till the end of February, when, if I can get no more money, I must stop."

Ten days later he writes to Jay that his solicitations make him appear insatiable, that he gets no assurances of aid, but that he is " very sensible " of Jay's " unhappy situation," and therefore manages to send him $30,000, though he knows not how to replace it. In the sad month of March, 1782, Lafayette nobly helped Franklin in the disagreeable task of begging, but to little purpose ; for at length there seemed a general determination to furnish no more money to the States. The fighting was over, and it seemed reasonable that the borrowing should be over likewise.

In February, 1782, Franklin says that Mr. Morris supposes him to have a sum " vastly greater than the fact," and has " given orders far beyond my abilities to comply with." Franklin was regarded as a miraculous orange which, if squeezed hard enough, would always yield juice ! It could not have been reassuring, either, to have one of the American agents at this time ask to have 150,000 livres advanced to him *at once ;* especially since the frankly provident gentleman based his pressing haste upon the avowed fear that, as business was going on, Franklin's embarrassments in money matters were likely to increase.

February 13, 1782, Livingston wrote a letter

which must have excited a grim smile. He comforts himself, in making more "importunate demands," by reflecting that it is all *for the good of France!* which thought, he says, may enable Franklin to "press them with some degree of dignity." Franklin's sense of humor was touched. That means, he says, that I am to say to de Vergennes : "Help us, and we shall not be obliged to you." But in some way or another, probably not precisely in this eccentric way, he so managed it that in March he wheedled the French government into still another, and a large, loan of 24,-000,000 livres, payable quarterly during the year. March 9 he informs Morris "pretty fully of the state of our funds here, by which you will be enabled so to regulate your drafts as that our credit in Europe may not be ruined and your friend killed with vexation."

He now engaged to pay all the drafts which Jay should send to him, so that Jay could extricate himself honorably from those dread engagements which had been giving that harassed gentleman infinite anxiety at Madrid. Some of his acceptances had already gone to protest ; but Franklin soon took them all up. By the end of March he began to breathe more freely ; he had saved himself and his colleagues thus far, and now he hoped that the worst was over. He wrote to Morris : "Your promise that after this month no more bills shall be drawn on me keeps up my spirits and affords me the greatest satisfaction." By the following summer the accounts between France and the States were in course of liquidation, and Franklin called the attention of Livingston to the fact that the king practically made the States a further present "to the value of near two millions. These, added to the free gifts before made to us at different times, form an object of at least twelve millions, for which no returns but that of gratitude and friendship are expected. These, I hope, may be everlasting." But liquidation, though a necessary preliminary to payment, is not payment, and does not preclude a continuance of borrowing; and in August we find that Morris was still pressing for more money, still drawing drafts, in happy forgetfulness of his promises not to do so, and still keeping Franklin in anxious dread of bankruptcy. By the same letter it appears that Morris had directed Franklin to pay over to M. Grand, the banker, any surplus funds in his hands! "I would do it with pleasure, if there were any such," said Franklin; but the question was still of a deficit, not of a surplus.

December 14, 1782, finds Franklin still at the old task, preferring "the application so strongly pressed by the Congress for a loan of $4,000,000." Lafayette again helped him, but the result remained uncertain. The negotiations for peace were so far advanced that the ministers thought it time for such demands to cease. But probably he succeeded, for a few days later he appears to be remitting a considerable sum. Peace, however, was at hand, and in one respect at least it was peace for Franklin as well as for his country, for even Congress could no longer expect him to continue borrowing. He had indeed rendered services not less gallant though less picturesque than those of Washington himself, vastly more disagreeable, and scarcely less essential to the success of the cause.

CHAPTER XIII.

HABITS OF LIFE AND OF BUSINESS: AN ADAMS INCIDENT.

JOHN ADAMS wielded a vivid and vicious pen; he neglected the Scriptural injunction: "Judge not," and he set honesty before charity in speech. His judgments upon his contemporaries were merciless; they had that kind of truthfulness which precluded contradiction, yet which left a sense of injustice; they were at once accurate and unfair. His strictures concerning Franklin are an illustration of these peculiarities. What he said is of importance because he said it, and because members of the Adams family in successive generations, voluminous contributors to the history of the country, have never divested themselves of the inherited enmity toward Franklin. During Adams's first visit to France the relationship between him and Franklin is described as sufficiently friendly rather than as cordial. December 7, 1778, in a letter to his cousin Samuel Adams, John thus described his colleague: —

"The other you know personally, and that he loves his Ease, hates to offend, and seldom gives any opinion till obliged to do it. I know also, and it is necessary that you should be informed, that he is overwhelmed with a correspondence from all quarters, most of them upon trifling subjects and in a more trifling style, with unmeaning visits from Multitudes of People, chiefly from the Vanity of having it to say that they have seen him. There is another thing that I am obliged to mention. There are so many private families, Ladies and gentlemen, that he visits so often, — and they are so fond of him, that he cannot well avoid it, — and so much intercourse with Academicians, that all these things together keep his mind in a constant state of dissipation. If indeed you take out of his hand the Public Treasury and the direction of the Frigates and Continental vessels that are sent here, and all Commercial affairs, and entrust them to Persons to be appointed by Congress, at Nantes and Bordeaux, I should think it would be best to have him here alone, with such a Secretary as you can confide in. But if he is left here alone, even with such a secretary, and all maritime and Commercial as well as political affairs and money matters are left in his Hands, I am persuaded that France and America will both have Reason to repent it. He is not only so indolent that Business will be neglected, but you know that, although he has as determined a soul as any man, yet it is his constant Policy never to say 'yes' or 'no' decidedly but when he cannot avoid it."

This mischievous letter, not actually false, yet misrepresenting and misleading, has unfortunately survived to injure both the man who wrote it and the man about whom it was written. It is quoted in order to show the sort of covert fire in the rear to which Franklin was subjected throughout his term of service. It is astonishing now, when the evidence is all before us and the truth is attainable, to read such a description of such a patriot as Franklin, a man who went through labors and anxieties for the cause probably only surpassed by those of Washington, and whose services did more to promote success than did the services of any other save only Washington. How blind was the personal prejudice of the critic who saw Franklin in Paris and could yet suggest that the charge of the public treasury should be taken from him! To whom else would the Frenchmen have unlocked their coffers as they did to him, whom they so warmly liked and admired? John Adams and Arthur Lee and every other American who endeavored to deal with the French court got himself so thoroughly hated there that little aid would have been forthcoming at the request of such representatives. It was to Franklin's personal influence that a large portion of the substantial help in men, ships, and especially in money, accorded by France to the States, was due. He was as much the right man in Europe as was Washington in America.

Nevertheless this attribution of traits, so maliciously penned, has passed into history, and though the world does not see that either France or the States had cause " to repent " keeping Franklin in Paris in general charge of affairs, and unwatched by a vigilant secretary, yet all the world believes that in the gay metropolis Franklin was indolent and given over to social pleasures, which flattered his vanity. Undoubtedly there is foundation in fact for the belief. But to arrive at a just conclusion one must consider many things. The character of the chief witness is as important as that of the accused. Adams, besides being a severe critic, was filled to the brim with an irrepressible activity, an insatiate industry, a restlessness and energy, all which were at this period stimulated by the excitement of the times to an intensity excessive and abnormal even for him. To him, in this condition of chronic agitation, the serenity of Franklin's broad intellect and tranquil nature seemed inexplicable and culpable. But Franklin had what Adams lacked, a vast experience in men and affairs. Adams knew the provinces and the provincials; Franklin knew the provinces and England and France, the provincials, Englishmen, Frenchmen, and all ranks and conditions of men, — journeymen, merchants, philosophers, men of letters, diplomatists, courtiers, noblemen, and statesmen. The one was an able colonist, the other was a man of the world, of exceptionally wide personal experience even as such. Moreover Franklin's undertakings were generally crowned with a success which justifies us in saying that, however much or little exertion he visibly put forth, at least he put forth enough. Adams sometimes was for putting forth too much. Franklin, when he arrived in France, was in his seventy-first year; his health was in the main good, yet his strength had been severely tried by his journey to Canada and by the voyage. He was troubled with a cutaneous complaint, of which he makes light, but which was abundant evidence that his physical condition was far from perfect; he was a victim of the gout, which attacked him frequently and with great severity, so that he was often obliged to keep his bed for days and weeks; when he was appointed sole minister of the States to France he remarked that there was " some incongruity in a *plenipotentiary* who could neither stand nor go;" later on he suffered extremely from stone and gravel; with all these diseases, and with the remorseless disease of old age gaining ground every day, it is hardly surprising that Franklin seemed to the hale and vigorous Adams not to be making that show of activity which would have been becoming in the chief representative of the United States during these critical years. Yet except that he was careless about his papers and remiss in his correspondence no definite allegations are made against him prior to the treating for peace; no business of importance was ever said to have failed in his hands, which should be a sufficient vindication of his general efficiency. The amount of labor which was laid upon him was enormous: he did as much business as the managing head of a great banking-house and a great mercantile firm combined; he did all the diplomacy of the United States; he was also their consul-general, and though he had agents in some ports, yet they more often gave trouble than assistance; after the commercial treaty with

France he had to investigate French laws and tariffs and give constant advice to American merchants upon all sorts of questions as to statutes, trade, customs, dues, and duties. What he did concerning the war ships, the privateers, and the prizes has been hinted at rather than stated ; what he did in the way of financiering has been imperfectly shown ; he was often engaged in planning naval operations either for Paul Jones and others in European waters or for the French fleet in American waters. He had for a perpetual annoyance all the captiousness and the quarrels of the two Lees, Izard, and Thomas Morris. When business had to be transacted, as often occurred, with states at whose courts the United States had no representative, Franklin had to manage it ; [1] especially he was concerned with the business in Spain, whither he would have journeyed in person had his health and other engagements permitted. Moreover he was adviser-general to all American officials of any and every grade and function in Europe ; and much as some of these gentlemen contemned him, they each and all instinctively demanded his guidance in every matter of importance. Even Arthur Lee deferred to him rather than decide for himself ; Dana sought his instructions for the mission to Russia ; men of the calibre of Jay and independent John Adams sought and respected his views and his aid, perhaps more than they

[1] For example, with Norway, with Denmark, and with Portugal.

themselves appreciated. Surely here was labor
enough, and even more responsibility than labor;
but Franklin's great, well-trained mind worked
with the ease and force of a perfectly regulated machine whose smoothness of action almost conceals
its power, and all the higher parts of his labor
were achieved with little perceptible effort. For
the matters of account-keeping and letter-writing, he
neglected these things; and one is almost provoked
into respecting him for so doing when it is remembered that during all the time of his stay in France
Congress never allowed to this aged and over-tasked
man a secretary of legation, or even an amanuen-
sis or a copyist. He had with him his grandson,
Temple Franklin, a lad of sixteen years at the time
of his arrival in France, and whom it had been
intended to place at school. But Franklin could
not dispense with his services, and kept this young-
ster as his sole clerk and assistant. It should be
mentioned also in this connection that it was not
only necessary to prepare the customary duplicates
of every document of importance, but every paper
which was to be sent across the Atlantic had to be
copied half a dozen extra times, in order to be
dispatched in as many different ships, so great
were the dangers of capture. It was hardly fair
to expect a minister plenipotentiary to display unwearied zeal in this sort of work. Adams himself
would have done it, and grumbled; Franklin did
not do it, and preserved his good temper. In conclusion it may be said that, if Franklin was indo-

lent, as in some ways he probably was, he had at least much excuse for indolence, and the trait showed itself only on what may be called the physical side of his duties ; upon the intellectual side, it cannot be denied that during the period thus far traversed he did more thinking and to better purpose 'than any other American of the day.

In saying that Franklin was fond of society and pleased with the admiration expressed for him by the ardent and courteous Frenchmen and by other continental Europeans, Adams spoke correctly. Franklin was always social and always a little vain. But much less would have been heard of these traits if the distinction made between him and his colleagues had been less conspicuous and less constant. That men of the size of the Lees and Izard should inflate themselves to the measure of harboring a jealousy of Franklin's preëminence was only ridiculous; but Adams should have had, as Jay had, too much self-respect to cherish such a feeling. It was the weak point in his character that he could never acknowledge a superior, and the fact that the world at large estimated Washington, Franklin, and Hamilton as men of larger calibre than his own kept him in a state of exasperation all his life. Now the simple truth, forced in a thousand unintended ways upon the knowledge of all American envoys during the Revolution, was, that in Europe Franklin was a distinguished man, while no other American was known or cared for at all. Franklin received deference, where others received

civility; Franklin was selected for attentions, for
flattery, for official consultations and communications, while his colleagues were "forgotten entirely
by the French people." Jay, Dana, and Carmichael accepted this situation in the spirit of sensible gentlemen, but Adams, the Lees, and Izard
were incensed and sought an offset in defamation.
Compare Carmichael's language with what has been
quoted from Adams: he says: "The age of Dr.
Franklin in some measure hinders him from taking
so active a part in the drudgery of business as his
great zeal and abilities would otherwise enable him
to execute. He is the Master, to whom we children
in politics look up for counsel, and whose name is
everywhere a passport to be well received." Still
it must have been provoking to be customarily
spoken of as " Dr. Franklin's associates." When
Franklin was appointed minister plenipotentiary
he was obliged to explain that he was not the " sole
representative of America in Europe." De Vergennes always wished to deal only with him, and
occasionally said things to him in secrecy so close
as to be exclusive even of his "associates." Adams
honestly admitted that "this court have confidence
in him alone." When a favor was to be asked, it
was Franklin who could best seek it; and when it
was granted it seemed to be vouchsafed to Franklin. In a word, Franklin had the monopoly of the
confidence, the respect, and the personal regard of
the French ministry. It was the same way also
with the English; when they made advances for

conciliation or peace, they too selected Franklin for their communications.

Adams was not sufficiently familiar with the modes of political life in Europe to appreciate what a substantial value Franklin's social and scientific prestige among the "ladies and gentlemen" and the "academicians" had there. All those tributes which the great "philosopher" was constantly receiving may have been, as Adams said, pleasant food for his vanity, but they were also of practical worth and service, signifying that he was a man of real note and importance in what European statesmen regarded as "the world." If Franklin relished the repast, who among mortals would not? And was his accuser a man to have turned his back on such viands, had he also been bidden to the feast of flattery? Franklin's vanity was a simple, amiable, and harmless source of pleasure to himself; it was not of the greedy or envious type, nor did its gratification do any injury to any person, or any interest. Jay, a man of generous temper, understood the advantage reaped by the States from being represented at the French court by a man whose greatness all Europe recognized. More than once he bore this testimony, honorable alike to the giver and to him for whom it was given.[1]

Pleasant as were many of the features of Franklin's residence in France, and skillfully as he may have evaded some of the more irksome labors im-

[1] See, for example, Franklin's *Works*, vii. 25.', note.

posed upon him, the attraction was not always sufficient to make him reluctant to have done with the
place. Its vexations and anxieties wore upon him
grievously. He knew that unfriendly representations concerning him were often made in America,
and that these induced some men to distrust him,
and caused others to feel anxious about him. He
heard stories that he was to be recalled, other
stories that there was a cabal to vent a petty ill-
will by putting an end to the clerkship of his
grandson. This cut him to the quick. "I should
not part with the child," he said, "but with the
employment;" and so the ignoble scheme miscar-
ried; for Congress was not ready to lose Franklin,
and did not really feel any extreme dread of harm
from a lad who, though the son of a loyalist, had
grown up under Franklin's personal influence. At
times homesickness attacked him. When he heard
of the death of an old friend at home he wrote
sadly: "A few more such deaths will make me a
stranger in my own country." He was not one
of those patriots who like to live abroad and protest love for their own country. Generally he preserved the delightful evenness of his temper with
a success quite wonderful in a man troubled with
complaints which preëminently make the sufferer
impatient and irascible. Only once he said, when
he was being very unreasonably annoyed about
some shipping business: "I will absolutely have
nothing to do with any new squadron project. I
have been too long in hot water, plagued almost to

death with the passions, vagaries, and ill-humors and madnesses of other people. I must have a little repose." A very mild outbreak this, under all his provocations, but it is the only one of which any record remains. His tranquil self-control was a very remarkable trait; he was never made so angry by all the calumny and assaults of enemies peculiarly apt in the art of irritation as to use any immoderate or undignified language. He never retaliated, though he had the fighting capacity in him. Before the tribunal of posterity his patient endurance has counted greatly in his favor.

By March, 1781, he had definitively made up his mind to resign, and wrote to the president of Congress a letter which was unmistakably earnest and in parts even touching.[1] When this alarming communication was received all the depreciation of the Lees, Izard, and the rest went for nothing. Without hesitation Congress ignored the request, with far better reason than it could show for the utter indifference with which it was wont to regard pretty much all the other requests which Franklin ever made. Its behavior in this respect was indeed very singular. He recommended his grandson to it, and it paid absolutely no attention to the petition. He repeatedly asked the appointment of consuls at some of the French ports; it created all sorts of other officials, keeping Paris full of useless and costly " ministers " accredited to

[1] Franklin's *Works*, vii. 207; the letter is unfortunately too long to quote. See also his letter to Lafayette, Ibid., 237.

courts which would not receive them, but appointed no consul. He urged hard, as a trifling personal favor, that an accountant might be appointed to audit his nephew Williams's accounts, but Congress would not attend to a matter which could have been disposed of in five minutes. He never could get a secretary or a clerk, nor even any proper appointment of, or salary for, his grandson. He seldom got an expression of thanks or approbation for anything that he did, though he did many things wholly outside of his regular functions and involving great personal risk and responsibility. Yet when he really wanted to resign he was not allowed to do so; and thus at last he was left to learn by inference that he had given satisfaction.[1]

No sooner had Adams got comfortably settled at home than he was obliged to return again to Europe. Franklin, Jay, Laurens, Jefferson, and he were appointed by Congress commissioners to treat for peace, whenever the fitting time should come; and so in February, 1780, he was back in Paris. But peace was still far away in the future, and Adams, meanwhile, finding the intolerable incumbrance of leisure upon his hands, exorcised the demon by writing long letters to de Vergennes upon sundry matters of interest in American affairs. It was an unfortunate scheme. If Nature had maliciously sought to create a man for the express purpose of aggravating de Vergennes, she

[1] See letter to Carmichael, *Works*, vii. 285.

could not have made one better adapted for that service than was Adams. Very soon there was a terrible explosion, and Franklin, invoked by both parties, had to hasten to the rescue, to his own serious injury.

On May 31, 1780, in a letter to the president of Congress, Franklin said : " A great clamor has lately been made by some merchants, who say they have large sums on their hands of paper money in America, and that they are ruined by some resolution of Congress, which reduces its value to one part in forty. As I have had no letter explaining this matter I have only been able to say that it is probably misunderstood, and that I am confident the Congress have not done, nor will do, anything unjust towards strangers who have given us credit." Soon afterward Adams got private information of the passage of an act for the redemption of the paper money at the rate of forty dollars for one in silver. At once he sent the news to de Vergennes. That statesman took fire at the tidings, and promptly responded that foreigners ought to be indemnified for any losses they might suffer, and that Americans alone should " support the expense which is occasioned by the defense of their liberty," and should regard " the depreciation of their paper money only as an impost which ought to fall upon themselves." He added that he had instructed the Chevalier de la Luzerne, French minister to the States, " to make the strongest representations on this subject " to Congress.

Adams was alarmed at the anger which he had excited, and besought de Vergennes to hold his hand until Franklin could " have opportunity to make his representations to his majesty's ministers." But this gleam of good sense was transitory, for on the same day, without waiting for Franklin to intervene, he composed and sent to de Vergennes a long, elaborate defense of the course of the States. It was such an argument as a stubborn lawyer might address to a presumably prejudiced court ; it had not a pleasant word of gratitude for past favors, or of regret at the present necessity ; it was as undiplomatic and ill-considered as it certainly was unanswerable. But its impregnability could not offset its gross imprudence. To exasperate de Vergennes and alienate the French government at that period, although by a perfectly sound presentation, was an act of madness as unpardonable as any crime.

Upon the same day on which Adams drew up this able, inexcusable brief for his unfortunate client, the Congress, he wrote to Franklin begging him to interfere. On June 29 he followed this request with a humbler note than John Adams often wrote, acknowledging that he might have made some errors, and desiring to be set right. On June 30 de Vergennes also appealed to Franklin, saying, amid much more : " The king is so firmly persuaded, sir, that your private opinion respecting the effects of that resolution of Congress, as far as it concerns strangers and especially Frenchmen, dif

fers from that of Mr. Adams, that he is not appre-
hensive of laying you under any embarrassment by
requesting you to support the representations which
his minister is ordered to make to Congress."

Franklin, receiving these epistles, was greatly
vexed at the jeopardy into which the rash zeal of
Adams had suddenly plunged the American interests in France. His indignation was not likely to
be made less by the fact that all this letter-writing
to de Vergennes was a tacit reproach upon his own
performance of his duties and a gratuitous intrench-
ment upon his province. The question which presented itself to him was not whether the argument
of Adams was right or wrong, nor whether the distinction which de Vergennes sought to establish
between American citizens and foreigners was practicable or not. This was fortunate, because, while
Adams in the States had been forced to ponder
carefully all the problems of a depreciating paper
currency, Franklin in France had neither necessity,
nor opportunity, nor leisure for studying either the
ethics or the solution of so perplexing a problem.
He now hastily made such inquiries as he could
among the Americans lately arrived in Paris, but
did not pretend "perfectly to understand" the subject. To master its difficulties, however, did not
seem essential, because he recognized that the obvious duty of the moment was to say something which
might at least mitigate the present wrath of the
French ministry, and so gain time for explanation and adjustment in a better state of feeling.

He had once laid down to Arthur Lee the principle : " While we are asking aid it is necessary to gratify the desires and in some sort comply with the humors of those we apply to. Our business now is to carry our point." Acting upon this rule of conciliation, he wrote, on July 10, to de Vergennes : —

" In this I am clear, that if the operation directed by Congress in their resolution of March the 18th occasions, from the necessity of the case, some inequality of justice, that inconvenience ought to fall wholly upon the inhabitants of the States, who reap with it the advantages obtained by the measure ; and that the greatest care should be taken that foreign merchants, particularly the French, who are our creditors, do not suffer by it. This I am so confident the Congress will do that I do not think any representations of mine necessary to persuade them to it. I shall not fail, however, to lay the whole before them."

In pursuance of this promise Franklin wrote on August 9 a full narrative of the entire matter ; it was a fair and temperate statement of facts which it was his duty to lay before Congress.[1] Before sending it he wrote to Adams that de Vergennes, " having taken much amiss some passages in your letter to him, sent the whole correspondence to me, requesting that I would transmit it to Congress. I was myself sorry to see those passages. If they were the effects merely of inadvertence, and you do not, on reflection, approve of them, perhaps you

[1] Franklin's *Works,* vii. 110–112.

may think it proper to write something for effacing the impressions made by them. I do not presume to advise you; but mention it only for your consideration." But Adams had already taken his own measures for presenting the case before Congress.

Such is the full story of Franklin's doings in this affair. His connection with it was limited to an effort to counteract the mischief which another had done. Whether he thought that the "inconvenience" which "*ought* to fall" only on Americans could be arranged to do so, does not appear; probably he never concerned himself to work out a problem entirely outside his own department. As a diplomatist, who had to gain time for angry people to cool down for amicable discussion, he was content to throw out this general remark, and to express confidence that his countrymen would do liberal justice. So far as he was concerned, this should have been the end of the matter, and Adams should have been grateful to a man whose tranquil wisdom and skillful tact had saved him from the self-reproach which he would ever have felt had his well-intentioned, ill-timed act borne its full possible fruit of injury to the cause of the States. But Adams, who knew that his views were intrinsically correct, emerged from the imbroglio with an extreme resentment against his rescuer, nor was he ever able to see that Franklin did right in not reiterating the same views. He wished not to be saved but to be vindicated. The consequence has been unfortunate for Franklin, because the affair has furnished material for one of the counts in the indictment which the Adamses have filed against him before the bar of posterity.

It may be remarked here that the few words which Franklin ever let drop concerning paper money indicate that he had given it little thought. He said that in Europe it seemed " a mystery," " a wonderful machine; " and there is no reason why he should have understood it better than other people in Europe. He also said that the general effect of the depreciation had operated as a gradual tax on the citizens, and " perhaps the most equal of all taxes, since it depreciated in the hands of the holders of money, and thereby taxed them in proportion to the sums they held and the time they held it, which is generally in proportion to men's wealth." [1] The remark could not keep a place in any very profound discussion of the subject; but it should be noted that in this point of view the contention of de Vergennes might be logically defended, on the ground that a foreigner ought not to be taxed like a citizen; but the insuperable difficulty of making the distinction practicable remained undisposed of.

[1] See also Franklin's *Works*, vii. 343.

CHAPTER XIV.

THE war had not been long waging before overtures and soundings concerning an accommodation, abetted and sometimes instigated by the cabinet, began to come from England. Nearly all these were addressed to Franklin, because all Europe persisted in regarding him as the one authentic representative of America, and because Englishmen of all parties had long known and respected him far beyond any other American. In March, 1778, William Pulteney, a member of Parliament, came under an assumed name to Paris and had an interview with him. But it seemed that England would not renounce the theory of the power of Parliament over the colonies, though willing by way of favor to forego its exercise. Franklin declared an arrangement on such a basis to be impossible.

A few months later there occurred the singular and mysterious episode of Charles de Weissenstein. Such was the signature to a letter dated at Brussels, June 16, 1778. The writer said that independence was an impossibility, and that the English title to the colonies, being indisputable,

would be enforced by coming generations even if
the present generation should have to " stop awhile
in the pursuit to recover breath; " he then sketched
a plan of reconciliation, which included offices or
life-pensions for Franklin, Washington, and other
prominent rebels. He requested a personal interview with Franklin, and, failing that, he appointed to be in a certain spot in Notre Dame at a
certain hour, wearing a rose in his hat, to receive
a written reply. The French police reported the
presence at the time and place of a man obviously
bent upon this errand, who was traced to his hotel
and found, says John Adams, to be " Colonel Fitz-
something, an Irish name, that I have forgotten."
He got no answer, because at a consultation between the American commissioners and de Vergennes it was so decided. But one had been written by Franklin, and though de Weissenstein and
Colonel Fitz-something never saw it, at least it has
afforded pleasure to thousands of readers since that
time. For by sundry evidence Franklin became
convinced, even to the point of alleging that he
" knew," that the incognito correspondent was the
English monarch himself, whose letter the Irish
colonel had brought. The extraordinary occasion
inspired him. It is a rare occurrence when one
can speak direct to a king as man with man on
terms of real equality. Franklin seized his chance,
and wrote a letter in his best vein, a dignified, vigorous statement of the American position, an eloquent, indignant arraignment of the English meas-

ures for which George III. more than any other
one man was responsible. In language which was
impassioned without being extravagant, he mingled
sarcasm and retort, statement and argument, with
a strenuous force that would have bewildered the
royal " de Weissenstein." To this day one cannot read these stinging paragraphs without a feeling of disappointment that de Vergennes would
not let them reach their destination. Such a bolt
should have been sent hotly home, not dropped to
be picked up as a curiosity by the groping historians of posterity.

The good Hartley also was constantly toiling to
find some common ground upon which negotiators
could stand and talk. One of his schemes, which
now seems an idle one, was for a long truce, during
which passions might subside and perhaps a settlement be devised. Franklin ever lent a courteous
ear to any one who spoke the word Peace. But
neither this strong feeling, nor any discouragement
by reason of American reverses, nor any arguments
of Englishmen ever induced him to recede in the
least from the line of demands which he thought
reasonable, nor to abate his uncompromising plain-
ness of speech.

With the outbreak of war Franklin's feelings towards England had taken on that extreme bitterness which so often succeeds when love and admiration seem to have been misplaced. " I was fond
to a folly," he said, " of our British connections,
. . . but the extreme cruelty with which we have

been treated has now extinguished every thought of returning to it, and separated us forever. You have thereby lost limbs that will never grow again." English barbarities, he declared, " have at length demolished all my moderation." Often and often he reiterated such statements in burning words, which verge more nearly upon vehemence than any other reminiscence which survives to us of the great and calm philosopher.

Yet in the bottom of his heart he felt that the chasm should not be made wider and deeper than was inevitable. In 1780 he told Hartley that Congress would fain have had him " make a school-book " from accounts of " British barbarities," to be illustrated by thirty-five prints by good artists of Paris, " each expressing one or more of the different horrid facts, . . . in order to impress the minds of children and posterity with a deep sense of your bloody and insatiable malice and wickedness." He would not do this, yet was sorely provoked toward it. " Every kindness I hear of done by an Englishman to an American prisoner makes me resolve not to proceed in the work, hoping a reconciliation may yet take place. But every fresh instance of your devilism weakens that resolution, and makes me abominate the thought of a reunion with such a people."

In point of fact the idea of an actual reunion seems never from the very outset to have had any real foothold in his mind. In 1779 he said : " We have long since settled all the account in our own minds. We know the worst you can do to us, if you have your wish, is to confiscate our estates and take our lives, to rob and murder us; and this . . . we are ready to hazard rather than come again under your detested government." [1] This sentiment steadily gained strength as the struggle advanced. Whenever he talked about terms of peace he took a tone so high as must have seemed altogether ridiculous to English statesmen. Independence, he said, was established; no words need be wasted about that. Then he audaciously suggested that it would be good policy for England "to act nobly and generously; . . . to cede all that remains in North America, and thus conciliate and strengthen a young power, which she wishes to have a future and serviceable friend." She would do well to "throw in" Canada, Nova Scotia, and the Floridas, and "call it . . . an indemnification for the burning of the towns."

Englishmen constantly warned him of the blunder which the colonies would commit, should they "throw themselves into the arms" of France, and they assured him that the alliance was the one "great stumbling-block in the way of making peace." But he had ever the reply, after the fashion of Scripture: By their fruits ye shall know them. France was as liberal of friendship and good services as England was of tyranny and cruelties. This was enough to satisfy Franklin; he

[1] See also a strong statement in letter to Hartley of October 14, 1777; *Works*, vii. 106.

saw no Judas in the constant and generous de Vergennes, and could recognize no inducement to drop
the substance France for the shadow England.[1]
To his mind it seemed to concern equally the honor
and the interest of the States to stand closely and
resolutely by their allies, whom to abandon would
be " infamy ; " and after all, what better bond
could there be than a common interest and a common foe ? From this view he never wavered to
the hour when the definitive treaty of peace was
signed.[2]

Such was Franklin's frame of mind when the
surrender at Yorktown and the events incident
to the reception of the news in England at last
brought peace into really serious consideration.
The States had already been forward to place
themselves in a position for negotiating at the first
possible moment. For in 1779 Congress had received from France an intimation that it would be
well to have an envoy in Europe empowered to
treat; and though it was seizing time very much
by the forelock, yet that body was in no mood to
dally with so pleasing a hint, and at once nominated John Adams to be plenipotentiary. This,
however, by no means fell in with the schemes of
the French ministry, for de Vergennes knew and
disliked Mr. Adams's very unmanageable character.
Accordingly the French ambassador at Philadelphia

[1] See Franklin's *Works*, vi. 303.
[2] See Franklin's *Works*, vi. 151, 303, 310; vii. 3, for examples
of his expressions on this subject.

was instructed to use his great influence with Congress to effect some amelioration of the distasteful arrangement, and he soon covertly succeeded in inducing Congress to create a commission by appointing Adams, Jay, Franklin, Jefferson, who never went on the mission, and Laurens, who was a prisoner in England and joined his colleagues only after the business had been substantially concluded. Adams promptly came to Paris, created a great turmoil there, as has been in part narrated, and passed on to Holland, where he still remained. Jay, accredited to, but not yet received by, the Spanish court, was at Madrid. Franklin therefore alone was on hand in Paris when the great tidings of the capture of Cornwallis came.

It was on November 25, 1781, that Lord North got this news, taking it " as he would have taken a ball in his breast." He recognized at once that " all was over," yet for a short time longer he retained the management of affairs. But his majority in Parliament was steadily dwindling, and evidently with him also " all was over." In his despair he caught with almost pathetic eagerness at what for a moment seemed a chance to save his ministry by treating with the States secretly and apart from France. He was a man not troubled with convictions, and having been obstinate in conducting a war for which he really cared little, he was equally ready to save his party by putting an end to it with the loss of all that had been at stake. Franklin, however, decisively cut off that hope.

America, he assured Hartley, would not forfeit the world's good opinion by " such perfidy ; " and in the incredible event of Congress instructing its commissioners to treat upon " such ignominious terms," he himself at least " would certainly refuse to act." So Digges, whom Franklin described as " the greatest villain I ever met with," carried back no comfort from secret, tentative errands to Adams in Holland and to Franklin in France. Simultaneous furtive advances to de Vergennes met with a like rebuff. France and America were not to be separated ; Lord North and his colleagues were not to be saved by the bad faith of either of their enemies. On February 22, 1782, an address to the king against continuing the American war was moved by Conway. It was carried by a majority of nineteen. A few days later a second, more pointed, address was carried without a division. The next day leave was granted to bring in a bill enabling the king to make a peace or a truce with the colonies. The game was up; the ministry held no more cards to play ; on March 20 Lord North announced that his administration was at an end.

In his shrewd, intelligent fashion, Franklin was watching these events, perfectly appreciating the significance of each in turn. On March 22 he seized an opportunity which chance threw in his way for writing to Lord Shelburne a short note, in which he suggested a hope that the " returning good disposition " of England towards America would " tend to produce a general peace." It was a note of a few lines only, seemingly a mere pleasant passage of courtesy to an old friend, but significant and timely, an admirable specimen of the delicate tact with which Franklin could meet and almost create opportunity. A few days later the cabinet of Lord Rockingham was formed, composed of the friends of America. In it Charles Fox was secretary for foreign affairs, and Lord Shelburne had the home department, including the colonies. No sooner were the new ministers fairly instated than Shelburne dispatched Richard Oswald, a retired Scotch merchant, of very estimable character, of good temper, reasonable views, and sufficient ability, to talk matters over with Franklin at Paris. Oswald arrived on April 12, and had satisfactory interviews with Franklin and de Vergennes. The important fact of which he became satisfied by the explicit language of Franklin was, that the hope of inducing the American commissioners to treat secretly and separately from France was utterly groundless.[1] After a few days he went back to London, carrying a letter from Franklin to Shelburne, in which Franklin expressed his gratification at these overtures and his hope that Oswald might continue to represent the English minister. Oswald also carried certain " Notes for Conversation," which Franklin had written out ; " some loose

[1] About the same time Laurens was released on parole and sent to confer with Adams in Holland, concerning a separate treating, and brought from Adams the like response as Oswald brought from Franklin.

thoughts on paper," as he called them, "which I intended to serve as memorandums for my discourse, but without a fixed intention of showing them to him." As matters turned out later, it would have been better if Franklin had not been quite so free with these "memorandums," which contained a suggestion that the English should cede Canada and the Americans should recoup the losses of the royalists. Indeed, no sooner had the paper left his hands than he saw his error, and was "a little ashamed of his weakness." The letter only was shown to the whole cabinet.

On May 5 Oswald was again in Paris, charged to discuss terms with Franklin. But on May 7 there arrived also Thomas Grenville, deputed by Fox to approach de Vergennes with the design not only of treating with France, but also of treating with the States through France. The double mission indicated a division in the English cabinet. Fox and Shelburne were almost as hostile to each other as were both to Lord North; and each was aiming to control the coming negotiations with the States. Which should secure it was a nice question. For English purposes of classification the States, until independence was acknowledged, remained colonies, and so within the charge of Shelburne. Hence came Fox's scheme for reaching them indirectly through France, also his avowed willingness to recognize their independence immediately, for foreign business belonged to him. Shelburne, on the other hand, strenuously resisted this; at worst, as he thought, independence must come through a treaty, and with equivalents. Moreover it seems that he cherished an odd, half-defined notion, apparently altogether peculiar to himself, that he might escape the humiliation of a grant of full independence, and in place thereof might devise some sort of " federal union." Perhaps it was out of this strange fancy that there grew at this time a story that the States were to be reconciled and joined to Great Britain by a gift of the same measure of autonomy enjoyed by Ireland.

When Oswald and Franklin next met, they made at first little progress ; each seemed desirous to keep himself closed while the other unfolded. The result was that Franklin wrote, with unusual *naïveté :* " On the whole I was able to draw so little of the sentiments of Lord Shelburne . . . that I could not but wonder at his being again sent to me." At the same time Grenville was offering to de Vergennes to acknowledge the independence of the United States, provided that in other respects the treaty of 1763 [1] should be reinstated. That is to say, France was to agree to a complete restoration of the *status quo ante bellum* in every respect so far as her own interests were concerned, and to accept as the entire recompense for all her expenditures of money and blood a benefit accruing to the American States. This was a humorous assumption of the ingenuousness of her most disinterested

---

[1] Made between England and France at the close of the last war, in which France had lost Canada.

protestations. The French minister, we are told, "seemed to smile" at this compliment to the unselfishness of his chivalrous nation,[1] and replied that the American States were making no request to England for independence. As Franklin happily expressed it: "This seems to me a proposition of selling to us a thing that was already our own, and making France pay the price they [the English] are pleased to ask for it." But the design of weaning the States from France, in the treating, was obvious.

Grenville, thus checked, next tried to see what he could do with Franklin in the way of separate negotiation. But he only elicited a statement that the States were under no obligations save those embodied in the treaties of alliance and commerce with France, and a sort of intimation, which might be pregnant of much or of little, that if the purpose of the former were achieved through the recognition of independence, then the commercial treaty alone would remain. This somewhat enigmatical remark doubtless indicated nothing more than that the States would not continue active and aggressive hostilities in order to further purely French designs. Clearly it would depend upon the demands of France whether the States might not find themselves in a somewhat delicate position. Their obligation to make no separate peace with England had been contracted upon the basis that

[1] "The Peace Negotiations of 1782-83," etc., by John Jay; in Winsor's *Narr. and Crit. Hist. of America*, vol. vii.

France should ally herself with them to obtain their independence ; and the injury expected to result therefrom to England, with the chance of commercial advantages accruing to France, had been regarded as a full consideration. Yet it would seem ungrateful, to say the least, to step out of the fight and leave France in it, and to refuse to back her demands for the recoupment of some of the losses which she had suffered in the previous war. But now the French alliance with Spain threatened grave complications ; she had joined France in the war, and the two powers were held closely together by the Bourbon family interests. Spain now had demands of her own in the way of territory on the American continent, where she had made extensive conquests, and even for the cession of Gibraltar. But the States owed little to Spain, vastly less, indeed, than they had tried to owe to her ; for their incessant begging had elicited only small sums, and they were more irritated at their failure to obtain much than thankful for the trifles they had extorted. So they now easily and gladly took the position of entire freedom from any obligation, either by treaty or of honor, towards that power. But in the probable event of France standing by Spain, peace might be deferred for the benefit of a country with which the States had no lien, unless the States could treat separately. It was not within the purview of the treaty that they should remain tied to France for such purposes ; and to this purport Fox wrote to Grenville. But though it might be tolerably easy to enunciate a theory by which the States could justly control their own affairs, with no regard to France, it was only too probable that the application of that theory to circumstances would be a very nice and perplexing task. It strongly behooved a new country to preserve its good name and its friendships.

If Fox had been able to carry his point, matters might have moved more expeditiously. But pending the struggle between him and Shelburne no advance could be made at Paris. Grenville and Oswald could not work in unison. Franklin and de Vergennes became puzzled and suspicious, having only an imperfect inkling by report and gossip concerning the true state of affairs. They suspected, with good show of evidence, that the real object of English diplomacy was to drive in a wedge between the allies. Amid these perplexities, on April 22, Franklin wrote to Jay, begging him to come to Paris : " Here you are greatly wanted, for messengers begin to come and go, . . . and I can neither make nor agree to conditions of peace without the assistance of my colleagues. . . . I wish therefore you would . . . render yourself here as soon as possible. You would be of infinite service." Jay arrived on June 23, to Franklin's " great satisfaction," and the meeting was cordial. Jay was thirty-seven years old, and Franklin was seventy-six, but Jay says : " His mind appears more vigorous than that of any man of his age I have known. He certainly is a valuable minister and an agreeable companion."

The deadlock continued. Grenville showed a commission to treat with France and " any other prince or state." But the " enabling act," giving the king authority to acknowledge the independence of the States, had not yet been passed by Parliament; and it did not appear that England recognized the ex-colonies as constituting either a prince or a state. Oswald had no commission at all. Franklin, though he found himself " in some perplexity with regard to these two negotiations," strove to set things in motion. He preferred Oswald to Grenville, and intimated to Lord Shelburne his wish that Oswald should receive exclusive authority to treat with the American commissioners. He at the same time suggested sundry *necessary* articles to be disposed of by the treaty, namely : independence, boundaries, and the fisheries ; and sundry *advisable* articles, namely : an indemnity to be granted by England to the sufferers by the war ; an acknowledgment of her error by England, and the cession of Canada.

But the duel between Shelburne and Fox must first be settled, and it was now about to be settled suddenly and in an unexpected manner. On July 1, 1782, Lord Rockingham died, and the crown, as Walpole facetiously remarked, thereby descended to the king of England. The monarch at once, though very reluctantly, requested Shelburne to accept the post of prime minister, regarding him as in some degree less obnoxious than Fox. Thereupon Fox and his friends retired in high dudgeon from

office, and Grenville promptly asked to be recalled.
His opportune request was granted very readily,
and his place was given to Fitzherbert, who brought
personal letters to Franklin, but who was not accredited to treat with the States. It seemed that
this business was now again to fall into the hands
of Oswald, and accordingly, though he still remained without any definite authority, active discussion was resumed between him and Franklin.
Early in August both believed that an understanding upon all important points had been reached.
Jay had been ill almost ever since his arrival in
Paris, and was only now recovering; Adams was
still in Holland; so that Franklin and Oswald had
had the whole matter between themselves.

Just at this time Parliament rose; and Shelburne sent Vaughan to Paris to give private assurance to Franklin that there would be no change in
policy towards America. A commission was at the
same time drawn up and sent to Oswald empowering him to treat with commissioners of the "colonies or plantations, and any body or bodies corpo-
rate or politic, or any assembly or assemblies."
This singular phraseology at once produced trouble. Jay indignantly repudiated the colonial condition imputed by this language, and resolutely
said that independence must be no item in any
treaty, but must be recognized before he would
even begin to treat. The point was discussed by
him with de Vergennes and Franklin. The French
minister at first had "objected to these general

words as not being particular enough;" but now
he changed his mind and advised not to stickle ;
for independence must be the result of the treaty,
and it was not to be expected that the effect should
precede the cause.   Franklin, with evident hesitation and reluctance,[1] gave his opinion that the
commission " would do."   Oswald then showed his
instructions, which directed him to concede "the
complete independence of the thirteen States."
Unfortunately the enabling act had not even
yet passed, so that there was some doubt as to the
power of the ministers to agree to this.   Jay's determination remained unchanged ; for he suspected
that the motives of de Vergennes were not disinterested, and thought that Franklin was hood-
winked by his French predilections.   Franklin, on
the other hand, thought that the minister wished
only to expedite the negotiation as much as possible, a matter in which he himself also was very
zealous ; for he understood the English political
situation and knew that Shelburne's tenure of
power was precarious, and that any possible successor of Shelburne would be vastly less well-disposed to the States.   This induced him to stretch
a point in order to go on with the treating.   Parliament was to meet on November 26, and unless
peace could be concluded before that time, the
chance for it thereafter would be diminished almost to the point of hopelessness.   But Adams
wrote from Holland that he also disapproved the

---

[1] Franklin's *Works*, viii. 99, 101, 150, note.

unusual form of the commission, though a commission to treat with envoys of " the United States of America " would satisfy him, as a sufficient implication of independence without an explicit preliminary acknowledgment of it.

About the middle of August Jay drew up a letter, suggesting very ingeniously that it was incompatible with the dignity of the king of England to negotiate except with an independent power ; also that an obstacle which meant everything to the States, but nothing to Great Britain, should be removed by his majesty. Franklin thought that the letter expressed too positively the resolve not to treat save upon this basis of pre-acknowledged independence. He evidently did not wish to bolt too securely the door through which he anticipated that the commissioners might in time feel obliged to withdraw. Moreover Jay thought that at this time " the doctor seemed to be much perplexed and fettered by our instructions to be guided by the advice of this court," a direction correctly supposed to have been procured by the influence of the French envoy at Philadelphia.

Jay's suspicions concerning the French minister happened now to receive opportune corroboration. On September 4th Rayneval, secretary to de Vergennes, had a long interview with Jay concerning boundaries, in which he argued strongly against the American claims to the western lands lying between the Alleghanies and the Mississippi. This touched Jay nearly, for the navigation of the Mis-

sissippi was the one object which he had especially
at heart.   Six days later the famous letter of Mar-
bois, de la Luzerne's secretary, which had been
captured *en route* from Philadelphia to de Vergennes at Paris, was put into the hands of Jay
through the instrumentality of the English cabinet.   This outlined a scheme for a secret understanding between England and France to deprive
the Americans of the Newfoundland fisheries.
This evidence seemed to prove Jay's case; yet
Franklin remained strangely unshaken by it, for
he reflected that it came from the British ministry
and was infected with suspicion by this channel.
But still another occurrence came to strengthen
Jay's conviction of some latent hostility in the
French policy, for he learned that Rayneval was
making a rapid and secret journey to London.   He
felt sure that this errand was to intimate to Shelburne that France did not incline to support the
demands of her American allies.   In the fullness
of his faith he took a courageous, very unconventional, but eminently successful step.   He persuaded Vaughan to hasten to London, and to present sundry strong arguments going to show that
it was the true policy of England to grant the demands of the States rather than to fall in with the
subtle plans of France.   He felt with regret that
he could not consult Franklin regarding this proceeding, which he undertook upon his own sole responsibility.   It put Shelburne in a singular position, as arbiter between two nations enemies of

England and allies of each other, but each ma-
nœuvring to secure its own advantage at the cost
of its friend, and to that end presuming to advise
him upon English interests. He did not ponder
long before accepting the American arguments as
the better, and deciding that the English policy
was rather to be liberal towards a kindred people than to unite with a traditional foe in curtailing their prosperity. He said to Vaughan : " Is
the new commission necessary ? " " It is," replied
Vaughan ; and his lordship at once gave orders for
making it out. Had he fallen in with the French
ideas, he would, upon the contrary, have cherished
this disagreement for a while, in order finally to
sell out a concession on this point at the price of
some such substantial matter as the fisheries or
the western lands. Forthwith Vaughan was on his
way back to Paris, accompanied by a messenger
who carried the amended document empowering
Oswald to treat with the commissioners of the
" Thirteen United States of America, viz. : New
Hampshire," etc., naming them all. " We have put
the greatest confidence, I believe, ever placed in
man, in the American commissioners. It is now
to be seen how far they or America are to be depended upon. . . . There never was such a risk
run ; I hope the public will be the gainer, else our
heads must answer for it, and deservedly." Such
were the grave and anxious words of the prime
minister.

Upon the receipt of this commission negotiations

were actively resumed, Franklin and Jay on one side, Oswald alone on the other. The old ground was gone over again. On October 5–8, both parties assented to a sketch of a treaty, which Oswald transmitted to London for consideration by the ministry. But the raising of the siege of Gibraltar, and reflection upon the probable results of the incipient estrangement between American interests and those of France and Spain, now induced the English to hope for more favorable terms in some particulars. So instead of adopting this draft they sent over Mr. Strachey, a man especially well informed concerning the disputed boundaries, to reinforce Oswald in an effort to obtain modifications on these points.

Meantime another serious difference of opinion was developed between Franklin and Jay. The influence of de Vergennes at Philadelphia had by no means been exhausted in securing colleagues for Mr. Adams. He had further desired to have the American envoys instructed that no American demands outside of independence must be allowed to interpose obstacles in the way of French purposes. In this he had been wholly successful. Of the demands which Congress had at first intended to insist upon, one after another was reduced to a mere recommendation, until at last independence alone was left as an absolute and definitive ultimatum. Moreover the closing paragraph of the instructions actually bade the envoys to maintain constant communication with their generous

ally the king of France, and in the last resort to
be governed in all matters by his advice. This ser-
vility had raised the ire of Jay almost to the point
of inducing him to refuse a post so hedged around
with humiliation. With his views concerning the
intentions of de Vergennes it now seemed to him
intolerable to jeopard American interests by placing them at the mercy of a cabinet which unmistakably, as it seemed to him, designed to sacrifice them to its own ends. Accordingly he was
for disobeying this unworthy instruction of Congress, and for conducting the negotiation in strict
secrecy as towards the French minister. But
Franklin was no less resolute on the other side.
His established and grateful confidence in de Vergennes remained unshaken, and he saw no error
in consulting the wisest, and by all proofs the best
and truest friend whom the States had ever had.
Moreover he saw that the orders of Congress were
imperative. It was a serious division. Fortunately it was soon settled by the advent of John
Adams, about the end of October. That gentleman, prompt, fearless, and suspicious, at once fell
in with Jay's views. In a long evening's talk he
apparently read Franklin a pretty severe lecture,
and certainly ranged himself very positively on
Jay's side. Franklin listened to his vehement colleague, and at the moment held his peace in his
wise way. It was true that Adams brought the
casting vote, though Franklin of course might resist, and could make his resistance effectual by com-

municating to de Vergennes all which passed, and in so doing he would be backed by the authority and orders of Congress. But he determined not to pursue this course. When next they all met for conference he turned to Jay and said: " I am of your opinion, and will go on without consulting this court." This was all that passed when thus for a second time Franklin surrendered. Nothing indicates by what motives he was influenced. Some writers suggest that he had a lurking notion that Jay's views were not altogether ill-founded; but later he declared the contrary.[1] Others fancy that he simply yielded to a majority vote. To me it seems more probable that, weighing comparative importance, he gave in to what he conceived to be the supreme necessity of advancing to a speedy conclusion; for, as has been said, he keenly appreciated that time was pressing. Parliament was to meet in a few weeks, on November 26, and it daily became more evident that if a treaty was to be made at all, it must be consummated before that date. Now, as in the question concerning the preliminary acknowledgment of independence, peace overruled all considerations of minor points.

If this was indeed his end, he achieved it, for negotiations were now zealously pushed. The important question of the western boundaries and the navigation of the Mississippi was the especial concern of Jay. Spain covertly wished to see the States worsted upon these demands, and confined

[1] Franklin's *Works*, viii. 305, 306.

between the Alleghanies and the sea; and the
Bourbon family compact influenced France to concur with the Spanish plans. But in the secret
treating Jay prevailed. The fisheries were the
peculiar affair of Adams, as the representative of
New England. France would fain have had the
States shut out from them altogether; but Adams
carried the day. Some concessions were made concerning the collection of debts owing in the States
to Englishmen, and then there remained only the
matter of indemnification to American royalists.
Upon this the fight was waged with zeal by all;
yet Franklin had the chief responsibility to bear.
For there now arose to plague him that unfortunate proposition of his for the cession of Canada
and the restoration of confiscated tory property in
the States. This encouraged the English and gave
them a sort of argument. Moreover the indemnification was "uppermost in Lord Shelburne's
mind," because, unlike other matters, it seemed a
point of honor. With what face could the ministry meet Parliament with a treaty deserting all
those who had been faithful to their king? It
was indeed a delicate position, and the English
were stubborn; but no less so was Franklin, upon
the other side. With the great province of Canada as an offset, or *quasi* fund, the States might
have assumed such an obligation, but without it,
never. Further the American commissioners reiterated the explanation often given: that Congress
had no power in the premises, for the matter lay

within the sovereign jurisdiction of each state. This argument, however, really amounted to nothing ; for if the fact was so, it behoved the states to give their agent, the Congress, any power that was necessary for making a fair treaty ; and England was not to be a loser by reason of defects in the American governmental arrangements. For a while it really seemed that the negotiation would be wrecked upon this issue, so immovable was each side. As Vaughan wrote : " If England wanted to break, she could not wish for better ground on *her* side. *You* do not break, and therefore I conclude you both sincere. But in this way I see the treaty is likely of *itself* to break."

Franklin now ingeniously counteracted his earlier imprudence by reviving an old suggestion of his, that immense claims might be preferred against England on behalf of Americans whose property had been wantonly destroyed, especially by the burning and plundering of towns, and he actually presented an article providing for such compensation, and an elaborate written paper sustaining it.[1] At last the Englishmen sought final instructions from Lord Shelburne. He replied with spirit that it should be understood that England was not yet in a position to submit to " humiliation," least of all at the hands of Americans ; but finally he so far yielded as to say that indemnification need not be absolutely an ultimatum. This settled the matter ; the negotiators who *could* yield

[1] Franklin's *Works*, viii. 218, text and note.

must yield, and they did so. A sort of compromise article was inserted: "that Congress should recommend to the state legislatures to restore the estates, rights, and properties of real British subjects." The American envoys knew that this was worthless, and the English negotiators certainly were not deceived. But the article sounded well, and gave at least a standing ground for the ministry to defend themselves.[1] On November 30 the articles were at last signed, with the stipulation that they were for the present merely preliminary and provisional, and that they should be executed as a definitive treaty only simultaneously with the execution of a treaty of peace between France and England.

The business was finished none too soon. In order to cover it the meeting of Parliament had been postponed until December 5. The danger which had been escaped, and which would not have been escaped had Franklin had a less correct ap-

---

[1] It is not without interest in this connection to remark that Franklin was very ill-disposed towards the "loyalists," having scant toleration for their choice of a party. For a man of his liberality and moderation his language concerning them was severe. He objected to calling them "loyalists," thinking "royalists" a more correct description. To indemnification of their losses by Parliament he had "no objection," for the damnatory reason that "even a hired assassin has a right to his pay from his employer." Franklin's *Works*, ix. 133. He often spoke in the like tone about these people See, for example, *Works*, ix. 70, 72. But when the war was over and the natural mildness of his disposition could resume its sway, he once at least spoke more gently of them. Ibid., 415

preciation of relative values in the negotiation, at once became apparent. The howl of condemnation swelled loud in the House of Commons; it was felt that the ministry had made not a treaty but a "capitulation." The unfortunate Shelburne was driven out of power, pursued by an angry outcry from persons altogether incapable of appreciating the sound statesmanship and the wise forecast of the future advantage of England which he had shown in preferring to give the colonies a chance to become a great, English-speaking, English-sympathizing, commercial people, rather than to feed fat the aspirations of France and Spain. These proceedings would have been good evidence, had evidence been wanting, that the American commissioners had done a brilliant piece of work. De Vergennes also added his testimony, saying: "The English have bought the peace rather than made it."

If the original instructions given to Oswald are compared with the treaty it will be found that England had conceded much; on the other hand the Americans, with no ultimatum save independence, had gained in substance all that they had dared seriously to insist upon. One would think that Franklin, Jay, and Adams had fairly won warm gratitude at the hands of their countrymen. Posterity, at least since the publication of long suppressed private papers and archives has shown what powerful occult influences were at work to thwart them, regards their achievement with unlimited admiration. But at that time a different feeling prevailed.

No sooner were the preliminary or provisional articles signed than Franklin informed de Vergennes of the fact. That minister was much surprised. He had been quietly biding his time, expecting to be invoked when the English and the Americans should find themselves stopped by that deadlock which he had done his best to bring about by his secret intimations to England. He was now astonished to learn that England had not availed herself of his astute suggestions, but had given terms which the Americans had gladly accepted. The business was all done, and the clever diplomat had not had his chance. At first he said nothing, but for a few days pondered the matter. Then on December 15th he disburdened his mind in a very sharp letter to Franklin. "I am at a loss," he wrote, "to explain your conduct and that of your colleagues on this occasion. You have concluded your preliminary articles without any communication between us, although the instructions from Congress prescribe that nothing shall be done without the participation of the king. You are about to hold out a certain hope of peace to America, without even informing yourself of the state of the negotiation on our part. You are wise and discreet, sir ; you perfectly understand what is due to propriety ; you have all your life performed your duties ; I pray you consider how you propose to fulfill those which are due to the king."

Franklin found himself in a painful position; for he could by no means deny that he had duties, or at least something very near akin to duties, to the king, imposed upon him by numerous and weighty obligations which at his request had been conferred upon him and accepted by him on behalf of the American people. The violation of the instructions of Congress gave to the secret treating too much the air of an insulting distrust, of the throwing over a friend when he had been sufficiently used; for whatever might be suspected, it could by no means be proved that de Vergennes was not still the sincere friend which he certainly long had been. This bore hard upon Franklin. The policy which in fact had been forced upon him against his will by his colleagues was now made a matter of personal reproach against him especially, because he was persistently regarded as the head and front of the commission; no European yet dreamed of considering any other American as of much consequence in any matter in which Franklin was concerned. During long years de Vergennes had been his constant and efficient adviser and assistant in many a day of trial and of stress, and Franklin believed him to be still an honest well-wisher to the States. Moreover it actually was only a very few weeks since Franklin had applied for and obtained a new loan at a time when the king was so pressed for his own needs that a lottery was projected, and bills drawn by his own officials were going to protest. All this made the secrecy which had been practiced seem almost like duplicity on Franklin's part, and he felt keenly the ill light in which he was placed. It is true that if he had known then all that we know now, his mind would have been at ease; but he did not know it, and he was seriously disturbed at the situation into which he had been brought.

But his usual skill did not desert him, and his reply was aptly framed and prompt. "Nothing," he said, "had been agreed in the preliminaries contrary to the interests of France ; and no peace is to take place between us and England till you have concluded yours. Your observation is, however, apparently just that, in not consulting you before they were signed, we have been guilty of neglecting a point of *bienséance.* But as this was not from want of respect for the king, whom we all love and honor, we hope it will be excused, and that the great work which has hitherto been so happily conducted, is so nearly brought to perfection, and is so glorious to his reign, will not be ruined by a single indiscretion of ours. And certainly the whole edifice sinks to the ground immediately if you refuse on that account to give us any further assistance. . . . It is not possible for any one to be more sensible than I am of what I and every American owe to the king for the many and great benefits and favors he has bestowed upon us. . . . *The English, I just now learn, flatter themselves they have already divided us.* I hope this little misunderstanding will, therefore, be kept a secret, and that they will find themselves totally mistaken."

This letter in a measure accomplished its soothing errand. Yet de Vergennes did not refrain from writing to de la Luzerne that "the reservation retained on our account does not save the infraction of the promise, which we have mutually made, not to sign except conjointly ; " and he said that it would be "proper that the most influential members of Congress should be informed of the very irregular conduct of their commissioners in regard to us," though "not in the tone of complaint." "I accuse no person," he added, "not even Dr. Franklin. He has yielded too easily to the bias of his colleagues, who do not pretend to recognize the rules of courtesy in regard to us. All their attentions have been taken up by the English whom they have met in Paris."

So soon as the facts were known in the States expressions of condemnation were lavished upon the commissioners by members of Congress who thought that the secrecy as towards France was an inexcusable slight to a generous and faithful ally. Livingston, as secretary for foreign affairs, wrote to the envoys, commending the treaty, but finding fault with the manner of attaining it. Jay, angered at the injustice of a reproof which belonged more especially to him, drew up an exculpatory statement. But Franklin, showing his usual good sense and moderation, sought to mitigate Jay's indignation, drew all the sting out of the document, and insisted upon leaving the vindication to time and second thoughts. For his own part Franklin not only had to take his full share of the reproaches heaped upon the commissioners for insulting France, but upon the other hand he was violently assaulted on the quite opposite ground, that he had desired to be too subservient to that power. Many persons insisted that he "favored, or did not oppose," the designs of France to rule out the States from the fisheries, and to curtail their boundaries; and that it was only due to the "firmness, sagacity, and disinterestedness" of Jay and Adams that these mischiefs were escaped.

Such were the fault-findings and criminations to which the diplomatic complexities, which it was impossible then to unravel, gave rise. Fortunately they were soon rendered mere personal and abstract disputes, of little practical consequence, by the simultaneous execution of definitive treaties by France and the United States with Great Britain on September 3, 1783. Many efforts had been made to insert additional articles, especially as to commercial matters; but they were all abortive. The establishment of peace had exhausted the capacity of the States and England to agree together; and the pressure of war being removed, they at once fell into very inimical attitudes. So the definitive treaty was substantially identical with the provisional one.

Franklin, after a while, finding that these charges of his having preferred France to his own country were being reiterated with such innuendoes as to bring his integrity into serious question, felt it necessary to appeal to his colleagues for vindication. He wrote to them a modest, manly letter,[1] and in reply received from Jay a generous testimonial,[2] and from Adams a carefully narrow acquittal.[3] The subsequent publication of Franklin's papers written at, and long before, the time of the negotiation, show that he was inclined to demand from Great Britain fully as much as any American upon either side of the ocean.

In taking leave of the subject it is interesting to know that in point of fact the secret action of the American commissioners was very nearly fraught with serious injury to France. For when the States were practically eliminated from active war by the signing of the provisional articles, five members of Shelburne's cabinet were in favor of breaking off negotiations with France, and continuing the contest with her.[4]

During the negotiation Franklin wrote to Laurens: "I have never yet known of a peace made that did not occasion a great deal of popular dis-

---

[1] *Works*, viii. 340; and see Ibid., 353.

[2] Ibid., 350.   [3] Ibid., 354.

[4] I have not endeavored to give a detailed account of this negotiation, though the narrative would be very interesting, because it seems to me that the proper place for it will be furnished by the *Life of Jay*. That volume will soon appear in this Series, and will contain a very full and accurate presentation of this entire affair, drawn from those sources which have only very recently become public, and which go far to remove former questions out of the realm of discussion.

content, clamor, and censure on both sides, . . . so that the blessing promised to peacemakers, I fancy, relates to the next world, for in this they seem to have a greater chance of being cursed." The prognostication was fulfilled. The act which gave peace to the warring nations, brought anything but good will among the American negotiators. Jay was so just, conscientious, and irreproachable a gentleman in every respect that he escaped unvexed by any personal quarrel; moreover he was not so distinguished as to have become the victim of envy and jealousy. But the antipathy previously so unhappily existing between Franklin and Adams became greatly aggravated, and their respective advocates in historical literature have not to this day reached an accord. Adams was a relentless hater, and has bequeathed bitter diatribes, which, as they can never be obliterated, can never cease to excite the ire of the admirers of Franklin. On the other side, Franklin has at least the merit of having left not a malicious line behind him. I have no mind to endeavor to apportion merits and demerits between these two great foemen, able men and true patriots both, having no room for these personalities of history, which, though retaining that kind of interest always pertaining to a feud, are really very little profitable. Perhaps, after all, the discussion would prove to be not unlike the classic one which led two knights to fight about the golden-silver shield.

Yet one dispute, which has been long waged,

no longer admits of doubt.   The suspicions of the good faith of de Vergennes which Jay first entertained, which Adams adopted, and which Franklin rejected, were undoubtedly correct.   As the years go by and collections of private papers and of hitherto suppressed public archives find their way to the light, the accumulated evidence to this effect has become overwhelming.   Such being the case, it must be admitted that the vital merit in the conduct of this difficult negotiation rests with Jay; that Adams has the credit belonging to one who accepts a correct view when presented to him ; and that Franklin did more wisely than he knew in twice assenting to a course which seemed to him based upon erroneous beliefs.

There is abundant evidence that from the very outset Franklin was not less resolute than was Adams about the fisheries; and that he was in perfect accord with Jay about the western boundaries and the Mississippi; though Adams and Jay did most of the talking concerning these subjects, respectively.   When it came to the even more difficult matter of the royalists, Franklin in turn took the laboring oar.   So far therefore as the three cardinal points of the negotiation were concerned honors were very evenly divided.   But the value of Franklin's contribution to the treating is not to be measured either by his backwardness in supporting Jay in certain points, or by his firm attitude about boundaries, royalists, and fisheries.   All these things he had outlined and arranged with

Oswald at an early stage in the negotiating. Later he fell seriously ill and was for a long while in no fit condition for work. Yet the treaty seemed to be made under his auspices. In reading the great quantity of diaries and correspondence which relate to the transactions, many a passage indicates the sense of respect with which he was looked up to. The high opinion entertained of his ability, integrity, and fair-mindedness influenced very powerfully the minds of the English ministry and their envoys. " I am disposed," said Shelburne, " to expect everything from Dr. Franklin's comprehensive understanding and character." The like feeling, strengthened by personal confidence and regard, went far to keep de Vergennes from untimely intermeddling and from advancing embarrassing claims of supervision. Altogether, it was again the case that Franklin's prestige in Europe was invaluable to America, and it is certainly true that beneath its protection Jay and Adams were able to do their work to advantage. Had they stood alone they would have encountered difficulties which would have seriously curtailed their efforts.[1] It is truth and not theory that Franklin's mere name and presence were sufficient to balance the scale against the abilities and the zeal of both his coadjutors.

It seems hardly necessary to endeavor to palliate Franklin's error in failing to detect the dupli-

[1] See, for example, Franklin's *Works*, viii 29, 67, note, 69, 70, 77, 109, 112, note, 133, note, 260.

city of de Vergennes. On the contrary, it would
give a less agreeable idea of him had he been
ready to believe so ill of an old and tried friend.
For years Franklin had been the medium through
whom had passed countless benefits from France to
the States, benefits of which many had. been costly
and inconvenient for the giver; he had been treated
with high consideration at this court, when no
other court in all Europe would even receive an
American ambassador; he had enjoyed every possible token of esteem and confidence both personally
and in his official capacity; he had ever found
fair words backed by no less fair deeds. In short,
the vast mass of visible evidence seemed to him
to lie, and in fact did lie, all on one side. On
September 13, 1781, writing to the president of
Congress, he said that de Vergennes had just read
to him a copy of the instructions prepared by Congress for the commissioners, and that the minister
" expressed his satisfaction with the unreserved
confidence placed in his court by the Congress, assuring me that they would never have cause to regret it, for that the king had the honor of the
United States at heart, as well as their welfare
and independence. Indeed, this has been already
manifested in the negotiations relative to the pleni-
potentiaries; and I have already had so much experience of his majesty's goodness to us, in the
aids afforded us from time to time, and by the sincerity of this upright and able minister, who never
promised me anything that he did not punctually

perform, that I cannot but think the confidence
well and judiciously placed, and that it will have
happy effects." Every event in the history of
many years made it natural and right for Franklin
to feel in this way; and it surely was no cause for
distrust that de Vergennes had had the interest of
France in mind as an original motive for aiding
America, when throughout the war Franklin had
witnessed France straining every nerve and taxing
every resource to aid her ally, in perfect sincerity;
and when also, upon the suggestion of negotiations,
he had just seen de Vergennes adhere rigidly to
his word to do no treating save collaterally with
the Americans, and refuse to take advantage of
Grenville's efforts to reach the Americans through
the French minister. Even though de Vergennes
had disapproved the delay caused by Jay's objection to the form of the commission, still he had
honorably stayed his own negotiation until that
matter was favorably settled. Early in the negotiations Grenville said to Franklin that the States
owed no gratitude to France, since she had in fact
only promoted her own interests. The remark excited Franklin's indignation, and he says: " I told
him I was so strongly impressed with the kind assistance afforded us by France in our distress, and
the generous and noble manner in which it was
granted, without extracting or stipulating for a single privilege or particular advantage to herself in
our commerce, or otherwise, that I could never suffer myself to think of such reasonings for lessening

the obligation, and I hoped, and indeed did not doubt, but my countrymen were all of the same sentiments." The words do his heart none the less honor, because it has been since discovered that his confidence was too implicit. In truth de Vergennes had been extremely scrupulous and delicate throughout, in all matters which could fall within the observation of the Americans. At the outset he said to Franklin: the English "want to treat with us for you; but this the king will not agree to. He thinks it not consistent with the dignity of your state. You will treat for yourselves; and every one of the powers at war will make its own treaty. All that is necessary is that the treaties go hand in hand, and are all signed on the same day." Thus, to one who could believe de Vergennes, everything seemed fair and sincere, and Franklin at least had a right to believe de Vergennes.

Furthermore it was not until negotiations actually began that the previous condition of French relationship, as Franklin had well known it for many years, underwent a sudden and complete change. Then at last were presented new temptations before which friendship and good faith could not stand, and each nation, keeping a decorous exterior, anxiously studied its own advantage. It was the trying hour when the spoils were to be divided. The States themselves preferred the profit of their enemy England to that of their half-friend Spain. Franklin did not appreciate this quick turning of the kaleidoscope, with the instant change of all the previous political proximities; in view of his age, his infirmities, his recent experience in France, and his habitual generous faith in his fellow-men, this failure should give rise neither to surprise nor censure.

In 1782, after signing the preliminary articles, Franklin a second time sent to Congress his resignation. He received no reply to this communication, and again, therefore, after the execution of the definitive treaty, he renewed his request to be relieved. But still Congress delayed. They wished to enter into commercial treaties with the European nations, and in spite of the rebukes which their chairman of the committee for foreign affairs had administered to Franklin, Jay, and Adams, they now showed no readiness to remove these gentlemen from the diplomatic service. Franklin accordingly remained in Paris, probably with no great reluctance, for he was attached to the place and the people, and his affection was warmly returned. It was a light labor to conduct the negotiations for the desired commercial treaties. Sweden, Denmark, Portugal, and even Morocco, all made advances to him almost immediately after the signing of the treaty of peace. For the most part he had the gratification of success. His last official act, just before his departure from Paris, was the signature of a treaty with Prussia, in which it was

agreed to abolish privateering,[1] and to hold private
property by land and sea secure from destruction
in time of war.   It was pleasant thus to be introducing his country to the handshaking, so to speak,
of the old established nations of the world.   So his
life glided on agreeably.   He was recognized as one
of the most illustrious men living ; and to enjoy
such a reputation in Paris in those days, especially
when it was supplemented by personal popularity,
was to find one's self in the enjoyment of all which
the world could bestow to make delightful days.

In August, 1784, Jefferson arrived to assist in
the commercial business.   But it was not until
March, 1785, that Congress at last voted that
Franklin might " return to America as soon as convenient," and that Jefferson should succeed him as
minister at the French court.   Jefferson has borne
good testimony to Franklin's situation, as he observed it.   A few years later, in February, 1791,
he wrote :   " I can only therefore testify in general that there appeared to me more respect and
veneration attached to the character of Dr. Franklin in France, than to that of any other person in
the same country, foreign or native.   I had opportunities of knowing particularly how far these sentiments were felt by the foreign ambassadors and
ministers at the court of Versailles. . . . I found
the ministers of France equally impressed with the
talents and integrity of Dr. Franklin.   The Count
de Vergennes particularly gave me repeated and

[1] See letter to Hartley, Franklin's *Works*, viii. 287.

unequivocal demonstrations of his entire confidence in him." When Jefferson was asked : " C'est vous, Monsieur, qui remplace le Docteur Franklin ?" he used to reply : " No one can replace him, sir ; I am only his successor ; " and we may be sure that the Frenchmen appreciated and fully agreed with an expression of courtesy which chimed so well with their own customs of speech. Later, in 1818, Jefferson wrote an interesting letter concerning the calumnies from which Franklin's reputation still suffered : —

" Dr. Franklin had many political enemies, as every character must which, with decision enough to have opinions, has energy and talent to give them effect on the feelings of the adversary opinion. These enmities were chiefly in Pennsylvania and Massachusetts. In the former they were merely of the proprietary party. In the latter they did not commence till the Revolution, and then sprung chiefly from personal animosities, which, spreading by little and little, became at length of some extent. Dr. Lee was his principal calumniator, a man of much malignity, who, besides enlisting his whole family in the same hostility, was enabled, as the agent of Massachusetts with the British government, to infuse it into that State with considerable effect. Mr. Izard, the doctor's enemy also, but from a pecuniary transaction, never countenanced these charges against him. Mr. Jay, Silas Deane, Mr. Laurens, his colleagues also, ever maintained towards him unlimited confidence and respect. That he would have waived the formal recognition of our independence, I never heard on any authority worthy notice. As to the fisheries, England was urgent to retain them exclusively, France neutral, and I believe that, had they ultimately been made a *sine quâ non,* our commissioners (Mr. Adams excepted) would have relinquished them rather than have broken off the treaty. To Mr. Adams's perseverance alone, on that point, I have always understood we were indebted for their reservation. As to the charge of subservience to France, besides the evidence of his friendly colleagues before named, two years of my own service with him at Paris, daily visits, and the most friendly and confidential conversation, convince me it had not a shadow of foundation. He possessed the confidence of that government in the highest degree, insomuch that it may truly be said that they were more under his influence than he under theirs. The fact is that his temper was so amiable and conciliatory, his conduct so rational, never urging impossibilities, or even things unreasonably inconvenient to them, in short so moderate and attentive to their difficulties, as well as our own, that what his enemies called subserviency I saw was only that reasonable disposition which, sensible that advantages are not all to be on one side, yielding what is just and liberal, is the more certain of obtaining liberality and justice. Mutual confidence produces of course mutual influence, and this was all which subsisted between Dr. Franklin and the government of France." [1]

When at last, in the summer of 1785, Franklin took his farewell of the much-loved land of France, the distinguished attentions which he received left no doubt of the admiration in which he was held. Indeed, many persons pressed him to remain in

[1] Jefferson's *Works,* vii. 108.

France, and three offered him homes in their own families, telling him that not even in America could he expect esteem and love so unalloyed as he enjoyed in France, and warning him also that he might not survive the voyage. But he said: "The desire of spending the little remainder of life with my family is so strong as to determine me to try at least whether I can bear the motion of the ship. If not, I must get them to set me ashore somewhere in the Channel and content myself to die in Europe." When the day of departure from Passy came "it seemed," said Jefferson, "as if the village had lost its patriarch." His infirmities rendered the motion of a carriage painful to him, and the king therefore placed at his disposal one of the queen's litters, which bore him by easy stages to the sea coast. He carried with him the customary complimentary portrait of the king; but it was far beyond the ordinary magnificence, for it was framed in a double circle of four hundred and eight diamonds, and was of unusual cost and beauty. On July 18 he arrived at Havre, and crossed the Channel to take ship at Portsmouth. The British government offset the discourtesy with which it was irritating Mr. Adams by ordering that the effects of Dr. Franklin's party should be exempt from the usual examination at the custom house. His old friend, the Bishop of St. Asaph, "America's constant friend," came to see him. So also did his tory son, the ex-governor of New Jersey, with whom a sort of reconciliation had been patched up. He sailed with Captain, afterward Commodore, Truxton, who found him a most agreeable companion.

Of all things in the world a sea voyage most induces to utter idleness, and it is a striking proof of the mental industry of this aged man that during the seven weeks of this summer passage across the Atlantic he wrote three essays, which remain among his best. But he never in his life found a few weeks in which his mind was relieved from enforced reflection upon affairs of business that he did not take his pen in hand for voluntary tasks. During the last eighteen months of his life in Paris all the social distractions incident to his distinguished position had not prevented his writing some of the best papers which he has bequeathed to literature.

CHAPTER XV.

On September 12, 1785, the ship brought Franklin into Delaware Bay, and the next morning he rejoiced to find himself "in full view of dear Philadelphia." A multitude, filling the air with huzzas of salutation, greeted his landing and escorted him to his door. Private welcomes and public addresses poured in upon him. His health had been much improved by the sea air and rest, and he rejoiced, as his foot touched the streets of the town which after all his wanderings was his home, to feel himself by no means yet a worn-out man, though in fact he had seventy-nine years of a busy life behind him. His fellow-citizens evidently thought that the reservoir which had been so bountiful could not yet be near exhaustion, and were resolved to continue their copious draughts upon it. They at once elected him to the State Council, of which he was made President; and, as he said, "I had not firmness enough to resist the unanimous desire of my country folks; and I find myself harnessed again in their service for another year. They engrossed the prime of my life. They have eaten my flesh,

and seem resolved now to pick my bones." A visible and a natural pleasure lurks in the words; old
age finds nothing sweeter than a tribute to the
freshness of its powers; and especially Franklin
saw in this honor a vindication against his malign-
ers. From it he understood that, however some individuals might indulge in dislike and distrust, the
overwhelming mass of his fellow-citizens esteemed
him as highly as he could wish. The distinction,
however, cost posterity an unwelcome price, for it
prevented further work on the autobiography, which
otherwise would probably have been finished.[1]

He came into office as a peacemaker amid warring factions, and in the fulfillment of his functions
gave such satisfaction that in 1786 he was unanimously reëlected; and the like high compliment
was paid him again in the autumn of 1787. It was
like Washington and the presidency : so long as he
would consent to accept the office, no other candidate was thought of. He also took substantially
the same course which had been taken by Washington as commander-in-chief concerning his pay ;
for he devoted his whole salary to public uses. He
had the good fortune to be able to carry out his
somewhat romantic, and for most persons impracticable, theory in this respect, because his private affairs were prospering. His investments in real estate in Philadelphia had risen greatly in value and
in their income-producing capacity since the war,
and he was now at least comfortably endowed with
worldly goods.

[1] Franklin's *Works*, ix. 459.

He still continued to ply his pen, and the just but annoying complaints which came from Great Britain, that English creditors could not collect their *ante-bellum* debts from their American debtors, stimulated him to a bit of humor at which his own countrymen at least were sure to laugh, however little droll it might seem to Englishmen, who reasonably preferred good dollars to good jokes. "We may all remember the time," he wrote, "when our mother country, as a mark of her parental tenderness, emptied her gaols into our habitations, '*for the better peopling*,' as she expressed it, '*of the colonies.*' It is certain that no due returns have yet been made for these valuable consignments. We are therefore much in her debt on that account; and as she is of late clamorous for the payment of all we owe her, and some of our debts are of a kind not so easily discharged, I am for doing, however, what is in our power. It will show our good will as to the rest. The felons she planted among us have produced such an amazing increase that we are now enabled to make ample remittance in the same commodity," etc., etc.

Nevertheless these English assaults nettled him not a little; and further he dreaded their possible influence in the rest of Europe outside of England. The English newspapers teemed with accounts of the general demoralization and disintegration of the States; it was said that they had found their ruin in their independence, and the unwillingness of American merchants to pay their debts was in one paragraph attributed to their dishonesty, and in the next to the hopeless poverty which was described as having possession of the country. It was in good truth what Mr. John Fiske has called it, "The Critical Period of American History." But Franklin was at once too patriotic and too sanguine to admit that matters were so bad as they seemed. His insight into the situation proved correct, and the outcome very soon showed that the elements of prosperity which he saw were substantial, and not merely the phantoms of a hopeful lover of his country. During these years of humiliation and discouragement he was busy in writing to many friends in England and in France very manly and spirited letters, declaring the condition of things in the States to be by no means so ill as it was represented. Industry had revived, values were advancing, the country was growing, welfare and success were within the grasp of the people. These things he said repeatedly and emphatically, and in a short time the accuracy of his knowledge had to be admitted by all, whether friends or enemies. He would not even admit that the failure to arrange a treaty of commerce with England was the serious misfortune which most Americans conceived it to be. In his usual gallant fashion of facing down untoward circumstances he alleged again and again that the lack of such a treaty was worse for Great Britain than for the States. If British merchants could stand it, American merchants, he avowed, could stand it much better. He was for showing no more concern about it. " Let the merchants on both sides treat with one another. *Laissez les faire*," he said. The presence of such a temper in the States, in so prominent a man, was of infinite service in those troubled years of unsettled, novel, and difficult conditions.

Dr. Franklin was not at first elected a member of the deputation from Pennsylvania to the convention which framed the Constitution of the United States. But in May, 1787, he was added in order that, in the possible absence of General Washington, there might be some one whom all could agree in calling to the chair.[1] It was fortunate that even an unnecessary reason led to his being chosen, for all future generations would have felt that an unpardonable void had been left in that famous assemblage, had the sage of America not been there. Certainly the " fitness of things," the historical picturesqueness of the event, imperatively demanded Dr. Franklin's venerable figure in the constitutional convention of the United States of America.

As between the two theories of government which divided that body, Franklin ranged himself with the party opposed to a strong and centralized government endowed with many functions and much power.[2] The simplest government seemed to him

[1] Parton's *Life of Franklin*, ii. 565.

[2] But later he remarked : " Though there is a general dread of giving too much power to our *governors*, I think we are more in danger from too little obedience in the *governed*."

the best; and he substantially gave in his allegiance to those democratic ideas which afterward constituted the doctrines of the Jeffersonian school in American politics. It was natural that he should do so; he was a cheerful optimist all his life long, and few men have ever so trusted human kind as he did; so now he believed that the people could take care of themselves, as indeed the history of the past few years and the character of the population of the States at that time indicated that they could. He attended regularly all the sessions, and gave his opinions freely; but they are only dimly revealed in the half-light which enfolds in such lamentable obscurity the debates of that interesting body. What little is known can be briefly stated.

The same theory which he was practicing concerning his own salary he wished to see introduced as an article of the Constitution. The President, he thought, should receive no salary. Honor was enough reward; a place which gave both honor and profit offered too corrupting a temptation, and instead of remaining a source of generous aspiration to " the wise and moderate, the lovers of peace and good order, the men fittest for the trust," it would be scrambled for by " the bold and the violent, the men of strong passions and indefatigable activity in their selfish pursuits." [1] In our day such a notion and such arguments would be quickly sneered out of the de-

[1] Franklin's *Works*, ix. 418. See, also, letter to Bishop of St. Asaph, Franklin's *Works*, viii. 270.

bate; but they were in keeping with the spirit of that era when the first generation which for ages had dared to contemplate popular government was carried away by the earliest romantic fervor of inexperienced speculation.

It is familiar that the gravest question which perplexed the convention was whether the larger and the smaller states should stand upon terms of equality, or whether some proportion should be established. After a discussion, recurred to at intervals during many weeks, had failed to develop any satisfactory solution of this problem, pregnant with failure, Franklin moved that the daily proceedings should be opened with prayer.[1] But Hamilton said that a resort to prayer would indicate to the people that the convention had reached a desperate pass; and either this or some other reason was so potent that scarcely any one voted yea on the motion. What could be more singular than to see the skeptical Franklin and the religious Hamilton thus opposed upon this question! Franklin next suggested a compromise: an equal number of delegates for all states; an equal vote for all states upon all questions respecting the authority or sovereignty of a state, and upon appointments and confirmations; but votes to be apportioned according to the populations of the states respectively upon all bills for raising and spending money. He was in favor of a single legislative chamber, and his plan was designed to be applied

---

[1] Franklin's *Works*, ix. 428.

to such a system. Its feasibility would probably have been defeated through the inevitable complexity which would have attended upon it in practice.[1] Nevertheless it was a suggestion in the right direction, and contained the kernel of that compromise which later on he developed into the system of an equal representation in the Senate, and a proportionate one in the House. This happy scheme may be fairly said to have saved the Union.

Upon the matter of suffrage Franklin voted against limiting it to freeholders, because to do so would be to " depress the virtue and public spirit of our common people," for whose patriotism and good sense he expressed high esteem. He opposed the requirement of a residence of fourteen years as a preliminary to naturalization, thinking four years a sufficient period. He thought that the President should hold office for seven years, and should not be eligible for a second term; he should be subject to impeachment, since otherwise in case of wrongdoing recourse could be had only to revolution or assassination; he should not have the power of an absolute veto.

When at last the long discussions were over and the final draft was prepared, Franklin found himself in the position in which also were most of his associates, disapproving certain parts, but thinking adoption of the whole far better than rejection. He was wise enough and singular enough to admit

---

[1] One becomes quite convinced of this upon reading his presentation of his scheme. *Works*, ix. 423 ; see, also, Ibid., 395.

that he was not infallibly right. "Nothing in human affairs and schemes is perfect," he said, "and perhaps that is the case of our opinions." He made an excellent speech,[1] urging that at the close of their deliberations all should harmonize, sink their small differences of opinion, and send the document before the people with the prestige of their unanimous approbation. While the last members were signing, relates Madison, "Dr. Franklin, looking toward the president's chair, at the back of which a rising sun happened to be painted, observed to a few members near him that painters had found it difficult to distinguish in their art a rising from a setting sun. 'I have,' he said, 'often and often in the course of the session, and the vicissitudes of my hopes and fears as to its issue, looked at that behind the president without being able to tell whether it was rising or setting; but now at length I have the happiness to know that it is a rising and not a setting sun.'"

He did what he could to secure the adoption of the instrument by the people; and when that end was happily achieved he joined his voice to the unanimous cry with which the American nation nominated George Washington as the only possible candidate for the presidency. He said: "General Washington is the man whom all our eyes are fixed on for President, and what little influence I may have is devoted to him."

It was about the time of the election that he him-

[1] Franklin's *Works*, ix. 431.

self took his farewell of public life. The third year of his incumbency in the office of president of Pennsylvania expired in the autumn of 1788, and his physical condition precluded all idea of further official labors. Nature could not have committed such an incongruity, such a sin against æsthetic justice, as not to preserve Benjamin Franklin's life long enough to enable him to see the United States fairly launched as a real nation, with an established government and a sound constitution giving promise of a vigorous career. But evidently with this boon the patience of nature was exhausted; for Franklin's infirmities now increased upon him terribly. He endured extreme pain during periods steadily increasing in length and recurring at ever-shortening intervals. He bore his suffering, which too often became agony, with heroic fortitude; but it was evident that even his strong frame could not long hold out against the debilitating effects of his merciless disease. Yet while it racked his body it fortunately spared his mental faculties; and indeed so lively did his interest in affairs remain that it seemed to require these physical reminders to show him how old he was; save for his body, he was still a man in his prime. He once said: " I often hear persons, whom I knew when children, called *old* Mr. Such-a-one, to distinguish them from their sons, now men grown and in business; so that by living twelve years beyond David's period, *I seem to have intruded myself into the company of posterity, when I ought to have*

been abed and asleep," — words which should take
their place among the fine sayings of the ages.

He was courageous and cheerful. In November,
1788, he wrote: "You kindly inquire after my
health. I have not of late much reason to boast of
it. People that will live a long life and drink to
the bottom of the cup must expect to meet with
some of the dregs. However, when I consider how
many more terrible maladies the human body is
liable to, I think myself well off that I have only
three incurable ones: the gout, the stone, and old
age; and, those notwithstanding, I enjoy many
comfortable intervals, in which I forget all my ills,
and amuse myself in reading or writing, or in conversation with friends, joking, laughing, and telling merry stories, as when you first knew me, a
young man about fifty." [1] He does not seem to
have taken undue credit to himself; there is no
querulousness, or egotism, or senility in his letters, but a delightful tranquillity of spirit. His
sister wrote to him that the Boston newspapers
often had matter in his honor. "I am obliged to
them," he wrote; "on the other hand, some of our
papers here are endeavoring to disgrace me. I
take no notice. My friends defend me. I have
long been accustomed to receive more blame, as
well as more praise, than I have deserved. It is
the lot of every public man, and I leave one account to balance the other." So serene was the

[1] He habitually wrote in this vein· see, for example, *Works*,
ix. 266, 283, and *passim*.

aged philosopher, a *real* philosopher, not one who, having played a part in life, was to be betrayed in the weakness and irritability of old age. He felt none of the mental weariness which years so often bring. He was by no means tired of life and affairs in this world, yet he wrote in a characteristic vein to the Bishop of St. Asaph : " The course of nature must soon put a period to my present mode of existence. This I shall submit to with the less regret, as, having seen during a long life a good deal of this world, I feel a growing curiosity to be acquainted with some other." It was characteristic that in these closing days it was the progress of mankind in knowledge and welfare which especially absorbed his thoughts. When he reflected on the great strides that were making he said that he almost wished that it had been his destiny to be born two or three centuries later. He was one of the few men who has left on record his willingness to live his life over again, even though he should not be allowed the privilege of "correcting in the second edition the errors of the first."

The French Revolution excited his profoundest interest. At first he said that he saw " nothing singular in all this, but on the contrary what might naturally be expected. The French have served an apprenticeship to liberty in this country, and now that they are out of their time they have set up for themselves." [1] He expressed his hope

that "the fire of liberty, . . . spreading itself over
Europe, would act upon the inestimable rights of
man as common fire does upon gold : purify without destroying them ; so that a lover of liberty may
find *a country* in any part of Christendom." The
language had an unusual smack of the French revolutionary slang, in which he seems in no other instance to have indulged. But as the fury swelled
his earlier sympathies became merged in a painful
anxiety concerning the fate of his many good old
friends.

Franklin's last act was a memorial addressed to
Congress, signed by him in his capacity as president of the abolition society, and praying that
body : " That you will devise means for removing
this inconsistency from the character of the American people ; that you will promote mercy and justice towards this distressed race ; and that you will
step to the very verge of the power vested in you
for discouraging every species of traffic in the persons of our fellow-men." He had always spoken
of slavery with the strongest condemnation, and
branded the slave-trade as " abominable," a "dia-
bolical commerce," and a " crime."

A large part of the last year or two of his life
was passed by Franklin in his bed. At times
when his dreadful suffering seemed to become intolerable, it was quelled, so far as possible, by
opium. But at intervals it left him, and still whenever he thus got a respite for a few days he was
again at work. It was in such an interval that he

wrote his paper condemning the liberty, which was becoming the license, of the press. If the law permitted this sort of thing, he said, then it should restore also the liberty of the cudgel. The paper is not altogether antiquated, nor the idea altogether bad!

It was even so late as March 23, 1790, that he wrote the humorous rejoinder to the pro-slavery speech delivered in Congress by Jackson of Georgia. But the end was close at hand; and when this brilliant satire was composed, there lacked but a few days of the allotted term when that rare humor was to be stilled forever, and that broad philanthropy was to cease from the toil in which it had never tired alike for the free and the oppressed.

On April 12, 1790, a pain in the chest and difficulty of breathing, which had been giving him much trouble, ceased for a short while, and he insisted upon getting up in order to have his bed re-made; for he wished to "die in a decent manner." His daughter expressed the conventional wish that he might yet recover and live many years. "I hope not," he replied. Soon afterward the pain returned, and he was advised to change his position, so that he could breathe more easily. "A dying man can do nothing easy," he said; and these are the last words which he is known to have uttered. Soon afterward he sank into a lethargy, and so remained until at eleven o'clock, P. M., on April 17, 1790, he died.

A great procession and a concourse of citizens

escorted his funeral, and Congress voted to "wear
the customary badge of mourning for one month."
The bits of crape were all very well, a conventional, insignificant tribute; but unfortunately the
account of the country, or at least of Congress as
representing the country, did not stand very honorably, to say nothing of generously, with one of
its oldest, most faithful, and most useful servants.[1]
Again and again Franklin had asked for some
modest office, some slight opening, for his grandson, Temple Franklin. The young man's plans
and prospects in life had all been sacrificed to the
service of Franklin as his secretary, which was in
fact the service of the country; yet he had never
been able to collect even the ordinary salary pertaining to such a position. Throughout a long life
of public service, often costly to himself in his own
affairs, Franklin had never asked any other favor
than this, which after all was rather compensation than favor, and this was never given to him.
When one reflects how such offices are demanded
and awarded in these days, one hardly knows
whether to be more ashamed of the present or of
the past. But this was not all nor even the worst;
for Franklin's repeated efforts to get his own accounts with the government audited and settled
never met with any response. It needed only that

[1] One of the most painful letters to read which our annals
contain is that written by Franklin to Charles Thomson, secretary
of Congress, November 29, 1788, *Works*, viii. 26, 30. It is an
arraignment which humiliates the descendants of the members of
that body.

Congress should appoint a competent accountant to examine and report. Before leaving France Franklin had begged for this act of simple, business-like justice, which it was the duty of Congress to initiate without solicitation; he had the fate of the "poor unhappy Deane" before his eyes, to make him uncomfortable, but in this respect he was treated no better than that misused man. After his return home he continued his urgency during his last years, not wishing to die leaving malignant enemies behind him, and accounts open which he could no longer explain and elucidate. Indeed, stories were already circulating that he was "greatly indebted to the United States for large sums that had been put into [his] hands, and that [he] avoided a settlement;" yet this request was still, with unpardonable disregard of decency and duty, utterly ignored. He never could get the business attended to, and Benjamin Franklin actually could not extort from an indifferent Congress the small satisfaction of having his accounts passed. The consequence was that when he died the United States appeared his debtor, and never extricated itself from that painful position.[1] It was only in this matter that he ever showed the slightest anxiety concerning his reputation with posterity. He wanted to leave the name of an honest man ; but otherwise he never was at the trouble of preparing a line to justify any of his actions, therein differing from many of his contemporaries.

[1] Parton's *Life of Franklin*, ii. 596.

France showed a livelier affection and warmer appreciation toward the great dead than did his own countrymen. At the opening of the National Assembly, June 11, 1790, Mirabeau delivered an impassioned eulogy in the rhetorical French fashion ; and the motion to wear mourning for three days was carried by acclamation. The president of that body, M. Siéyes, was instructed to communicate the resolution to Washington. At the celebration of the municipality of Paris the citizens generally wore a mourning badge ; and the grain market, where the oration was delivered, was draped in black. The Academy of Sciences of course did formal honor to his memory, as did likewise the revolutionary clubs. A street at what was in his day Passy, but is now included in Paris, near the Trocadéro, perpetuates by his name the admiration which France felt for him.

Among illustrious Americans Franklin stands preëminent in the interest which is aroused by a study of his character, his mind, and his career. One becomes attached to him, bids him farewell with regret, and feels that for such as he the longest span of life is all too short. Even though dead, he attracts a personal regard which renders easily intelligible the profound affection which so many men felt for him while living. It may be doubted whether any one man ever had so many, such constant, and such firm friends as in three different nations formed about him a veritable host. In the

States and in France he was loved, and as he grew into old age he was revered, not by those who heard of him only, but most warmly by those who best knew him. Even in England, where for years he was the arch-rebel of all America, he was generally held in respect and esteem, and had many constant friends whose confidence no events could shake. It is true, of course, that he had also his detractors, with most of whom the reader has already made acquaintance. In Pennsylvania the proprietary party cherished an animosity which still survives against his memory, but which does not extend far beyond those who take it as an inheritance. It does him no discredit with persons who understand its source. In New England a loyalty to those famous New Englanders, John Adams and Samuel Adams, seems to involve in the minds of some persons a depreciation of Franklin. In English historical literature the patriotic instinct stands in the way of giving Franklin quite his full due of praise. But the faults and defects of character and conduct which are urged against him appear little more than the expression of personal ill-will, when they are compared with the affection and the admiration given to him in liberal measure by the great mass of mankind both in the generations which knew him as a living contemporary and in those which hear of him only as one of the figures of history. It is not worth while to deify him, or to speak with extravagant reverence, as if he had neither faults nor limitations. Yet it seems ungracious to recall these concerning one who did for his fellow-men so much as Franklin did. Moral, intellectual, and material boons he conferred in such abundance that few such benefactors of the race can be named, though one should survey all the ages. A man of a greater humanity never lived; and the quality which stood Abou Ben Adhem in good stead should suffice to save Franklin from human criticism. He not only loved his kind, but he also trusted them with an implicit confidence, reassuring if not extraordinary in an observer of his shrewdness and experience. Democrats of the revolutionary school in France and of the Jeffersonian school in the United States have preached an exaggerated gospel of the people, but their words are the dubious ones of fanatics or politicians. Franklin was of a different kind, and had a more genuine and more generous faith in man than the greatest democrat in politics who ever lived.

Franklin's inborn ambition was the noblest of all ambitions : to be of practical use to the multitude of men. The chief motive of his life was to promote the welfare of mankind. Every moment which he could snatch from enforced occupations was devoted to doing, devising, or suggesting something advantageous more or less generally to men. His detractors have given a bad, but also a false coloring to this trait. They say that the spirit of all that he did and taught was sordid, that the motives and purposes which he set before men were selfish, that his messages spoken through the mouth

of Poor Richard inculcated no higher objects in
life than money-getting. This is an utterly unfair
form of stating the case. Franklin was a great
moralist: though he did not believe in the Christian religion according to the strait-laced orthodox
view, he believed in the virtues which that religion
embodies; and he was not only often a zealous
preacher, but in the main a consistent exemplar
of them. Perhaps he did not rest them upon precisely the same basis upon which the Christian
preacher does, but at least he put them on a basis
upon which they could stand firm. In such matters, however, one may easily make mistakes, breed
ill blood, and do harm; and his wisdom and good
sense soon led him to put forth his chief efforts
and to display especial earnestness and constancy
in promoting the well-being of all men. It was an
object sufficiently noble, one would think, worthy
of the greatest brain and the largest heart, and
having certain very commendable traits in the way
of practicability and substantial possibilities. His
desire was to see the community prosperous, comfortable, happy, advancing in the accumulation of
money and of all physical goods, but not to the
point of luxury; it was by no means the pile of
dollars which was his end, and he did not care to
see many men rich, but rather to see all men well
to do. He was perfectly right in thinking that
virtuous living has the best prospects in a well-to-
do society. He gave liberally of his own means
and induced others to give, and promoted in pro-

portion to the ability of the community a surprising number of public and *quasi* public enterprises;
and always the fireside of the poor man was as
much in his thought as the benefit of the richer
circle. Fair dealing and kindliness, prudence and
economy in order to procure the comforts and sim-
pler luxuries of life, reading and knowledge for
those uses which wisdom subserves, constituted the
real essence of his teaching. His inventive genius was ever at work devising methods of making
daily life more agreeable, comfortable, and wholesome for all who have to live. In a word, the service of his fellow-men was his constant aim; and
he so served them that those public official functions which are euphemistically called " public services" seemed in his case almost an interruption of
the more direct and far-reaching services which he
was intent upon rendering to all civilized peoples.
Extreme religionists may audaciously fancy that
the judgment of God upon Franklin may be severe; but it would be gross disloyalty for his own
kind to charge that his influence has been ignobly
material.

As a patriot none surpassed him. Again it was
the love of the people that induced this feeling,
which grew from no theory as to forms of government, no abstractions and doctrines about " the
rights of man." He began by espousing the cause
of the people of the Province of Pennsylvania
against proprietary despotism, and for many years
he was a patriot in his colony, before the great

issue against England made patriotism common. His patriotism had not root in any revolutionary element in his temper, but was the inevitable outcome of his fair-mindedness. That which was unfair as between man and man first aroused his ire against the grinding proprietaries; and afterward it was the unfairness of taxation without representation which especially incensed him; for an intellect of the breadth and clearness of his sees and loves justice above all things. During the struggle of the States no man was more hearty in the cause than Franklin; and the depth of feeling shown in his letters, simple and unrhetorical as they are, is impressive. All that he had he gave. What also strikes the reader of his writings is the broad national spirit which he manifested. He had an immense respect for the dignity of America; he was perhaps fortunately saved from disillusionment by his distance from home. But be this as it may, the way in which he felt and therefore genuinely talked about his nation and his country was not without its moral effect in Europe.

Intellectually there are few men who are Franklin's peers in all the ages and nations. He covered, and covered well, vast ground. The reputation of doing and knowing various unrelated things is wont to bring suspicion of perfunctoriness; but the ideal of the human intellect is an understanding to which all knowledge and all activity are germane. There have been a few, very few minds which have approximated toward this ideal, and among them

Franklin's is prominent. He was one of the most distinguished scientists who have ever lived. Bancroft calls him "the greatest diplomatist of his century." [1] His ingenious and useful devices and inventions were very numerous. He possessed a masterly shrewdness in business and practical affairs. He was a profound thinker and preacher in morals and on the conduct of life ; so that with the exception of the founders of great religions it would be difficult to name any persons who have more extensively influenced the ideas, motives, and habits of life of men. He was one of the most, perhaps the most agreeable conversationist of his age. He was a rare wit and humorist, and in an age when "American humor" was still unborn, amid contemporaries who have left no trace of a jest, still less of the faintest appreciation of humor, all which he said and wrote was brilliant with both these most charming qualities of the human mind. Though sometimes lax in points of grammar, as was much the custom in his day, he wrote as delightful a style as is to be found in all English literature, and that too when the stilted, verbose, and turgid habit was tediously prevalent. He was a man who impressed his ability upon all who met him ; so that the abler the man and the more experienced in judging men, the higher did he rate Franklin when brought into direct contact with him ; politicians and statesmen of Europe, distrustful and sagacious, trained readers and valu-

[1] Bancroft, *Hist. U. S.*, ix. 134.

ers of men, gave him the rare honor of placing confidence not only in his personal sincerity, but in his broad fair-mindedness, a mental quite as much as a moral trait.

It is hard indeed to give full expression to a man of such scope in morals, in mind, and in affairs. He illustrates humanity in an astonishing multiplicity of ways at an infinite number of points. He, more than any other, seems to show us how many-sided our human nature is. No individual, of course, fills the entire circle; but if we can imagine a circumference which shall express humanity, we can place within it no one man who will reach out to approach it and to touch it at so many points as will Franklin. A man of active as well as universal good-will, of perfect trustfulness towards all dwellers on the earth, of supreme wisdom expanding over all the interests of the race, none has earned a more kindly loyalty. By the instruction which he gave, by his discoveries, by his inventions, and by his achievements in public life he earns the distinction of having rendered to men varied and useful services excelled by no other one man; and thus he has established a claim upon the gratitude of mankind so broad that history holds few who can be his rivals.

INDEX.

———

ADAMS, Abigail, on Franklin, 208.
Adams, John, 109, 217, 281, 284, 353, 367, 378, 383, 391, 395, 414 ; at the conference with Lord Howe, 212–214 ; remarks concerning Franklin, 232, 234, 333, 340 ; in the Williams quarrel, 262 ; concerning rum, 273 ; feeling toward France, 283 note ; arrival in Paris, and extreme activity there, 290–292 ; share in the quarrels there, 292 ; advises to break up the French commission, 293, 294 ; returns home, 294 ; letter to, 318 ; drafts on, and financial labors in Holland, 326–328 ; unpopular at the French court, 335 ; relations with Franklin, 336, 337, 338, 340, 341, 342 ; return to Paris as peace commissioner, 355, 357 ; trouble with de Vergennes, 345–349 ; consequent wrath against Franklin, 350 ; disapproves Oswald's commission, 368 ; approves of treating without communication with de Vergennes, 373 ; his part in the negotiations, 375, 386, 394 ; testimony in behalf of Franklin, 384 ; feud with Franklin, 385.
Adams, Samuel, 106, 109, 333, 414 ; opposes Franklin's nomination as agent for Massachusetts, 136 ; projects a New England Confederacy, 209.
"Alliance," officers of, 313.
Arnold, General, 208.
"Art of Virtue," scheme for book, 30–32.
Austin, J. L., brings news of Burgoyne's defeat, 267 ; secret mission to England, 268.

Bache, Richard, marries Franklin's daughter, 201.
Bancroft, Edward, 258 ; tells story about Franklin's coat, 189, 280 ; a spy, 221, 227.
Beaumarchais, Caron de, early career, 222 ; meets Arthur Lee, 222 ; espouses colonial cause, 223 ; establishes firm of Hortalez & Co., 226–228 ; relations with Deane, 234, 235, 237 ; suspected by Lee, 235 ; at Burgoyne's surrender, 267 ; claims on cargoes of rice and indigo, 305, 306.
Bedford, Duke of, 113 ; opposed to raising a colonial army, 51.
Bollan, Mr., agent for council of Massachusetts Bay, 153 ; in affair of the Hutchinson letters and privy council hearing, 183, 185.
"Bon Homme Richard," 297, 298.
Bond, Dr., aided by Franklin in establishing hospital, 40.
Braddock, General, 50 ; visited by Franklin, 52 ; expedition, 50 et seq. ; praises Franklin, 54.
Bradford, ——, editor of rival newspaper, 12.
Burgoyne, General, 264, 269 ; news of defeat, 267 ; effect of, 331.
Burke, Edmund, 113 ; on Franklin's French mission, 230.
Burke, William, pamphlet in favor of retaining Guadaloupe rather than Canada in 1760, 78, 79.
"Busybody" papers, 31.
Bute, Earl of, 104, 113, 211.

Camden, Marquis of, counsel for Penns, 67 ; predicts an American revolt, 81 ; befriends the colonies, 117 ; enters cabinet, 146.
Canada, question whether to retain it at peace of 1763, 77–82.
Carmichael, William, 217, 317 ; praises Franklin, 341.
Charles, Mr., agent for colonies, executes agreement as to taxation, 69.
Chatham, Earl of. See *Pitt*.
Chaumont, M. Ray de, lends his house to Franklin, 232.
Choiseul, Duke de, predicts American independence, 82.
Colden, letter to, 39.
Conway, General, receives office, 113 ; moves repeal of Stamp Act, 131 ;

enters cabinet, 146 ; advises adoption of Franklin's ideas, 281 ; motion, after news of Yorktown, 359.

Conyngham, the privateersman, 245, 246 *et seq.*

"Cool thoughts on the Present Situation," etc., published, 90.

Cooper, Sir Grey, on Franklin's French mission, 230.

Cooper, Samuel, letter as to Franklin's appointment as agent for Massachusetts, 137.

Cornwallis, Lord, surrender, 358.

Cumberland, Duke of, forms cabinet, 113 ; dies, 115.

Cushing, Thomas, letter to, as to Hutchinson's letters, 177.

Dana, Francis, reliance on Franklin, 338, 341.

Dartmouth, Lord, succeeds Hillsborough in charge of colonies, 164 ; relations with Franklin, 164 ; annoyed at Governor Hutchinson's behavior, 165 ; discusses situation with Franklin, 165–167 ; petition to, for removal of Hutchinson, etc., 181 ; achieves nothing for colonies, 191 ; Franklin's memorial to, 197.

Deane, Silas, 217, 229, 272, 412 ; character and career, 219 ; arrival in France, 220, 227 ; instructions, 221 ; relations with Bancroft, 221, 227 ; relations with Beaumarchais, 234, 235, 237 ; traduced by Arthur Lee, 235, and by Izard, 286 ; defended by Franklin, 236, 286 ; sends foreign officers to the States, 238–240 ; favors strong appeal to France, 266 ; return home, 286, 290 ; friendly to Franklin, 393.

Declaration of rights, 123.

De Grey, Lord Chief Justice, 184.

De la Luzerne, minister to States, 346, 357, 382.

Denham,——, offers Franklin a clerkship, 9 ; dies, 10.

Despencer, Lord le, breakfast party at his house, 134.

D'Estaing, Admiral, sails, 282.

De Weissenstein, letter from, and reply, 352–354.

Dickinson, John, 170 ; speech of, 93 ; opposition to election of Franklin as agent for Pennsylvania, 96, 97 ; desires to petition Parliament, 204, 215.

Digges, rascality of, 260, 359.

"Dissertation on Liberty and Necessity, Pleasure and Pain," published, 9 ; Franklin's subsequent opinion of, 25.

Dubourg, Dr., letter to Franklin, 228.

Dunning, Mr., counsel for Franklin, 185, 186.

East India Company, suffers by English legislation, 173.

Fiske, John, 400.

Folger, Abiah, wife of Joseph Franklin, 2.

Folger, Peter, 2, 3.

Fox, Charles, 268, attacks Lord North about the French alliance, 277 ; in Rockingham cabinet, 360 ; differences with Shelburne, 361, 365, 366 ; retires from office, 366.

Franklin, Benjamin, lineage, 2 ; birth, 3 ; intended for the church, 3 ; apprenticed to his brother, 4 ; religious speculations, 5 ; runs away, 5 ; beginnings in Philadelphia, 6 ; returns home, 7 ; embarks for England, under auspices of Sir William Keith, 7 ; career in London, 8 ; infidelity, 9 ; returns home, 10 ; illness and epitaph, 10, 11 ; partnership with Meredith, 11 ; establishes a newspaper, 12, 23 ; matrimonial schemes, 13 ; married, 15 ; establishes a library, 20 ; publishes "Poor Richard's" almanac, 21 ; as a teacher of morality, 24 *et seq.* ; religious views, 24 *et seq.* ; scheme for "The Art of Virtue," 30–32 ; letter to President Stiles, 28 ; project for the "Society of the Free and Easy," 33 ; establishes the Junto, 33 ; studies languages, 35 ; clerk of the General Assembly, 35 ; postmaster at Philadelphia, 35 ; invents a stove, 35 ; founds a philosophical society, 36 ; interest in agriculture, 36 ; founds the University of Pennsylvania, 36 ; endeavors to reorganize the night watch, 37 ; establishes the Union Fire Company, 38 ; interest in military matters, 38 ; "Plain Truth," 39 ; takes a partner, 39 ; elected to various offices, 40 ; commissioner to treat with the Indians, 40 ; assists Dr. Bond to establish his hospital, 40 ; attends to lighting and cleaning streets, 42 ; postmaster general, 42 ; made Master of Arts of Harvard and Yale, 43 ; deputy to an Indian conference at Albany, 43 ; proposes a colonial confederation, 44 ; writes letters on Shirley's plan for assembly of governors, 46 ; early views on parliamentary taxation of colonies, 46 *et seq.* ; and concerning colonial representation in parliament, 48 ; visits Boston, 49 ; appointed to supervise military expenditures, 49 ; concerned in Braddock's campaign, 51–54 ; claims against the government for advances, 54 ; becomes a colonel, 54–56 ; scheme for planting colonies inland, 56; reputation among scientists in Europe, 58; his existence doubted, 58; deputed to represent Pennsylvania in England, 59, 62; opposed to the proprietaries, 61, 62; embarks, but is long detained, 63, 64; arrival in London, 65; interview with Lord Granville as to colonial conditions, 65; with the proprietaries, 66; and with their counsel, 67; finally substantially carries his point, 69–71; prolonged detention in England, 72; vain efforts to see Mr. Pitt, 73; social amenities, 73; friendship with Strahan, 74; university honors in England and Scotland, 74; fancy for living in England, 75, 76, 85; scheme for matrimonial alliance for his daughter, 75; and for his son, 75; efforts to induce England to retain Canada, 77–81; deprecates the idea of American independence, 80, 81; predicts the growth of the West, 82; return home and warm welcome, 83; chosen to the assembly, 83; voted an imperfect compensation, 83; unaffected by appointment of his son as governor of New Jersey, 84; postal journey, 85; prognostications concerning Governor Penn, 86; opposition to the murdering "Paxton boys," 86–89; relations with Governor Penn, 89; a leader on the popular side, 90; campaign literature, 90–94; chosen speaker, to sign petition, 93; opposed, and beaten at election for assembly in 1764, 95; chosen as agent for the colony, in England, 96–98; embarkation at Philadelphia and arrival in London, 99; position and business in England, 100, 101; instructed to oppose the Stamp Act, 104; interview with Grenville, 105; early opinion as to Stamp Act, 105–107; no idea of independence, 106; recommends Mr. Hughes to dispense stamps at Philadelphia, 107; consequent unpopularity at home, 108, 109; falls in with public opinion in the States, 110, 120; his usefulness in England, 109–112; a witness before the House of Commons, 118, 120; expresses American view as to principle of Stamp Act, 120, 122; willing to hunt and fish for a livelihood, 122; upon taxation without representation, 122; says Americans are not subjects of parliament, 123, 124; personal regard for George III., 124–126; views as to colonial representation in parliament, 126–128; on difference between internal and external taxes, 128–130; asserts willingness of colonies to bear their share of public burdens, 130; sudden return of popularity in Pennsylvania, 132; sends a gown to his wife, 132; efforts to instruct Englishmen concerning America, 133 *et seq.;* jest as to claim of king of Prussia to England, 134; "Rules for reducing a Great Empire to a small one," 135; communication with French government, 136; agent of New Jersey, Georgia, and Massachusetts, 136; opposed in Massachusetts, 137; position before Englishmen, 137; salary, 137; financial affairs, 138, 143; postmastership, 138; attempts at bribery, 139; slandered, 139; advises moderation, 144; on Hillsborough's appointment, 150; relations and interview with Hillsborough, 151–155; no longer recognized as agent for Massachusetts, 156, 157; on bad terms with Hillsborough, 156; views as to proper character of colonial agents, 157; works against Hillsborough, 158, and overthrows him, 158–162, and is snubbed by him, 162; argument addressed to Privy Council about a frontier province, 161; never gets the grant, 163; suggests Hillsborough's successor, 163; relations with Dartmouth, 164; again recognized as agent for Massachusetts, 164; conversation with Dartmouth about quarrel between Hutchinson and Massachusetts assembly, 165–167; desire to restore an earlier *status*, 167–169; forebodings of war, 169; counsels moderation, 170; faith in non-importation, 171–173, 174; on the result of the Stamp Act and the Customs Act, 173; sends the Hutchinson letters to Massachusetts, 176–178; exculpates Whately and Temple, 180; transmits petition to Lord Dartmouth, 181; notified of hearing before Privy Council, 182; remarks before the council, 183; assailed by Wedderburn, 186–188; his velvet coat, 188; deprived of office as postmaster, 190; resigns agency for Massachusetts, 190; blamed by Massachusetts Assembly, 191; speaks well of Arthur Lee, 192; personal danger, charges of treason, 192; on provincial government, 194; interview with Chatham, 194; views as to unity of the Empire, 195; complimented by Chatham in House of Lords, 195; irritated into addressing an angry memorial to Lord Dartmouth, 196–199; secret negotiations for conciliation, 199; last day in England, with Dr. Priestley, 200; return home, 200; letter to Priestley, after Lexington and Concord, 202; to Strahan, 203; services in Provincial Congress, as to new petition, 204; declaration for Washington, 204; jesting habit, 206; plan for a union of colonies, 206; postmaster general, 206; chairman of provincial committee of safety, 207; member of the assembly, 207; sent to confer with Washington at Cambridge, 207; sent to Canada, 208; member of Constitutional Convention of Pennsylvania, 209; connection with Declaration of Independence, 209, 210; opinion as to voting power of States in the confederacy, 210; correspondence with Lord Howe, 211; interview with him, 212–214; affected by bloodshed, 214; letters to Priestley, 215; fitness for diplomacy, 217 *et seq.;* gets news from France in September, 1776, 228; and is consequently sent thither, 228; his voyage, 229, 230; his arrival, 228, 230–232; takes quarters at Passy, 232; way of life, 232; audience given by de Vergennes, 233; in connection with the Deane-Beaumarchais business, 234, 236, 237; dealings with foreign military officers, 240–243; a political prophecy, 243; advises privateering, 245; connection with privateersmen in Europe, 246 *et seq.;* protects them against French governmental interference, 248; endeavors to effect exchange of prisoners with England, 250 *et seq.;* correspondence with Hartley on this subject, 253 *et seq.;* methods of business in this matter, 256, 257; remits money to prisoners, 254, 260; appoints Jonathan Williams naval agent, 261; consequent trouble, 261, 262; troubled by lack of news from the States, 264; keeps up his spirits, 264–266; gets news of Burgoyne's surrender, 267; sends J. L. Austin to England, 268; correspondence with Hartley about French alliance, 269, 270; negotiating treaties with France, 270–276; misunderstanding with Lee, 273–275; writes to Hartley about peace, 278; granted an audience by Louis XVI., 279; his costume, 280; hated by George III., 281; ideas as to conduct of warfare, 283, 284; meeting with Voltaire, 285; says a good word for Deane, 286; more assaults on the part of Lee, 287–290, 293, 294; ad-

vises establishing a single representative at Versailles, 293; appointed minister plenipotentiary to France, 294, 295; trouble with Lee about official papers, 296; relations with John Paul Jones, 296, 297; troubles with Landais and Lee, 298, 299; as American financier in Europe, 303, 305, 307; lends money to Congress, 304; yields two cargoes to Beaumarchais, 306; appeals to Thomas Morris, 306; writes a pamphlet on credit of the States, 307; agrees to meet interest on loan in the States, 307; annoyed by drafts, 308, 314, 316, 327, 329, 331; not advised concerning bills drawn, 309; vexed by demands of Lee and Izard, 310–313; aids the officers of the Alliance, 313; begging from France, 314, 320, 321, 323; annoyed by state agents seeking loans, 315; applied to by Jones, 315; assists Jay, 317, 318, 324, 329, 330; proposes furnishing supplies to French fleet, 318; urges self-help, 318; meets drafts on Laurens, 320, 322, 324; fragment of his diary, 322; secures a loan in Holland, 324; trouble about Jackson's purchases, 324–326; called upon to meet drafts on John Adams, 326; demands of Morris, 326, 329, 331; asks remittances from America, 327; antedated bills, 328; personal liability, 327, 328; demands from Livingston, 328, 329; warned by de Vergennes, 328; relations with John Adams, 333, 350; influence in France, 335; discussion of his official life in France, 336–342; annoyed by rumors from home, 343; patience, 343; effort to resign, 344; ill-treated by Congress, 344; invoked to aid Adams in his trouble with de Vergennes, 346–351; opinions as to paper money, 351; approached by Pulteney, as to peace, 352; share in the de Weissenstein episode, 352–354; approached by Hartley, as to truce, 354; feelings toward England, 354, 355; as to reunion with England, 355; as to choice between England and France, 356; one of the Commission to treat for peace, 358; refuses to treat separately from France, 358, 359; opportune note to Shelburne, 359; first interview with Oswald, 360; second interview, 362; refuses to negotiate separately from France, 363; urges Jay's presence, 365; asks to treat with Oswald, 366; agrees with Oswald, 367; opinion as to Oswald's commission, 368;

criticises Jay's letter, 369; differs with Jay, 370, 372–374; on compensation to American royalists, 375, 376; antipathy to American royalists, 377; correspondence with de Vergennes as to the secret treating, 379, 382; blamed by Congress, 382; and by others, 383; vindicated, 384; feud with the Adams family, 385; discussion of his part in making the treaty, 386–391; opinion of de Vergennes, 388; again resigns, 391; retained for commercial treaties, 391; leave to retire, 392; Jefferson's testimony as to his position in France, 392–394; departure from France, 395; voyage, 396; arrival at home, 397; councilor, 397; devotes salary to public use, 398; proposal for repaying British debts, 399; encouraging views, 400; member of the Constitutional Convention, 401–405; comes out for Washington, 405; physical ills, 406; feeling about French revolution, 408; anti-slavery efforts, 409, 410; condemns the liberty of the press, 409; last illness and death, 410; ill treatment experienced at the hands of Congress, 411, 412; French action concerning his death, 413; reflections on his character, abilities, and life, 413–420.

Franklin, Mrs. Deborah, receives Franklin's illegitimate son, 16; letter to, 74; dread of crossing the Atlantic, 75, 76; in the Stamp Act riots, 108; Franklin's present of a gown to, 132; dies, 201. See *Read*, Miss Deborah.

Franklin, James, early relations with Benjamin, 4, 5.

Franklin, Josiah, emigration and marriages of, 2; refuses to aid Franklin in setting up as a printer, 7.

Franklin, Sarah, offer of marriage, 75; and the Stamp Act riots, 108; marries, 201.

Franklin, Temple, his unrequited services, 243, 245, 339, 411.

Franklin, William, birth, 16; will not marry Mary Stevenson, 75; appointed governor of New Jersey, 83; and becomes a Tory, 84; last interview with his father, 396.

Gadsden, Christopher, 106, 109.

Galloway, Joseph, speech of, 93; defeated at election for Assembly, 96.

Gates, General, 269, 277, 295.

"Gentleman's Magazine," The, on Franklin's examination, 120.

George III., anxious for peace with France in 1759–60, 77; displaces Grenville, 113; Franklin's opinion of, 124–126; hatred of Shelburne, 147, 148; vexed with Hillsborough, 158; hatred of Franklin, 281; and de Weissenstein, 353; makes Shelburne prime minister, 366.

George IV., 268.

Gérard, M., negotiates with colonial commissioners, 270–276; liberal professions to them, 282; claims credit for ousting Arthur Lee, 294.

Gibbon, Edward, quoted, 276, 281.

Grand, M., the banker, 310, 322, 331.

Granville, Lord, interview with Franklin concerning colonial politics, 65, 66.

Greene, General, on Franklin, 207.

Grenville, George, 178; in the treasury department, 103; schemes concerning colonial taxation, 103, 104; interview with Franklin, 105; procures from Franklin nomination of stamp distributor, 107; and the Stamp Act, 112, 113, 142; on external and internal taxes, 128, 130.

Grenville, Thomas, mission to Paris, 361, 363–366; recalled, 367; remarks concerning obligations to France, 389.

Guadaloupe, question of retaining, 77 *et seq.*

Hall, David, fellow-workman of Franklin, 9; taken into partnership, 39.

Hamilton, Alexander, 340, 403.

Hamilton, Governor, superseded, 86.

Harrison, Benjamin, 207, 210.

Hartley, David, 252, 359; and the American prisoners, 253, 255–258; advice as to alliance with France, 269; and the conciliatory bills and peace, 278, 279; warning to Franklin, 284; proposes truce, 354; about a peace, 356.

Harvard College makes Franklin master of arts, 43.

Hawthorne, Nathaniel, 214, 280.

Henry, Patrick, 106, 109.

Hillsborough, Earl of, placed in charge of the colonies, 150; Franklin's opinion of, and relations with, 150 *et seq.*, 156; interview with Franklin, 152–156; precarious tenure of office, 158; vexes the king, 158; loses his place on the question of granting lands, 159–162; resentment against Franklin, 162; speaks ill of the colonists, 163, 164.

Hortalez & Co., firm of, 226, 227, 235.

Howe, Lord, efforts at conciliation, in England, 199; and in America, 211–214; captures Philadelphia, 264.

Hughes, nominated stamp distributor, 107.

Hume, David, 74.
Hunter, William, associated with Franklin in managing the post-office, 42.
Hutchinson, Anne, 176, note.
Hutchinson, Governor Thomas, 182, note, 183; quarrels with Massachusetts Assembly and irritates the ministry, 165; his letters, 175 *et seq.*; position in Massachusetts, 176, note; petition for his removal, 181; favors arrest of Franklin, 193.

Izard, 217, 290, 295; meddles in the treaty negotiations, 275; traduces Deane, 286; and Franklin, 286, 289, 294, 393; exorbitant demands for money rebuked by Franklin, 310–313.

Jackson, William, demands for money, 324, 325.
Jay, John, 217, 383, 391; financial trouble in Spain, 303, 316, 318, 326; aided by Franklin, 317, 327, 329, 330; feeling towards Franklin, 338, 341, 342, 365, 393; on peace commission, 358; comes to Paris, 365; ill, 367; objects to Oswald's commission, 367; letter on the subject, 369; suspicious of de Vergennes, 369, 370, 373; persuades Vaughan to go secretly to London, 370; desires to treat without communication with de Vergennes, 373; takes charge of boundaries and navigation of Mississippi, 374, 375; angry at congressional reproof, 382; testimony in behalf of Franklin, 384; his part in the negotiation, 386.
Jefferson, Thomas, and Declaration of Independence, 210; French mission, 229; on peace commission, 345, 358; tribute to Franklin, 392–394, 395.
Jones, John Paul, his doings and relations with Franklin, 296, 297; trouble with Landais, 298; applies for money, 315.
Junto, the, established, 33; aids in establishing fire companies, 38.

Kames, Lord, 74; letter to, as to "Art of Virtue," 31; letter to, on leaving England, 76; letter to, as to growth of the West, 82.
Kant, Immanuel, calls Franklin Prometheus, etc., 59.
Keimer, Franklin's employer, 6, 11; publishes a newspaper, and sells it, 12.
Keith, Sir William; behavior to Franklin, 6–8.
Knox, agent for Georgia, favors a Stamp Act, 104.

Lafayette, Marquis de, recommended by Franklin, 243; aids Franklin to raise money, 329, 331.
Landais, Captain, his misbehavior, 298, 299.
Laurens, Henry, 217, 384; complains of Franklin, 260; drafts on, 320, 322; on peace commission, 358; friendly towards Franklin, 393.
Laurens, John, expenses in Holland, 324.
Lee, Arthur, 183, 217, 270, 295; slanders Franklin, 139, 192, 288, 290, 291, 294, 299, 393; praised by Franklin, 192; succeeds Franklin, 200; meets Beaumarchais, 222; commissioner to France, 229; traduces Deane, 235, 237; vituperates Williams, 261; sides with Franklin, against Deane, 267; jealousy of Franklin, the cake story, 272; makes trouble about the alliance, 274, 275; not told of departure of Deane and Gérard, 286; comments upon, 287; general unpopularity, 288; excessive demands for money, 293, 310, 312; removed from French commission, 294, 295; bad behavior as to official papers of French commission, 295; return home, 299; spoils a loan, 313; relies on Franklin, 338.
Lee, John, counsel for Franklin, 185, 186.
Lee, William, 217; and the Williams affair, 261; meddles in the French mediations, 275; traduces Franklin, 294.
Lincoln, Abraham, 265.
Livingston, letters to, 319, 331; letters from, 328, 329, 382.
"London Chronicle," letters of Franklin published in, 46.
Loudoun, Lord, dispatched to the provinces, 63; his character and behavior, 63, 64.
Louis XVI., 222, 223, 225; polite speech to American commissioners, 279; civilities to Franklin, 395.
Lovell, James, letter to, 308.

Madison, James, story of the rising or the setting sun, 405.
Mansfield, Lord, interview with Franklin as to the disputes with the Penns, 69; supports principle of Stamp Act, 117.
Mason, J. M., 229, 230.
Mather, Cotton, 2.
Mauduit, Israel, 183.
Meredith, ——, Franklin's partner, 11, 12.
Mirabeau, Comte de, eulogy on Franklin, 113.
Morris, Robert, 300, 303; in matter of

Thomas Morris, 261; demands for money, 326, 328–331.

Morris, Thomas, 217, 260, 261, 306.

Necker, Jacques, loan to the States, 324.

"New England Courant," 5.

Noailles, Marquis de, announces alliance between France and United States, 280.

Norris, Isaac, speaker of Pennsylvania Assembly, 62; resigns rather than sign petition, 93.

North, Lord, 361; chancellor of exchequer, 150; at privy council hearing, 187; and conciliation, 199; and Hartley, 253; introduces conciliatory bills after Burgoyne's surrender, 277; admits the alliance with France, 278; receives news of Cornwallis's surrender, 358; resigns, 359.

Oliver, Lieutenant-Governor, 184; his letters, 175; petition for his removal, 181.

Oswald, Richard, opens talk about peace, 360; second interview, 362; difficulties as to his authority, 365–368; receives new commission, 371; and treats, 372 *et seq.*

Otis, James, 106.

Oxford, University of, makes Franklin doctor of laws, 74.

Parton, James, life of Franklin cited, 16, 23, 35, 206, 219, 229, 237, 238, 268, 278, 279, 280, 401, 408, 412.

"Paxton boys," massacre and riot, 86–88; the affair excites hostility toward Franklin, 89, 95.

Pelham, Henry, 103.

Penn, the family of, proprietaries, relations with the people, 49, 59–63; efforts of Franklin to negotiate with, 66 *et seq.*; their position concerning taxation, 67–70; beaten, 71; send one of their number to be governor, 86; Franklin's hostility to, mitigated, 94, note.

Penn, John, made governor, 86; behavior in the matter of the Paxton massacre and riot, 88; hostility toward Franklin, 89; his vetoes, 89, 90.

Penn, Richard, Franklin's famous epitaph for, 94.

Penn, Thomas, 49, 63, 86; Franklin's famous epitaph for, 94.

"Pennsylvania Gazette," published by Franklin, 12, 13, 23; articles in, 43.

Pitt, William, 73, 82, 103; opposes Stamp Act, 112, 115, 117; fails to form a cabinet, 113; will not take office, 116; reforms the Rockingham ministry, 146; backs Shelburne, 147; statue to, in America, 148; seclusion, 148, 149; Franklin's interview with, 194, 195; compliments Franklin in House of Lords, 195.

"Plain Truth" published, 39.

"Poor Richard's Almanac," 21–23.

Pownall, Governor, scheme for "barrier" colonies, 56.

Pratt, John J. See *Camden*, Marquis of.

Priestley, Dr., concerning privy council hearing, 187; passes day with Franklin, 200; letter to, at outbreak of war, 202; humorous letter to, 215; and Austin, 268.

Pulteney, William, mission about peace, 352.

Ray, Catherine, letter to, 14.

Rayneval, F. M. G. de, views as to western lands, 369; secret mission to London, 370.

Read, Miss Deborah, first sees Franklin, 6; subsequent career, 14, 15; marries Franklin, 15. See *Franklin*, Mrs. Deborah.

Rockingham, Marquis of; his cabinet, 113; position as to Stamp Act, 117; his cabinet revamped, 145, 146; on Franklin's French mission, 231; second cabinet, 360; death, 366.

Robertson, Dr., 74.

"Rules for reducing a Great Empire," etc., 135.

Rush, Dr., 228.

Rutledge, Edward, at conference with Lord Howe, 212–214.

Sandwich, Lord, assails Franklin, 195.

Serapis, The, 297, 298.

Shelburne, Earl of, enters cabinet, and his position therein, 146–148; backed by Pitt, 147; opposed by Townshend, 146–148; hated by George III., 147, 148; superseded, 150; entertains Austin, 268; letter of Franklin to, 359; in Rockingham cabinet, 360; opens talk about peace, 360; differences with Fox, 361, 366; scheme for "federal union," 362; prime minister, 366; his position in respect of the treaty, 367, 368; an arbiter between France and the States, 370, 371; earnest in behalf of American royalists, 375; but yields, 376; thrust from power, 378.

Shirley, William, Governor, plan for assembly of colonial governors, 46; for representation of colonies in Parliament, 48; appoints auditors for claims under Braddock's expedition, 54; qualifications as a soldier, 55.

Siéyes, Abbé E. J. de, 413.

Slidell, John, 229, 230.

" Society of the Free and Easy," 33.

Stamp Act, the, 101, 103, 104, 107, 112, 143, 145, 167, 168 ; passed, 105 ; Franklin's feeling about, 105 *et seq. ;* effect in England, 114 ; opposed by Pitt, 112, 115 ; Rockingham's position, 117 ; debate on principle of, 117 ; Franklin's examination in connection with, 120 *et seq. ;* repealed, 131 ; causes of repeal, 141 ; opinion as to repeal, 141, 142 ; financial results of, 173.

St. Andrews, University of, makes Franklin doctor of laws, 74.

St. Asaph, Bishop of, 278, 395, 402, note, 408.

Steuben, Baron, introduced by Franklin, 243.

Stevenson, Mary, 100 ; Franklin wishes his son to marry, 75 ; letter to, 85.

Stevenson, Mrs., 100.

Stiles, Ezra, letter to, 28.

Stormont, Lord, interferes with Beaumarchais, 227 ; on Franklin's reception in France, 231 ; reply to Franklin concerning exchange of prisoners, 250 ; leaves Paris, 281.

Strachey, Henry, sent to Paris, 372.

Strahan, William, 74 ; offers matrimonial alliance, 75 ; letter to, on leaving England, 76 ; letter to, as to welcome home, 83 ; letter of enmity to, 203.

Sullivan, General, 212.

Temple, ——, and the Hutchinson letters, 178–181.

Thomson, Charles, letters to, 105, 411.

Thornton, Major, agent to aid prisoners, 254.

Townshend, Charles, 104 ; in charge of colonial business, 102 ; his schemes, 102 ; succeeded by Grenville, 103 ; hostility to colonies, 115 ; favors repeal of Stamp Act, 142 ; chancellor of the exchequer, 146 ; position in hostility to Shelburne on colonial affairs, 146–148 ; proposal for colonial taxation, 149 ; dies, 150.

Truxton, Commodore, 396.

Turgot, views as to aiding the colonies, 224 ; displaced, 225 ; on French finances, 314.

Union Fire Company established, 38.

University of Pennsylvania, 37.

Vaughan, Benjamin, mission to Lord Shelburne, 370, 371 ; about the royalists question, 376.

Vergennes, Comte de, foresees American independence, 82 ; views as to aiding the colonies, 223, 225 ; arrangements with Beaumarchais, 226, 227 ; upon Franklin's arrival in France, 231 ; gives audience to colonial commissioners, 233 ; and the colonial privateers, 247, 248 ; charges of selfishness against, 249 ; secret interview with colonial commissioners, 270 ; liberal dealing with them, 282 ; as to Lee, 286, 288 ; financial applications to, 320, 323, 327, 328, 330 ; liking for Franklin, 342, 393 ; trouble with John Adams as to paper money, 345–349 ; and the de Weissenstein letter, 353 ; trusted by Franklin, 357, 388–390 ; dislikes Adams, 357 ; influence in matter of peace commission, 357 ; at first suggestions of peace, 359, 360 ; amused at English propositions, 363 ; puzzled, 365 ; opinion as to Oswald's commission, 367 ; suspicions against, 368–370, 380 ; on the treaty of peace, 378 ; anger at the secret treating, 379–382.

Voltaire meets Franklin, 285.

Walpole, Horace, on Franklin's embarkation, 229 ; and the French alliance, 277.

Walpole, Sir Robert, 103.

Walpole, Thomas, 277 ; advice to Franklin, 197–199.

Washington, George, 204, 241, 264, 295, 303, 304, 323, 335, 340, 353, 398, 413 ; visited by Pennsylvania delegation, 207 ; president, 405.

Wedderburn, Alexander, Solicitor-General, at the hearing before the privy council, 183, 184, 186, 187.

Weissenstein. See *de Weissenstein.*

Whately, Thomas, and the Hutchinson letters, 178–181 ; sues Franklin, 185.

Whately, William, and the Hutchinson letters, 178.

Williams, Jonathan, 217, 294, 322 ; receives appointment from Franklin, 261 ; displaced, 262 ; ill-treated, 263, 345.

Wyndham, Sir William, proposes to Franklin to teach swimming, 10.

Yale College makes Franklin master of arts, 43.

Yorke, Charles, counsel for Pennsylvania, 67.

AMERICAN MEN OF LETTERS

Biographies of our most eminent American Authors, written by men who are themselves prominent in the field of letters. Each volume, with portrait, 16mo, gilt top.

The writers of these biographies are themselves Americans, generally familiar with the surroundings in which their subjects lived and the conditions under which their work was done. Hence the volumes are peculiar for the rare combination of critical judgment with sympathetic understanding. Collectively, the series offers a biographical history of American Literature.

The following, each, $1.25

WILLIAM CULLEN BRYANT. By JOHN BIGELOW.
J. FENIMORE COOPER. By T. R. LOUNSBURY.
GEORGE WILLIAM CURTIS. By EDWARD CARY.
RALPH WALDO EMERSON. By OLIVER WENDELL HOLMES.
BENJAMIN FRANKLIN. By JOHN BACH MCMASTER.
WASHINGTON IRVING. By CHARLES DUDLEY WARNER.
MARGARET FULLER OSSOLI. By T. W. HIGGINSON.
EDGAR ALLAN POE. By GEORGE E. WOODBERRY.
GEORGE RIPLEY. By O. B. FROTHINGHAM.
WILLIAM GILMORE SIMMS. By WILLIAM P. TRENT.
BAYARD TAYLOR. By ALBERT H. SMYTH.
HENRY D. THOREAU. By FRANK B. SANBORN.
NOAH WEBSTER. By HORACE E. SCUDDER.
NATHANIEL PARKER WILLIS. By HENRY A. BEERS.

The following, each, $1.10, net; postage, 10 cents

NATHANIEL HAWTHORNE. By GEORGE E. WOODBERRY.
HENRY W. LONGFELLOW. By T. W. HIGGINSON.
FRANCIS PARKMAN. By H. D. SEDGWICK.
WILLIAM HICKLING PRESCOTT. By ROLLO OGDEN.
JOHN GREENLEAF WHITTIER. By GEO. R. CARPENTER.

The set, 19 volumes, $23.00; half polished morocco, $50.50.

In preparation

BRET HARTE. By HENRY C. MERWIN.
OLIVER WENDELL HOLMES. By S. M. CROTHERS.
Other titles to be added.

HOUGHTON MIFFLIN COMPANY

AMERICAN
COMMONWEALTHS

Volumes devoted to such States of the Union as have a striking
political, social, or economic history. Each volume, with Map
and Index, 16mo, gilt top, $1.25, *net ;* postage 12 cents. The set,
19 vols., $23.75 ; half polished morocco, $52.25.

*The books which form this series are scholarly and readable individually ;
collectively, the series, when completed, will present a history of the nation, setting
forth in lucid and vigorous style the varieties of government and of social life to
be found in the various commonwealths included in the federal union.*

CALIFORNIA. By JOSIAH ROYCE.
CONNECTICUT. By ALEXANDER JOHNSTON. (Revised Ed.)
INDIANA. By J. P. DUNN, JR. (Revised Edition.)
KANSAS. By LEVERETT W. SPRING. (Revised Edition.)
KENTUCKY. By NATHANIEL SOUTHGATE SHALER.
LOUISIANA. By ALBERT PHELPS.
MARYLAND. By WILLIAM HAND BROWNE. (Revised Ed.)
MICHIGAN. By THOMAS M. COOLEY. (Revised Edition.)
MINNESOTA. By WM. W. FOLWELL.
MISSOURI. By LUCIEN CARR.
NEW HAMPSHIRE. By FRANK B. SANBORN.
NEW YORK. By ELLIS H. ROBERTS. 2 vols. (Revised Ed.)
OHIO. By RUFUS KING. (Revised Edition.)
RHODE ISLAND. By IRVING B. RICHMAN.
TEXAS. By GEORGE P. GARRISON.
VERMONT. By ROWLAND E. ROBINSON.
VIRGINIA. By JOHN ESTEN COOKE. (Revised Edition.)
WISCONSIN. By REUBEN GOLD THWAITES.

In preparation

GEORGIA. By ULRICH B. PHILLIPS.
ILLINOIS. By JOHN H. FINLEY.
IOWA. By ALBERT SHAW.
MASSACHUSETTS. By EDWARD CHANNING.
NEW JERSEY. By AUSTIN SCOTT.
OREGON. By F. H. HODDER.
PENNSYLVANIA. By TALCOTT WILLIAMS.

HOUGHTON MIFFLIN COMPANY

DATE DUE

GAYLORD   PRINTED IN U.S.A.